A TREASURY OF PERSIAN CUISINE

A TREASURY OF PERSIAN CUISINE

Shirin Simmons

The Book Guild Ltd
Sussex, England

First published in Great Britain in 2002 by
The Book Guild Ltd
25 High Street,
Lewes, East Sussex
BN7 2LU

Typesetting in Garamond by
Keyboard Services, Luton, Bedfordshire

Printed in Great Britain by
Bookcraft (Bath) Ltd, Avon

A catalogue record for this book is
available from the British Library

ISBN 1 85776 675 X

To my darling late husband, Michael,
whom I lost tragically

CONTENTS

INTRODUCTION

1. GEOGRAPHY

Persia, with an area of some 1,680,000 square kilometres, is just under half the size of India and the fifth largest country in Asia. The Iranian plateau is a triangle set between two depressions, bordered by the Persian Gulf to the south and to the north by the states of Armenia, Azarbaijan and Turkemenistan (formerly of the USSR) and the Caspian Sea. To the east lie Afghanistan and Pakistan. As a bridge between central and western Asia, it forms a promontory which links the steppes of inner Asia to the plateau of Asia Minor and beyond to Europe. Geography can therefore account for the historic part which the plateau was called on to play in the course of thousands of years of human history.

The triangle is bounded by mountains rising round a central depression, a desert region formed by the bed of a dried-up sea. The western mountains, or Zagros range, run from north-west to south-east, over 620 miles in length and 120 in width. The chain rises to between 3,280 and 5,570 feet, and consists of numerous parallel folds, enclosing valleys 30 to 60 miles long and 6 to 12 miles wide. Below the pastures on the higher slopes of these mountains stretch the remains of what were once dense forests of oak, walnut, evergreen, wild almond and pistachio. Lower down in the high valleys grow vines, figs and pomegranates, and there is wide cultivation of wheat, barley, cotton and tobacco. Owing to the summer heat in the lower valleys, goats, sheep and horses, are taken up to the higher pastures. Therefore a large proportion of the population in that area lead a nomadic life, imposed on it by the climate and natural conditions.

From the central Zagros range, a spur runs westward into the Mesopotamian plain causing a bend in the Tigris, which at this point approaches the Euphrates. This spur has the shape of a hatchet which from aloft threatens the plain below and it was in the second millennium BC, that the Kassites invaded and dominated Babylon for over five centuries. The country now called Luristan, the northern part of the triangle, is surrounded by the chain of Alborz mountains, of which the highest peak Mt Damavand, rises to over 19,000 feet. Skirting the southern shore of the Caspian Sea, the Alborz range forms a high and narrow barrier which separates the coastal area with its luxuriant vegetation, from the desert regions of the interior. At their western end, the Alborz reach the Iranian part of Azarbaijan in the centre of which lies the salt lake of Uraemia, and in its valleys wheat, millet, cotton, rice, tobacco, castor-oil trees, and melon are cultivated. To the east is the mountain of Khorasan, not very high and easy to cross and with extremely fertile valleys in which grow wheat, barley, rice, cotton and vines.

This granary of Iran, owing to its geographical formation, is the second gateway for penetration into the plateau. Waves of invaders poured through it coming from the plains

2

of central Asia which stretch thousands of miles to the north, west and east. Like Azarbaijan, Khorasan is a crossroads of people, and was raided by the Turcomans down to the end of the 19th century. The valley of the Atrek and the plain of Gorgan between the Caspian Sea and the mountains, are natural oases for migration towards Iran and to defend themselves there the Sassanian kings built a brick wall many miles in length, the remains of which can still be seen. This north east district of Iran was the birth-place of several dynasties; the Arsacids, Safavi, and Ghajars (Kajars). Finally, the mountains bordering the Iranian triangle are completed by a southern chain, the Makran, a range pierced by two passes, one to Bandar Abbas, the other leading east to Baluchestan and Quetta. In the central part of the plateau, which is crossed by two inner mountain chains, lies a great desert depression, the most arid in the world.

This is divided into Dasht-e-Kavir to the north and Dasht-e-Lut to the south. The former is a series of mud and salt flats where nothing grows or lives. In some places life is possible round the hollows where the soil is less saline, and there are true oases. The Lut, on the contrary, is a completely dry basin, and the rare explorers who have had the courage to cross this inhospitable waste say that the great deserts of central Asia, such as the Gobi, are semi-fertile regions in comparison. Therefore life could develop on the plateau only in the valleys of the great peripheral ranges or in the oases. But it also made great progress on the wide plains of inner and outer Iran. The most important of these is the plain of Kusestan in the south west, ancient Susiana, which geographically is only an extension of the Mesopotamian plain.

Running up into the Zagros range, it forms a counterpoise to the mountainous salient of Lurestan, the Pusht-e-Kooh. Susiana was a country with a very old settled urban civilization and throughout the centuries influenced the nomadic and semi-nomadic hill people living along its borders. When the political frontiers of the Iranian Empire extended far to the west of Zagros, it was on this plain that the great capital city of Susa arose, an administrative centre linked by easy communications to Mesopotamia and Asia Minor.

All the capitals of Iran, ever since the rise of the first kingdom, have faced towards the desert. Lying along the two principle routes that skirt the inner edges of the two great ranges from west to east on the strategic trade route along the Alborz, stand Ecbatana (Hamadan) Ghazvin (Kazvine) Teheran, Ray, Damghan, and Herat. On the southern route lie Isfahan, Pasargadeh, Estakhr, Persepolis, and Shiraz. Research by archaeological investigation has shown that stone-age man, almost as soon as he came down from the mountain into the plain, settled along the same line, which describes an arc around the salt desert. The main sites so far identified are at Kashan, Ghom (Qum), Ray and Damghan. The religious centres of the country too lay along the same natural lines of communication, and indeed even today holy cities of Mashhad and Ghom (Qum), are situated respectively on the east-west and north-south routes.

3

Primarily an agricultural and stock-breeding country, Iran possesses rich and varied mineral resources. From the third millennium BC its quarries provided marble and alabaster for the Sumerian princes, who also drew supplies of building woods from the forests which at that period covered the mountains, though now they are practically denuded. Carnelian, turquoise and lapis lazuli were all exploited from the very earliest period. Iron, copper, tin and lead attracted the attention of the conquering Assyrians. Both slopes of the Zagros are of a gypsous rock and contain oil-bearing deposits which were already known in the time of Herodotus, and have been worked for the last fifty years.

The country is, in reality, open on all sides, to the plains of Mesopotamia and Russia as well as to India and the Persian Gulf. As it was the hub on the great lines of communication which link East and West, Iran was crossed by the oldest trade route, the Silk Road, which was also the path for invasions. For despite the protection of its mountains; and its impregnable appearance, Iran has known many conquerors. The country, physically disjointed and therefore not homogeneous, is ill shaped for defence. These features conditioned its intermittent periods of decadence and glory alike, for its people, although scattered in belts of cultivable soil and in oases, were endowed with the power to create a civilization. Ideas and customs, religious and artistic developments which had taken their rise in Iran left their mark on more than one foreign civilization.

Just under fifty years ago geological research showed that at the time when the greater part of Europe was covered in glaciers, the Iranian plateau was passing through a pluvial period. When even a great valley was under water. The central part of the plateau today remains as a great salt desert which thousands of years ago was an immense lake or great sea. Fossil fish and shells have been found in the desert and the valley, which shows physical aspects of the country from many thousands of years ago. From 15,000 to 10,000 BC there was slow change in the climate. Slowly the pluvial period was followed by a dry period, the rainfall became increasingly less, slowing down the current of the rivers and the streams as the valleys dried, and there were profound changes in the condition of man's existence. The main central lake shrank and became rich pasture and savannah. Animals moved from the mountains to the newly formed grasslands, with man who lived by hunting.

The Iranians are pastural people. They bring agriculture to the fore from out of the distant country. Their methods were medieval. They opened up new tracts of land – hitherto uncultivated land rich in iron and other minerals. Iron, being the chief natural resource of Persia, has been used for army warfare, farming and for industry. Persia traded with neighbours as far away as Spain, China and the Orient. Changes took place as never heard of in the annals of history.

Pottery – women were the ones with great ability in pottery, not the men. Women were the leaders, the inventors, the makers of pottery – men did nothing worth while, they were weak and useless. Women led the agricultural movement and were the inventors of many utilities in the early ages. Women were predominant in everything.

2. Agriculture & Irrigation

Another outer plain backs on to the mountains bordering the Caspian Sea. This high mountain barrier catches the clouds, bringing an abundant rainfall to a narrow strip of extraordinarily fertile land. It is tropical Iran, covered with forests. Lemons, mulberries, figs and pomegranates grow there and provide food for about a third of the country. The outer plains, however, played only a secondary part in the development of Iranian civilization. This, from earliest times, was centred in the scattered oases in the mountain ranges which encircled the plateau and caught the rain clouds. The centre of this area is a desert, except where the alluvial soil, in general very fertile, can be cultivated by means of artificial irrigation. Despite extremes of climate, intense cold in winter and heat in summer, the ground yields abundantly wherever man can bring water. At all times on the plateau, the question of water has been vital.

Irrigation

Iran is not watered by the rivers of the Nile, the Tigris or Euphrates, nor does it enjoy regular seasons of beneficial rains stimulating the earth to produce agriculture. Irrigation has been vital to successful agriculture in Iran. For men could settle only where irrigation is possible.

The country was artificially irrigated from prehistoric times and by the Achaemenian (Hakhameneshian) period by the ghanat or underground water channel – first seen in the central plateau at least 2000 years ago and still very much in use. To build a ghanat – which is a highly skilled, dangerous and well paid job in Iran – you need first to bore a well down to an underground water source which may be 100 metres deep. And it must be at a higher level than the point at which the water is to be collected. Then you dig a tunnel which can be about 25 miles long. Thousands of men work all the year round, digging new canals and clearing old ones. Thanks to this water, and thanks also to the favourable rainfall in the Zagros and Alborz mountains, these ranges are dotted with cultivated areas and oasis settlements.

After the death of Alexander the Great, Persia fell back into the hands of the Iranians, and the beginning of the Seleucid Empire, which included the Iranian world, ancient Babylon, the Phoenician towns and the cities of Asia Minor, a period which was marked by great increase in the cultivation of all kinds of plants. It was the period when the Orient, southern Europe and in particular Italy, acclimatized a number of new plants and domestic animals, imported from Asia. The defeated Orient subjugated Europe. Cotton, the lemon, the melon, sesame seeds, the oriental nut, olives, dates and figs, the duck, and the Asiatic ox brought about a real agrarian revolution in Italy.

By clearance and drainage of new districts, the Seleucids brought more land under cultivation. The needs of the market demanded rational methods and a scientific approach. Agricultural techniques developed in such an intensive manner that they were not surpassed until the Middle Ages, not even under Islam. New methods were introduced in the cultivation of vines, a new plough came into use, a triple rotation of crops was practised, and new techniques were applied in irrigation, forestry, and in the cultivation of orchards and gardens.

In agriculture came the domestication of the first animal. Then animals provided the Iranians with food and clothing and a source of transport, then came flocks of sheep and herds of larger animals, such as goats and cows. Large families came to settle, even the slaves, men, women and little children. At that time the economy was at its height with plentiful hunting, fishing, gardens, fields and live stock, greenery and the exploitation of manual resources.

3. HISTORY

During the 6th century BC Cyrus the Great appeared as the first notable Persian ruler. The Achaemenian Empire which he founded lasted from 558 to 330 BC and his successors, Dariush I and Xerxes, expanded all the way to India in the east and the Aegean sea in the west. Even Egypt came under Persian rule and the magnificent complex of Persepolis became the hub of the empire.

This led to the unification of the whole of Western Asia under the Achaemenian crown, and the division of this immense area into provinces or satraps with their administration under central control. The creation of land and sea routes linking the different parts of the Empire, a perfectly balanced system of tax collection, the flow of gold into the Government coffers – such were the powerful factors that gave an unprecedented impetus to the economic life of Iran. The introduction of weights and measures and above all, of coinage throughout the Empire stimulated foreign commerce, which greatly expanded owing to certain improvements in the national economy.

Small silver coins had appeared in the 7th century, but a true monetary system, bimetallic in gold and silver, was first introduced by Croesus in Lydia. This quickly spread through Asia Minor and was adopted by Dariush in his empire. The tablets from Persepolis, one group of which consists of wage lists of the men working on the construction of the palace, give a very vivid picture of the transitional period that followed the introduction of money in Iran. Previously wages had been paid in kind: meat, barley, wheat, wine and all kinds of food. In the time of Xerxes, two-thirds was still paid in kind and one-third in cash. Later in the reign of the same king, payment in kind was reduced to a third only. Thus it took about half a century for money to replace goods and for the new system to become established, despite the fact that from the beginning certain transactions were entirely in cash.

Throughout the country public works were undertaken to increase productive capacity. One of the achievements of the Achaemenian kings was the digging of subterranean canals, ghanats which were of vital importance on the plateau and in other areas where water was short, such as the Syrian desert or central Asian region. It seems certain that drainage of marshes was also undertaken in the Empire, since this was practised by the Greeks at the same period. Agriculture expanded and as a result of the wars, foreign countries learnt about the useful plants of Iran. Lucerne was grown in the valleys of Media and was an ideal fodder for horses. The Median wars brought it to Greece as fodder for the Persian cavalry, and it was then adopted there. Also introduced into Europe were the domestic fowl, the white dove, and peacock, all natives of Asia. The west owes tulips to the Persians.

Dariush took a personal interest in arboriculture and in the propagation of new species. There is a curious letter of his to the satrap Gadatas, in which he orders him to transplant eastern plants and trees to Asia Minor and Syria. 'I commend your plan,' wrote the king, 'for improving my country by the transplantation of fruit trees from the other side of the Euphrates in the further part of Asia.' This was not merely the desire of a satrap to gratify the caprice of a prince. It was part of an economic policy, deliberately pursued by the Persian administration with the object of spreading as widely as possible plants that would improve the standard of living for the subject of the Empire. Thus we learn that at Damascus the Persians tried to plant a type of vine that was highly esteemed at their court. That they introduced the first pistachios in Aleppo and that around this period, the famous nut of pontus appeared in Greece. It was the Achaemenians who imported sesame into Egypt; and rice into Mesopotamia and in pursuing a similar policy on a large scale the Hellenistic kings were only following the example set by the Persians monarchs.

Being interested in the cultivation of plants, the Persians were also concerned with the equally vital question of the exploitation of forests. It is not, of course, correct to speak of scientific exploitation, but there must have been a measure of planning. The cedar of Lebanon and teak-wood in particular were required for the royal building projects. Timber was also extensively used for housing and building boats, war chariots, carts and weapons. Asia Minor,

Crete and the island of Cyprus were, with the Lebanon and India, the main centre of the timber trade.

The Empire was as self-sufficient in metals as in timber. Cyprus yielded silver, copper and iron, Asia Minor, copper and silver and the same metals were also found in Palestine. Copper and iron came from the Lebanon and the upper Tigris and Euphrates valleys, the Kerman region yielded gold and silver, Seistan was noted for its tin and the southern Caucasus for silver and iron, which came also from the southern shore of the Black Sea.

Work in the quarries increased as a result of the gigantic building programme undertaken by the kings to adorn their capitals. The foundation charter of the palace of Susa informs us that building-stone was quarried in the mountains of Elam and that lapis lazuli, probably from Bakak-Shan, and turquoise and carnelian from the mines of Khorasan were used.

Hunting and above all fishing were much more important in antiquity than they are today. A very large proportion of the population of the ancient world, both rich and poor, lived on bread, fish, a little oil and wine. The fisheries of the Persian Gulf and of the Tigris and Euphrates exported salted, dried, cured fish in jars to a considerable distance and we know from Herodotus that part of the imperial tribute paid by Egypt consisted of the profits from the fisheries.

Agricultural production during the Achaemenian period continued to be based on the large estate worked by serfs attached to the land and bought and sold with it, and also by the slave brought back from successful wars. Agriculture was the key industry of the Iranian state, and was considered the natural occupation of a freeman. The small estate existed, but was probably relatively unimportant in comparison with the great estates with closed economies. It was above all in Fars, the country of the master people, exempt from taxes and dues, that peasants, being free, owned land. Wheat and barley, grapes and olives were grown, cattle, sheep and goats were raised as well as draught animals, the donkey, mule and horse. Bee-keeping was much practised, as honey was the only form of sweetener.

ARTAXERXES III

Fate seemed to offer Persia a last chance of salvation by bringing to the throne a man who, though without doubt cruel and brutal, possessed a will of iron and the authority of a statesman. His accession was steeped in the blood of all his brothers and sisters, to the number of several dozen. Was this too high a price to pay for re-establishing the unity of the Empire, which faced by one menace after another, was on the downward path and could save itself only by accident?

He put down the revolt of the Cadusians with great firmness and also that of the satraps. Athens, which had lent support to some of them, was given a severe warning and under the threat of war withdrew its troops. The king directed his efforts towards the reconquest of Egypt, but his first attempt was a failure. Sidon, allied to Egypt, rebelled. The king burnt the city, its thousands of inhabitants and left it in ruins. A new campaign against Egypt with fresh contingents of mercenaries resulted in total victory.

The pharaoh fled to Ethiopia. Its cities were captured and their walls razed. Its temples were pillaged. The priests could ransom themselves only by the payment of enormous sums. The Empire was completely restored. It seemed to be stronger that at any time since Dariush.

Greece was hit hard by this rapid revival of Persia. For some time past, patriotic spirits, such as Socrates, had been appealing to the Hellenes to unite in the struggle against Persia and a new note had crept into their harangues. Not only descendants of Greeks were Hellenes but all those who shared in their civilization. The struggle they preached passed from a defence of city states to a conflict between cultures and principles of civilization, but Greece, exhausted by its long wars, lacked strength to realize the unity essential for this new crusade. This was nevertheless achieved in spite of Greece under the compulsion of the Macedonians, a vigorous people of non-Hellenic descent but of Greek culture. Since 360 BC the efforts of Philip of Macedonia had been directed to annexing to his kingdom the countries situated north of the Peloponnese, Thrace and Thessaly. He became a dominant personality among the Greeks and was regarded as the leader who would direct the crusade against Asia, which was more prosperous than Europe, where the barbarians were richer than the Greeks.

Philip was cautious, and seeing Artaxerxes reconquer Egypt, he preferred to put the enemy on the wrong scent and negotiate with Persia, which was suppressing all revolts, even in Cyprus. In Athens, Demosthenes violently opposed the pro-Macedonian policy, seeing on the contrary the salvation of his country in an alliance with the Great King. When reproached for betraying the Asiatic Greeks, he replied with the hard truth.

'Are we really interested in these Greeks of Asia? Does not each Athenian general demand his "benevolent" contribution? An Athenian embassy was sent to Susa and an alliance concluded?' Secure on the Athenian front, the king dispatched an army which threw Philip out of Perinthus. Only danger could result for Macedonia from this alliance, and Philip decided to finish with Greece, by force if necessary. Supported by his son, Alexander, he won a decisive victory over Athens and its allies, putting an end to Greek independence (338 BC). In the same year Artaxerxes was poisoned. In striking down the king the murderer also struck a mortal blow at the Empire, which did not long survive him.

It would be inaccurate and unjust to consider the Achaemenian Persians as conquerors, imposing themselves on subject peoples of whom they demanded only blind obedience to their victorious might. It is true that underlying their policy was imperialism, the desire for power, domination and subjugation of those they conquered. In their time the world was divided into very different blocks, the Persian Empire and Greece, each with a civilised and economically balanced life, each with an inclination to extend its way of life to the rest of the world. They were the first to achieve Iranian unity just as they were first to establish the unity of the oriental world, or rather, of the civilized world, the diverse elements of which were brought into a closer relationship than ever before under one political control. The Iranian nation which came into being despite its ethnographical diversity, emerged triumphant from the chaos of languages and civilizations.

The Persians not only founded a world empire, but they also achieved a world civilization with a very wide influence.

The composite constitution of this empire should not be regarded as a sign of inferiority, for other great civilizations – for example, that of Rome – followed a like course. The Persians were as successful in administration as they were in their economy and commerce. Research has shown that outlying countries affected by Achaemenian expansion were profoundly transformed under their beneficent influence. Thus Chorasmia, as well as other eastern possessions, enjoyed nearly three and a half centuries of peace – a rare event in the history of eastern countries at this period – during which time it experienced real urban and agricultural development. At the same period there grew up an irrigation system, of subterranean canals, as in the oases of southern Egypt.

Achaemenian art spread far beyond the frontiers of Iran itself: its influence may be discerned in Egypt, Cyprus, on the coasts of the Black Sea, and in particular among the Scythians. The Achaemenians maintained an atmosphere favourable to the development of science, and we know that under Dariush a great Babylonian astronomer, Naburimanni, made a study of lunar eclipses and arrived at calculations more accurate than those of Ptolemy and Copernicus. Mention should also be made of another astronomer, Kidinnu of Sippar, who towards the end of the Empire discovered the precession of the equinoxes. He arrived at an exact calculation of the length of the equinoxes and arrived at an exact calculation of the length of the year, making an error of only seven minutes, sixteen seconds.

The assassination of Artaxerxes III caused political confusion across the known world at the very moment when a new force, Macedonia, took part. Philip, who had formed a united Greece, assembled a strong Macedonian army supported by the Greek fleet, against Persia, where the throne was occupied by a young prince. Philip was assassinated and his son Alexander the Great who succeeded him, carried on the task begun by his father, with the enthusiasm of youth.

The son of Artaxerxes had been poisoned and replaced by a relative, Dariush (Darius III, Codomannus), but this marked the end of the Achaemanian Empire.

There were changes in the character of commerce. The marketing of cheap goods, which had formed the bulk of merchandise in the preceding period, declined in volume to the advantage of luxury goods and fine wares. A new factor, Rome, had entered the circuit of world commerce with Iran and India supplying raw materials, such as wood and metals, in large quantities. Iran also exported clothing and ornaments, drugs, precious stones, carpets, seed corn, lead and pedigree dogs. Its abundant supplies of raw materials favoured its industrial development, in particular the manufacture of textiles, carpets, and toreutics, for which Iranian artists and craftsmen acquired a well-deserved reputation.

The country also sought to become independent of certain imported goods, such as papyrus, of which Egypt had the monopoly. Some attempt was made to grow plants locally or to substitute parchment. Animals replaced men in the mills, the craftsman increased his production of pottery objects, engraving on bone, and chasing and building, affected by the new trend, also increased.

The European expansion under Alexander and his successors enriched the material culture of Iran to such an extent that several generations were to subsist on its fruits. It left behind a great heritage in administrative organization and in urban development, the principles of the plan of Hippodamus even being adopted by the Sassanian kings, themselves great town builders. The Greeks laid the foundation of the urban life they succeeded in developing. They created a prosperous industry, intensive agriculture, and a flourishing commerce. They covered the country with a network of roads and communications, encouraged the arts and sciences, and introduced a calendar beginning with a new era.

The benefits of these civilizing activities were felt even in distant Chorasmia, where recent archaeological exploration has shown that this epoch was marked by the founding of towns and fortified villages, by advances in agriculture, by increased production of manufactured goods and the focusing of social life round houses of fire. During this expansion of Iranian civilization (the Sassanian), the national economy continued to be based on agriculture rather than trade. Although the Sassanian period ended in the collapse of the ancient order, the administration made notable cultural and political advances. Revenue increased, and there was a more equitable distribution of goods. In both the Roman and Sassanian Empires a process of levelling took place that affected every aspect of life and human activity. This part of the ancient world was undoubtedly in advance of southern, central and northern Europe.

In commerce, Sassanian coinage of silver and copper, more rarely of gold, circulated over a wide area. The bill of exchange appeared during this period and Jewish banking circles in Babylon and analogous Persian institutions played a leading part in its circulation. The bill had been known since the second millennium BC but its use had been limited, and in effect it was no more than the recognition of a debt fixing the date of repayment. In the Sassanian period it became a legally recognized title-deed. The banks of the empire run by Iranians or Jews employed a highly developed system of monetary exchange by writing. How many financiers and bankers know, for example, that the word 'cheque' or the term 'avaliser' come from the Pahlavi language and were invented by the Iranian banking institutions of this remote age? The Christian traders of Syria borrowed the bill from Iran, and introduced it into the west, where it was in use from the Merovingian period.

More money was in circulation in the towns, as is shown by the great number of silver dirhems found in Iran and neighbouring countries in rural districts. However, the wages of the peasant, soldier and official, and even the taxes, were paid in kind.

Commerce was subject to strict control. There were water supplies along the roads, rivers and canals. Officials specially allocated to this service inspected the frontier posts and sea-ports.

The state also established monopolies, of which the most important seems to have been that in raw silks from China. Silk was woven mainly in the Syro-Phoenician workshops, but a rival industry was established by the Sassanian kings on Iranian territory, and the workshops of Susa, Gundeshapur and Shushtar were famous for their products. Luxury china and glassware from the Syro-Palestinian and Alexandrian workshops were imported into Iran. There was considerable trade in textile and clothing. Amber came from the Black Sea, papyrus was still bought, but was increasingly replaced by parchment. The use of paper was not introduced from China until the Islamic period. There was a transit trade in spices from China and Arabia, and nard and pepper were exported from Media.

International trade encouraged the growth of colonies of merchants, particularly Jews and Syrians, who established themselves as far afield as India, Turkestan, Brittany and the Black Sea. The exporting houses became more specialized and confined their dealings to corn, cattle and manufactured goods.

Production improved and expanded, particularly in the silk and glass industries, and this also was marked by a greater degree of specialization. As the result of its monopolies the state became a producer and ran its own workshops. It also intervened in certain private industries, notably those that directly concerned the court, army and administration. It supervised the prices of raw materials and the wages and organization of the workers. New tendencies thus arose, which finally crystallized in the medieval guilds.

The great landowner had his own labourers, carpenters, blacksmiths, weavers, bakers and millers, his oil-press and water mill, the last coming into general use in the 4th century. Agricultural production expanded and innovations were introduced such as the cultivation of mulberry trees and breeding of silk worms which were of great importance in view of the great demand for silk. The great estates belonging to the state and nobility continued to be exploited by the old methods. Improvements could be introduced only on state lands, for there was too little economic liberty to encourage private enterprise.

Xerxes was defeated by the Greeks at Marathon in 490 BC. This marked the end of the Achaemenians and the great history of the Persian Empire. Alexander the Great invaded Persia during the 4th century and accidentally burned down the palace of Persepolis.

The Greek language had begun to spread in Iran when thousands of young aristocrats entered the cavalry formations of the army, while soldiers were recruited into the infantry. Marriages took place between Iranian women and Macedonian men, many of whom remained in Iran. The founding of colonies, as well as commerce, administration and justice, all contributed to the replacement of Aramaic, which had been the official language of the

Achaemenians, by Greek. The Sassanians ruled Persia from 224 to 638 AD, but throughout the centuries the history of Persia was conflict with the Roman Empire and later the Byzantine Empire.

Then between 637 and 642 all Persia was taken by the Arabs and a country which wholly followed the Zoroastrian religion was compulsorily converted to Islam. Many Zoroastrians fled to India and formed a Parsi community and as a result the present population of Zoroastrians in the world reaches only about 130,000.

The Arabs controlled Persia for almost 600 years, and it was only towards the end of this period that they were slowly supplanted by the Turkish Seljuq (Saljug) dynasty. It was the time the Turks absorbed the tattered remnants of the Byzantine Empire. The Seljuqs heralded a new era of Persian literature, art and science, by people such as the mathematician, poet Hakim Omar-Khayam. Then, in the year 1220, Chengiz Khan Moghol (Gengis Khan) swept the country with cold blood and the Seljuq period collapsed.

In the year 1380 there was another invasion by Tamelane (Timur-e-Lang), but in 1502 the Safavid period commenced under the Shah Abbas I (1587–1629). The Safavid period was hastened by an invasion from Afghanistan, but in 1736 Nader Shah overthrew the Afghans, Russians and Turks. On his return from India he was assassinated. Neither Zand or Ghajar periods were notable – only when under Karim Khan-e-Zand in Shiraz.

Then came the Pahlavi dynasty which started with Reza Khan, a former army officer who became Shah after a coup in the nineteen twenties. He was succeed by his son, Mohamad Reza Shah. The dynasty was short-lived and ended with Mohamed Reza Shah being overthrown by the Islamic revolution in 1979. Emam Khomeini, a Kashmiri born, then became the effective ruler of the country. The Islamic fundamentalists enforced a strict dress code for women in particular.

Despite the strength of the fundamentalists the other three major religions in the country, Christianity, Judaism and Zoroastrianism, were all allowed to practise their religions freely. Holy days such as the Christian Christmas, the Jewish Passover and Rosh Hashanah (New Year) and the Zoroastrian New Year (Novrooz) were all celebrated. The most ancient festival in the country, which was celebrated by Cyrus the Great, was Zoroastrian New Year, centuries before.

GENERAL SUMMARY

The great history of the Persian Empire began in Iran when there were two main tribes, the Meads and the Persians. The Meads went west to Media, establishing themselves in Kurdestan on the edge of the Begon valley and in the old valley of Elan (in Kurdestan). It was none the less from the Persian dynasty of the clan Medias that there descended the first king of Media of united Persia. This was Cyrus the Great and the conqueror of Babylon circa 549. He humbled the last king of the Meads and the Babylonian conquest followed, swallowing Babylon. Cyrus advanced through Asia Minor to the sea, dropping down to Syria and Palestine (now called Israel). But he was eventually killed fighting the Syrians.

Cyrus was a moralist who observed the traditions of other nations. He rebuilt the temple in Jerusalem. A Jewish prophet said it was the work of the most high and called Cyrus the Lord's anointed because Cyrus destroyed Babylon. Cyrus's name lives on. His works and traditions were copied throughout Asia and Europe. During that time there were periods of peace and plenty. There may have been plenty of set backs, but the treasures, the jewels, and gold bullion provided a tradition that lasted for two centuries and work for those in the near and far east.

Cyrus's son added Egypt to the Europeans, but he died before he could declare the pretender to the thrown. The restorer to Cyrus's hierarchy, who claimed allegiance to the Cardemonian descent, was Dariush. Although he did not achieve all he wished to in his life, his last words were 'I am Dariush, the Great King of Persia'.

Starting on the high Iranian plateau east of the Zagros mountains in around 4000 BC the kingdom of Media now became the major power of this stage of history. The Syrians took time to come to terms with them in the seventh century, meanwhile the reign of Bslaser, last of the Mesopotamian kings, soon came to an end.

ALL ABOUT THE INGREDIENTS

Juice healing has been one of the oldest remedies amongst the ancient Persians, Greeks and the Romans. Raw juice healing is used in conjunction with the doctor's treatment, and one should always seek a practitioner's advice. As a practice nurse I gathered experience of the beneficial effect of juice healing through working with Doctor Kaboli, who was also a homeopath.

An electric juice extractor is a part of every Persian household but before the electric juice extractor found its way to my mother's kitchen a hand grinder was used.

Raw juice is not the only form of treatment, but simply a natural, safe way to maintain the body in good health, revitalizing, reducing stress and strain. Research has shown that the intake of regular raw fruit and freshly extracted vegetable juice is the answer to restoring health and destroying toxins in the body.

To provide sufficient minerals Dr Kaboli's recommendation was 350ml/12floz carrot juice, the juice of one large raw beetroot of about 200ml/8floz, before breakfast, with the same amount of carrot juice and 150ml/$^1/_4$ pint mixed parsley, coriander and spinach juice before bed time.

To overcome nervous problems Dr Kaboli suggested 2–3 teaspoons of passion flower, brewed and strained, with a little candy sugar, traditionally served with nabat, obtainable in Persian supermarkets. He also suggested a mixture of 2–3 teaspoons of borage, the same amount of Valerian, and half a dried lime (limoo omani) also obtainable in Persian supermarkets, brewed and served with nabat. Camomile and lavender were recommended for a headache, also made as above. Yoghurt whey is an old remedy amongst all Persians as it brings drowsiness before bed time especially if eaten with cucumber (recipe for yoghurt is given in the Basics chapter).

Vegetable skin contains as much or more vitamin as the flesh itself. By cooking the vegetable with other ingredients such as meat, pulses, fish and grains (khoresht) the vitamins, minerals and other goodness remain in the cooking pot, rather than cooking the vegetables and draining them over the kitchen sink, when only a trace of vitamins are left behind. Historically a healthy diet has been achieved by keeping to raw fruit and vegetable juice, with vegetables lightly cooked.

Carbohydrate is part of the diet which produces everyday energy and is found in food such as rice, pulses, and grains and is used abundantly in Persian cooking. Sugar provides energy, white sugar is used in moderation in sweetmeats. Demerara sugar is best for cooking, although fruit contains natural sugar.

Brown bread bought in shops contains colour, whereas nan is made from wholemeal flour and contains natural fibre.

Fat provides twice as much energy as sugar. If too much fat is consumed bodyweight increases substantially. To reduce saturated fats the amount of pulses and grains should be increased to replace animal fat, which as we already know reduces the risk of arteriosclerosis and heart attack.

Always use corn, sunflower or olive oil. Maybe one of the least absorbing oils is rapeseed for frying.

Protein is essential for body growth and is rich in amino acids. One of the most important of these is histidine, which is needed for growing babies. Although egg, milk, meat and fish are some of the best sources of protein, a mixture of pulses, grains, seeds, nuts and legumes are all used in Persian cooking, making a perfect protein diet.

Minerals play a very important part in every diet and are found in some fruits and vegetables.

Obesity is a problem which is not often easy to control with a restricted and boring diet, although the following story illustrates how it can be achieved easily.

Babak was our hard-working cook, helping my mother when a large number of guests were invited. He had worked as a chef in Abadan, in the oil refinery and part of the time in the neighbouring country Iraq, but he was heavily overweight. He had returned after a few years, to settle near his family and friends. He had had a a slight heart attack. After several visits to the hospital he was eventually admitted for one week for observation. He was instructed to take care with his health and to take regular gentle exercise to reduce his weight. He was told to adopt a more healthy diet and to stop smoking.

It was difficult for Babak to follow the instructions as his appetite was enormous, mostly following his old diet. He visited Dr Kaboli in his search for a solution and was advised of Dr Kaboli's recommended remedy.

Begin each meal with a large glass of freshly extracted juice: 350ml/12floz carrot juice, the juice of one large lemon, 200ml/8floz cucumber juice, also the same amount mixture of watercress, spinach, parsley, coriander and celery juice. The idea of the vegetable cocktail is a natural way to satisfy the appetite and more filling than the calorific equivalent of cooked food. The amount of the juice was divided into three parts, and was kept in the fridge over night, to drink before each meal. For breakfast start with citrus juice or fruit, followed by a piece of wholemeal bread/nan, 25g/1oz of protein such as one egg, 25g/1oz low-fat cheese or lean meat or 15g/½oz of nuts. 150ml/¼ pint of low fat milk and the same amount of plain yoghurt was allowed each day. Fruit in moderation, about 3–4 pieces a day, at any time. For lunch a large bowl of salad, as much as he could possibly eat, with most kinds of vegetables, except peas and sweetcorn which had an allowance as for bread (25g/1oz bread was equal to 90g/3oz cooked pulses). Also allowed was tomato purée in moderation, and chicken or vegetable stock (cubes).

Recipe for khoresht (this quantity was for lunch and dinner)

½ teaspoon oil
1 medium onion, chopped

17

2 cloves of garlic, crushed (optional)
175g/6oz lean meat or chicken with skin and fat removed, or fish cut into cubes
$^1/_4$ teaspoon turmeric/cinnamon/saffron or any kind of spice
salt and pepper
as much vegetable, herbs and salad as he liked

Pour $^1/_2$ teaspoon oil into a large saucepan, add the onion and stir for one minute on a very low heat. Cover the pan and allow to cook in its own juice, stir in the garlic with the spices, add the chicken and 175–225ml/6–8floz water, simmer until tender, adding more water into the pan if necessary, add the tomato purée. Finally add the vegetables, simmer for an additional 4–5 minutes. Serve with steamed rice – follow the recipe for plain rice using only $^1/_2$ teaspoon oil for greasing the pan. The total allowance is 9oz for the day.

SPINACH
Esfenaj

The word spinach derives from the word Esfenaj, a Persian word where the vegetable originates from. Dr Kaboli did not consider spinach just as a vegetable, but as a very important treatment, which he often recommended for his patients. It is the best way to treat constipation, being roughage. He was confident that raw spinach juice would prevent any form of disease, 'for its richness and concentration of valuable minerals and vitamins of all sorts'.

Spinach juice is an effective and important substance in building up the blood. It is also one of the best remedies for preventing kidney stones, as it contains a high amount of oxalic acid, and often the juice would be drunk by the majority of the population in Yazd before the complication would occur, which had to be taken in a very large quantity.

Spinach contains vitamin C, E, and B6, with a very high amount of folic acid, which can be destroyed if the spinach is cooked too long, so it is best to add it into the ingredients at the end of cooking, just to mix before removing the pan from the heat.

Dr Kaboli often recommended spinach juice for his elderly and pregnant patients, children and patients suffering with bone disease such as rheumatic problems, in large quantity as it is rich in iron and calcium with an essential function of regenerating the red blood cells, cobalt and iodide.

Spinach juice should be consumed within one to two hours or deep frozen.

TURNIP
Shalgham

Turnip was a winter vegetable and grown on almost every cultivated land in Yazd. It was carefully chosen, complete with root and top, fresh from the farm. The root was cut into small strips and used in salad or as a dip, also delicious when fried in a little oil. The top is known to contain a great amount of calcium, and for the maximum beneficial value. It is best to drink the juice with a mixture of cabbage, spinach and watercress juice, with a pinch of cinnamon. It is also recommended for patients with coughs and colds, with a little lemon juice.

The raw top is also rich in vitamin C: 122mg in 100g. When cooked the amount of vitamin C is reduced by about 39% but the amount of calcium remains the same.

Dr Kaboli's recommendation for depression and prevention of kidney stones was turnip juice, a glass full of the juice was recommended for children every day, to receive enough calcium, accompanied by cabbage, spinach and watercress.

He found that those living in the mountain region, with a simple diet, consuming turnip, spinach and carrot, with plenty of fruit juice, had less risk of haemorrhoids. The length of the treatment was about 9 weeks. It was even more effective in preventing kidney stones if combined with walnuts.

The harsh winter days provided the best memories. Lightly boiled turnips with a sprinkle of salt for our breakfast before leaving for school, to receive our maximum amount of calcium.

Turnip top juice is as valuable as spinach juice.

RHUBARB
Rivas

Rhubarb is cooked at least twice a week when in season, with meat or chicken. It is also used for a medicinal herb in treatment of constipation, and in diarrhoea.

Rhubarb does not have a high vitamin content, and the leaves should not be eaten because they are poisonous.

ONION
Piyaz

Onion is indigenous to Iran, and contains many of the same essential values as garlic. The Persians, Romans and the Greeks used the juice for all digestive problems, and for purifying the blood.

One of the oldest remedies in Yazd was and still is a mixture of onion juice with milk to remove worms from children, also effective on the nervous system. One of the common remedies for catarrh, leading to cold, and a treatment for diseases of the respiratory tract, which includes coughs and cold with bronchitis,

was a mixture of onion juice with warm water and honey, which is still much in evidence today. Onion contains less vitamins and minerals and more sugar than many other vegetables, with few calories (8–9 calories per oz).

PARSLEY
Jaafary

Parsley is a widely known herb in almost all countries with slightly different varieties. Believed to have first been introduced to North America by the Vikings, it may be indigenous to the Mediterranean region.

Parsley is perhaps one of the most commonly used herbs in Iran. It has more vitamin C than any other standard vegetable in use today, with about 167mg per 100g (4oz), which is just over three times as much as citrus fruit. The herb is rich in manganese, calcium and potassium, and extremely high in iron. It was a remedy given by Dr Kaboli to women, to increase the menstruation and help to regulate the monthly period. It is also recommended for preventing kidney stones, as a diuretic and for rheumatism, and as a kind of stimulant. One of the old remedies during the ancient Persian Empire was the use of the plant to treat malaria. It is often given to patients with stomach problems, as it settles the tummy and brings appetite.

The Persians not only use parsley abundantly in cooking, but they also drink the juice to assist the absorption of iron. Because of its powerful quality, it is best to drink 50ml (2oz) of the juice three times a day, preferably mixed with other juices such as carrot juice.

When in season parsley is used by all members of the family, sorted out on a large copper tray and dried on large batik cloths, and stored in polythene bags or jars for winter use. It can also be frozen, which perhaps gives a better flavour to the dish, than dried parsley.

BEANS
Lubia

I felt almost like a stranger and yet very much at home, when I walked along the pavement of the long avenue under the high dusty beech tree in the heat of summer. I walked alone towards the Bazaar, it was difficult at first to recognise the area. My very recent visit after many years, in fact since I was a child.

The streets were typical of Yazd, some had not changed at all. I could even recognize some shop-keepers. Taghi had taken over the business, he was only a boy when I saw him last, working with his father. He used the same old faded wooden chair his father used to sit on, at the entrance to the shop.

There was a young woman whose face I could hardly see. She was wrapped in chador (the long cloth worn by Muslim woman). There was a little girl of only seven holding on to her mother, bearing a great resemblance to Taghi – you could see it was his daughter. I gave the woman and child a smile, the little girl clapped her hands over her face, looking so shy, and buried her face into her mother's clothes then whispered in her ears. My guess was right. I was invited in to take a closer look at the shop. The only display which had changed was the spices rather decoratively served in layers piled in a large bowl. I drifted back to my childhood days. I could almost see myself holding on to Meme's skirt as she chose her pulses. There was almost every type of bean on display, some in large sacks and some in tin bowls, such as black-eyed beans, red kidney beans, lima beans, pinto beans, rosococo beans, white beans. The major ingredients in Persian cuisine, which are all from the haricot bean family, originally from South America.

My research went further when I visited Peru last year to find out that the word haricot derives from the Aztec word Aycolt, going back more than 9,000 years and first introduced to the west by the Spanish during the 1500s.

But broad beans (Lima-Esque) originate from north America. During summer, when they are in season, the beans are boiled with their young skin, drained and served in a large plate with a sprinkle of salt, held with the fingers by the tail end as you would eat asparagus. A staple food for the poor across the Mediterranean.

The soy bean is very high in protein and a very important part of the diet world-wide. It originates from Southwest Asia, going back over 4,000 years.

The Persian diet is always rich in health, as shown by the thick soup 'Ash' with its major ingredients being various beans with a high amount of protein and hardly any fat.

French beans, known in France as haricots verts, have a short season in Iran, when a housewife does her best to feed the family with different dishes while in season.

With string beans it is best to cook them whole rather than cutting them in half or slicing them as they will lose their value during cooking.

As a juice remedy there is not a high content of vitamin in this vegetable, but it is richer in vitamin B6 than most other fruit and vegetables.

Although Iranians are known for drying their vegetables for winter use before the freezer was invented, there was never great satisfaction in drying French beans as they lose their flavour so they are best frozen.

A remedy by Dr Kaboli for diabetics and patients with nervous problems and gout, who of course were strictly controlled by his prescription and advice, was: a large glass of French bean juice – about 350ml/12floz was recommended – also a mixture of cabbage or Brussels sprouts, with a pinch of ground cinnamon and salt. The diet was continued until the end of the season.

GARLIC
Sir

Garlic, indigenous to Persia, is used abundantly, its history going back more than 5000 years. It is believed to be the remedy for restoring complete health. Garlic contains much of the quality of the onion, has a powerful effect on health, is an excellent vegetable and an effective disinfectant.

A dish from ancient Zoroastrian times that is still

popular in Zoroastrian homes today is rue and garlic sauce.

Garlic juice was often made with a mortar and pestle, until the electric juice extractor found its way into my mother's kitchen.

To extract the garlic juice you may need a spare juice extractor, because its strong essential oil is extremely difficult to remove from the machine.

During my nursing days practising with Dr Kaboli, research in natural food showed that garlic can destroy the bacterium staphylococcus, can improve the condition of arteriosclerosis (thickening and hardening of the walls of the arteries) and lower the blood pressure.

The old remedy in Yazd is still in evidence and used regularly for patients with cold, coughs and catarrh.

One tablespoon of garlic juice in a large glass of warm water is a cure for worms. It is also a remedy for patients who suffer with diarrhoea, dysentery, enterocolitis (inflammation of the intestine) and tuberculosis. Garlic is also an expectorant and helps asthma sufferers and patients with bronchitis.

Garlic is a common food source of germanium, and is also richer in selenium than any other fruit or vegetable.

HORSERADISH
Torob-E-Koohi

It all begins during spring. Herbs, vegetables and fruit have a great significance in a Persian family. Everyone queues to buy their share and more.

The shop is full of herbs wrapped in bundles piled high against the wall almost to the ceiling, looking just like a garnish. White spring onions, large purple radishes (Torob) with their long shape, some in creamy white, large in size with their delicate or peppery flavour in many different forms and shapes. But the most popular is the scarlet red radish: round and sweet with their crispy green leaves used in salad. Young radish pods are also edible with a spicy flavour.

The radish is believed to be indigenous to the Eastern Mediterranean. An important part of the Egyptian diet by 2000 BC, it found its way to China during 500 BC and was known in Japan in AD 700. Now it is widely cultivated almost all over the world.

The word radish derives from the Latin radix, meaning 'root', and is from the same species as mustard.

Horseradish (Torob-e-koohi) is a seasonal vegetable, a favourite salad dish for all Persians, and is much stronger than radish with a very sharp, peppery taste.

A remedy for patients suffering with sinus problems is to pound the horseradish with lime juice and a pinch of salt, which can be kept in a jar and refrigerated for about two weeks. One teaspoon is to be taken twice a day, once in the morning after breakfast. with nothing to eat or to drink for at least one hour, and once before bed time, after the evening meal, accompanied with 150ml/6fl oz juice of mixed radish, its leaves, carrot and juice of one lemon. It is recommended to stay in bed for at least one hour after taking this, because the strength of the vegetable will cause sweatiness with runny eyes. Sometimes it is necessary to continue the treatment for a few weeks for the best result. You may also find that horseradish sauce bought in supermarkets is effective for the common cold.

This remedy is also recommended as a regular drink to prevent kidney stones, and was given to patients with water retention.

Horseradish contains a high amount of vitamin C, potassium, and sulphur, and is also rich in calcium.

GINGER
Zanjafil

This herb, with its great value and enormous quality, acts as a remedy against cardiovascular disease. Very much like the Iris "bulb" by the name of Rhizome, it is believed to be indigenous to India, was next known in Egypt, then its popularity grew all over the west.

Ginger provides high protection from stroke and heart attack, because of its ability to prevent blood clotting. It is often recommended as an alternative to aspirin for those with irritation of the gastro-intestinal tract.

An old remedy in Chinese medicine as a tonic for digestive problems, ginger absorbs and neutralises the toxins in the stomach. It is also valuable for controlling the production and secretion of bile from the liver and gallbladder.

Dr Kaboli often recommended ginger for controlling the level of cholesterol in the body.

This versatile herb is also recommended for motion sickness and nausea, colds and coughs, stomach problems such as constipation, indigestion and flatulence, headaches and sinus congestion.

ALMONDS
Badam

Spring gave a spectacular colour to the sunken garden. My most vivid memory is the brilliant different-coloured roses beside the almond trees covered in blossom, the first colour to appear at the beginning of the season.

Almond trees grew everywhere, especially in the mountain region, their branches covered in blossoms, shadowed by the barren rocky hills being irrigated by the mountain stream which ran underneath the rocks.

Most almond kernels are sweet. But if they are bitter they have a minute amount of prussic acid when uncooked, which is made edible by heating to a high temperature, the same as some apricot and peach kernels (the bitter kernels were burned, pounded and placed over cut wounds). There is always fresh almond oil in a Persian home, made by a member of the family, a ready remedy for ear ache especially for children. The pulps are never discarded as they are mixed and pounded with sugar and ground cinnamon to make a delicious snack.

Almonds are also grown in parts of America such as California, also in Australia and South Africa and extensively in the Mediterranean. In America bitter almonds are used for flavouring liqueurs. Almonds are rich in protein and also contain calcium, folic acid, magnesium, potassium, vitamin E, riboflavin and fibre.

PERSIMMONS
Khormaloo

Almost every house in the capital city Tehran or a city with a similar climate, owns a persimmon tree. Ours was mature with the branches spreading, shading the balcony from the midday sun. The branches were laden with orange-coloured fruit, which did not ripen until late autumn, around October.

If the fruit is picked before it is ready, it is not pleasant at all as it covers the mouth with fluffy bits. If it is picked during harvesting time and still firm to touch, it is placed on the window ledge in a warm atmosphere, e.g. kitchen window, for a few days until soft. It is best to pick and eat the persimmon when it is over ripe and at its best.

It grows in many countries, such as the Gulf states and in the warmer climates of states such as California and the American south east. Japan also grows its own kind, which may have originated from China called KaKi and traditionally it is dried and only used by some families for New Year celebrations.

Persimmon is also cultivated in France, Africa and parts of South America such as Brazil. There are mixed feelings about the origins of Californian persimmons but it is widely believed they were introduced to the country from Asia during the 16th century.

Thanks to the Israelis we also have the sharon fruit from the same family, which can be eaten when firm to the touch.

LEMON
Limoo

For centuries the lemon has been known for its high amount of vitamin C. It is used in many Persian dishes, for its quality and beneficial value, and also as a summer drink. Lemonade was a popular refreshing drink during the time of Genghis Khan, and still is in Persian homes today.

During hot summer days a mixture of water,

lemon and sugar is not only drunk by the family, but the drink is always ready for unexpected guests, served in glasses held by silver holders. It is a drink known to bring the body temperature down, and especially to prevent dehydration.

If someone is suffering from a sore throat or fever it is best to add honey to the lemon juice instead of sugar.

The left over pulp from the lemon is excellent for the skin and is a quick remedy for a sting. A mixture of the pulp or a little of the juice with toilet water and glycerine is rubbed into the skin for a smooth result.

Demonstration has shown that extract of lemon when it is vaporized will neutralize the antibodies of meningococcus, typhoid, pneumococcus and staphylococcus in just over two hours. Dr Kaboli recommended lemon juice as an important tonic for cases of respiratory tract infection.

LETTUCE
Kahoo

Lettuce is one of the earliest vegetables to be cultivated. A family favourite in salad, the lettuce season begins during early spring. Cos lettuce is the most popular, and has been known since the Middle Ages. It is bought by the dozen, to allow two or three per person eaten as a mid-morning snack dipped in a mixture of lemon juice and golden syrup.

Lettuce oil applied on the forehead and temple is a treatment for headache.

Dr Kaboli recommends lettuce for his male patients who suffer from premature orgasm. It also has a calming effect on sexual ardour. And by increasing the intake of lettuce by male patients the level of fertility has been shown to increase.

The ancient Persians and the Greeks believed lettuce had a calming effect on the nervous system and digestive organs. The vitamin content includes a fair amount of carotene and a good spectrum of minerals. But it is essential to know that the outer leaves may contain fifty times more goodness than the white inner leaves.

ORANGES
Porteghal

Oranges have a modest amount of mineral but a ripe small fruit contains an average of 50mg of vitamin C in 100g (4oz). Concentrated orange juice has been known to reduce high blood pressure and is a helpful treatment for colds. A daily glass is therefore recommended, especially during the winter months, to store Vitamin C in the body.

APPLE
Sib

Cultivation of apples goes back more than three thousand years, with many thousands of different kinds, wild and edible. It is usually a suitable form of fruit to be grown in cool climates and is believed to be indigenous to the Baltic region.

There are many different varieties of apples in the USA, such as Washington State, May Queen, and so on. The English have their own such as Granny Smith, Golden Noble, Reinette, Ontario, King of the Pippins, Coxes and many others. The French are proud of their Golden Delicious. But the Persians also have their own special home-grown varieties, such as rosewater apple (or sib-e-golab), which is very small and green with a strong scent of rosewater; red apple (or sib-e-sorkh); yellow apples (or sib-e-zard); and sour apple (or sib-e-torsh) used for cooking.

In Yazd apples are grown mostly in the mountain region, as the city is arid and not suitable for growing the crop.

We always looked forward to our summer present from family or friends, when apples and other fruit were sent to us packed in large wooden boxes in between large vine leaves. Research has shown that the Vitamin C content varies according to variety. Varieties high in Vitamin C include Pippins, Golden Nobles, Bramleys and Coxes. Those with less include Rome Beauty and Laxton Superb while Golden Delicious seems to be in the middle range.

Apples have a very high mineral content, and also

contain pectins, malic acid and tannic acid, all very important elements to the intestines. They are also an important source of cleanser and for purifying the blood, a general tonic especially helpful for skin and liver. As the juice oxidises quickly is best to keep it in the refrigerator for a short while.

Apple has as little as 15 calories per oz. It contains vitamin C, thiamine, riboflavin, nicotinic acid, carotene, vitamin B6, biotin and folic acid. It also has a very small amount of sodium and is rich in potassium and phosphorous. One of the best refreshing drinks served as a family drink in Iran is apple juice, which is excellent in overcoming a liverish feeling, with helping the digestive system, and good for flushing the kidneys. Recommended by Dr Kaboli is a mixture of apple, beetroot and tomato juice to be taken daily to improve the complexion.

APRICOT
Zardaloo

It was on my very recent visit to Esfahan, the great city of the Saffavid dynasty, that I took a pleasurable walk along the Zayendeh Rood, with the river passing through this historical city. Then I decided to walk even further, amongst the hundreds and thousands of apricot trees just on the outskirts of the city. The trees were laden with fruit, and there was tranquillity in the surrounding area. The ripened fruit were smashed on to the hot ground, filling the atmosphere with their sweet scent. I picked them and ate more than my share. The fruit is known to have grown in the area for more than 2000 years, having been brought from neighbouring Armenia.

It was the Romans who took the first fruit back with them from Persia, spreading it throughout the western world.

Choose apricots when ripe or firm to the touch, as the carotene builds up in the final stages of the ripening period, at least 200 per cent more than when picked immature. It is best to eat the fruit fresh within one day and no longer, as they may lose the high amount of vitamins C and A.

The numerous apricot trees in our garden gave enough fruit for all the family, relations and neighbours. The juice was frozen for winter use, which often was mixed with other fruit and vegetable juices for variation. The fruit itself was also dried and stored for winter.

CARROTS
Havij

One of the most important vegetables, especially in the form of juice, is the carrot, which produces carotene from its yellow colour, which is pro vitamin A (rather than containing vitamin A) meaning when the vegetable reaches the body it will produce vitamin A. To increase the vitamin A in children Dr Kaboli recommends a mixture of carrot juice and milk, one of the safest ways to take in vitamin A.

For the best result the very yellow carrot juice (in Iran the very red) is recommended as it has the highest amount of carotene. The new crop and first in season are pale and have the lowest amount of carotene.

Dr Kaboli recommends expecting and nursing mothers to drink the juice as this will increase their milk production. Also to eat raw carrots as snacks, instead of butter and eggs, as they all contain the same vitamin A.

BEETROOT
Choghondar

The ancient Greeks and Persians believed that beetroot was good for relaxation and cooling the blood. They also used it to treat patients with signs of fever, and as a regular diet for children. The amount of iron in beetroot is not as high as has been presumed, and it has few calories.

If beetroot is boiled for around two hours it loses most of its vitamins, but retains its mineral content. It is best to drink raw beetroot juice, which has a stimulating effect on the nervous system, and is especially good for the intestine. The Persians even to this day use beetroot juice for malignant disease in large quantities.

Amongst the Zoroastrian population in Yazd a mixture of carrot, cucumber and beetroot juice was a part of a regular diet for building the blood and, for people of both sexes, a cure for sexual weakness. It can also be used to prevent kidney stones, and as therapy for gall-bladder, liver and prostate problems.

Beetroot can be kept longer than many other vegetables in a cool dry place. I have vivid memories of my childhood, when large quantities of beetroots were buried deep in the garden, to be used almost all the year around until the next season.

If beetroot is cooked whole in water just to eat as salad rather than with other ingredients, remove the grit and wash well before boiling, taking care not to break the skin. If peeled the red juice will escape and leave the vegetable pale.

A Persian housewife does not discard the green leaves, as they contain a high amount of carotene and minerals, and can be used in salad, cooked as an alternative to spinach or the juice can be extracted and drunk mixed with carrot juice.

CABBAGE
Kalam

Cabbage is an unusual vegetable, which comes in many colours and shapes. Some are green and others are red, some have smooth leaves, others are wrinkled. It is believed to be indigenous to western Europe from the coast of Mediterranean.

As research has shown, due to the natural oil in the plant, it has the similar result to garlic with its antibiotic properties. One of the major benefits of cabbage is its effect on patients with gastric ulcer or digestive problems.

Dr Kaboli recommends concentrated cabbage juice as more effective than eating the cabbage raw or slightly cooked. In the case of ulcers it is best to be taken for about two weeks and in more serious conditions longer – about 7–8 weeks. This also has been proved in the west with astonishing good results. Dr Kaboli prescribed cabbage juice in moderation for his patients, as in larger quantities it could lead to thyroid problems.

CUCUMBER
Khiyar

Cucumber is one of the most common seasonal vegetables in Persia. The harvesting begins in early spring when they have an extremely delicate flavour. In the form of gherkin (khiyar) it can be eaten in the morning for breakfast, with feta cheese, honey or golden syrup and Nan. The same menu can be used for a midday snack. Cucumber mixed with yoghurt makes a good starter for lunch and dinner, or can be used as a side salad or a garnish on fruit trays. Cucumber juice is recommended for its properties to increase the flow of urine, to help the kidneys and the digestive system, and a large quantity of cucumber juice is a remedy for rheumatic conditions. Cucumber is very low in calories and high in potassium. It contains about 4 calories per ounce (25g).

The juice and the skin are recommended to use on hands and face for smoother skin.

Khiyar chang is a long curly shape, with pale green skin, and is eaten a few at a time.

PEACH
Holoo

The botanical name for peach is prunus persica (named after Persia). It was first brought from China to Persia, maybe at the same time as oranges, by the Portuguese explorers.

It was first transplanted to Rome from Persia then spread through to the rest of Europe and eventually the Spanish immigrants took the fruit back to America with them, where it has been widely cultivated since.

CELERY
Karafs

It is a strong belief in Iran today – as it was during the ancient Persian era – that celery helped to prevent kidney stones, liver, and gall bladder problems, and was also a cure for constipation. The best parts of this vegetable are the leaves, the bulbous roots and the stem, which contain the highest medicinal properties. It contains minerals and vitamins and a high concentration of hormones and essential oils, which give celery its strong and characteristic smell. Its oil has a specific effect in helping to rid the body of water and has a good calming effect on the nervous system. Dr Kaboli's recommendation for people with sleeping and sexual disorders, is to take two dessertspoonfuls of honey in celery juice to relax and bring drowsiness and to improve sexual ability. It can also reduce appetite if sipped slowly before a meal. As celery helps in the control of arthritis and rheumatism, it is beneficial to eat it raw in salad or in the form of juice. It is also delicious when cooked. But take care not to over cook and just stir for one or two minutes – enough to fuse the flavour of the ingredients.

WATERMELON
Hendevaneh

In midsummer the cellar floor was covered with all kinds of melon, the number of watermelon alone reached thirty or more. Some had dark skin and some pale green, and they had already been tested by baba (father) at the farm he bought them from.

To test watermelon: if they feel hefty and make a crunchy sound when pressed between the palms of your two hands, they are sweet and fresh.

Once melon and watermelon are picked from their stems they are ready to eat, as they will not ripen further, the same as cucumber, courgettes, marrow and pumpkin as they are all the same family, with almost exactly the same blossom.

As a little girl I passed the cultivated land every morning. During spring the newly grown shoots would appear slowly, their crawling stems reaching a few metres in length, spreading over the especially raised ploughed land, which was irrigated by pur-chased water.

Melon or watermelon is not eaten sparingly in a Persian home. During the day each person can eat one whole fruit or even more as it is the best summer drink with 92 per cent liquid.

There are two kinds of watermelon. The more popular has a very rich red colour and occasionally yellow flesh.

Watermelon can be kept in a cool place for several weeks. The family would often keep watermelon to celebrate the longest night (Shab-E-Yalda). It is believed to originate from Africa.

CORIANDER
Geshnis

A herb indigenous to Persia and India, coriander is one of the basic herbs in Persian cooking. Almost every day it is used in some form, fresh, dried or frozen, usually for cooking rather than in a herb bowl.

It is best not to substitute parsley for coriander as it will not have the same flavour, and will not give the authentic taste to the dish. The seeds are also used in cooking, which are first roasted then ground and used in powder form.

The introduction of coriander into the west was by the Romans. First the seeds were used in flavouring bread and biscuits. Also it is common to use the roasted seeds in pickles, to give that special flavour. The powder is used in Persian cooking but is not as common as say turmeric or saffron.

DILL
Sheveed

Dill is native to Persia, western India and the Far East. It was first brought to Europe during AD 800 by the Roman emperor Charlemagne. Dill became a popular herb and was often used in salads and fish dishes. A popular dish in Scandinavia is salmon served with cucumber and dill salad.

Sir Anthony Sherley (1565–1635), who went to Persia as a politician and tradesman in the year 1599, and was the first ambassador to the country, was offered a dish cooked with dill almost on his arrival. He returned to Europe as the envoy of the shah abbass.

Dill is also used in pickles, and has a reputation for lowering the cholesterol level.

Although the leaves are very similar to fennel they have a completely different flavour and must not be mistaken.

FENUGREEK
Shanbelileh

Fenugreek is very strong in flavour, and used very occasionally in Persian cuisine. But it is a must as a major ingredient in lamb in herb sauce (khoresht-e-ghormeh sabsi) as without this herb the dish will never taste the same.

Fenugreek is used in a very small quantity otherwise it will give a very strong and unpleasant flavour to the dish. The use of fenugreek is meticulously stated in the recipes.

It is known for its medicinal quality, and said to be good for those with diabetes and hypertension. The herbs are dried for winter use. But in the west it is available throughout the year in Persian and Indian supermarkets. It can be chopped fine and frozen for use.

PEAS
Nokhod Farangi

One of my joys during the summer season was helping Memeh (mother) to clean herbs and vegetables, and maybe one of my favourite was podding the freshly picked peas, as I would eat them raw, almost like a meal. And baba (father) would tell me the history during summer break from school.

The history of peas goes back for centuries. It was a major part of the Roman diet, who grew nearly forty different varieties, and was eaten mostly in the form of soup. The Italian and French have had the triumph of growing their own kind, such as 'piselli novell' meaning new peas and the 'petit pois' meaning small peas in French – one of the popular kind sold frozen in most supermarkets today.

It is believed peas were brought to the west from central Asia or the near East, where they were eaten fresh, uncooked as is a common habit amongst Persians even to this day.

Fresh peas are seasonal in Persia. It was my joy as a child to stand on the flat roof of the house to watch the Muslim lady sakineh approaching, carrying her large batik cloth on her back filled with fresh peas. She was really very tired reaching the door, and was glad when Memeh decided to buy a few kilos off the weight before she would carry the rest to the next door neighbour.

SAFFRON
Zaaferon

Thick new-born violets a soft carpet spread
and clustring lotos swell'd the rising bed
and sudden hycinths the turf bestrow
and flow'ry crocus made the mountain glow

Tlida, book 4

The Greek called this plant KPOXOS or KPOXOV. The Romans called it crocus, after a beautiful youth, who was consumed by his impatient love for Smilax. Hercules, his father, changed him into the flower that still bears his name. Smilax was changed into a plant called smilax or bindweed.

This spice was known early to the Romans who used it as perfume and for scattering on the street when welcoming their honoured guests. It was also used for inflammatory conditions, especially those of the eyes. It was valued for use against ulceration of the stomach, breast and liver, and as a treatment for coughs, colds and pleurisy.

The physicians who visited Anthony and Cleopatra in Egypt recommended the use of saffron for clearing their complexion, as it would prevent jaundice.

The Greeks sprinkled it in their palaces to celebrate a special occasion. The Persians not only used it for dyeing their robes and bed clothes, but also for perfuming their palaces. It was recommended by physicians for patients suffering with heart problems.

The Persians always liked to use saffron for flavouring and garnishing their food, preparing and setting the dishes before the king's court and for special occasions.

In India after the death of the Buddha, the priests dyed their robes with saffron. Artists used it in their water colours.

Saffron is beneficial for many diseases if taken in moderation. But it is dangerous if taken in large doses. Dr James says the dosage for saffron for those who are not accustomed to it should not be increased half a scuple, but can be increased gradually to one drachm.

Saffron was intoduced from Persia to India and Egypt during 500 BC, then brought to Europe by the Romans, but as the Roman Empire declined, the use of saffron diminished.

My grandfather named saffron as one of the most expensive spices, as valuable as gold, and gave it as Novrooz (new year) presents to his friends. The best saffron is in full orange colour. My father often used a small quantity when making wine as it would give a reddish-yellowish colour. It is always best to use it fresh while it is not too dry or too moist, with a very firm, strong smell.

Saffron is a native of Persia, where it grows in the mountain region of Mashad, the holy city of Islam, where I watched the most labour-intensive production, with many men and women carefully gathering the pistils from each blossom from one bulb. Over 8,000 blossoms were to be picked to produce 455g (1lb) of dried saffron. It also grows in the southern extremities of Europe.

The best saffron can be bought in Persian shops, usually in the form of a very strong string of a very reddish colour. The best and most economical way to use saffron is to put a small oven proof dish or pan in a very hot oven or under the grill for 2–3 minutes then switch off the heat. Remove the pan from the heat, add in the saffron strings, return the dish to the cooling heat, and leave for about one minute. This will make the thread crisp. Crush the strings between two large spoons or, if using a large quantity, grind into powder in a coffee grinder.

CINNAMON
Darchin

Cinnamon is a form of brown bark favoured by the ancients because of its sweet odour.

Cinnamon is a native of the east Indies, which is confined to the Island of Ceylon. The value of the bark is for its rarity rather than its quality. It was at a very early date – around 1727 BC – when it was first introduced to Canaan at the time of Jacob. It is known that the Queen of Sheba carried a present of gold, precious stones and spices (cinnamon) with her wherever she went. King Solomon recognized cinnamon as a luxury which came from a long way away, over the dangerous roads of desert and sands, and he perfumed his bed with it. Recent research has shown that cinnamon has medicinal benefits, especially for those suffering from diabetes.

LENTILS
Adas

The ancient Zoroastrians were good warriors, fighting on horseback with bow and arrow. On one occasion when the Persians succeeded in defeating the Romans in 53 BC, it was believed their everyday diet of lentils kept their blood cool and nerves calm. This philosophy spread out to the rest of the east, following the Persian way of diet.

SPICES
Advieh

Many thousands of years ago Farsi language became popular in India, now the nearest is the Ordu language with a mixture of Persian alphabets, one of which has remained. The most popular term still used in cooking is Garm Masalah (Garm in Farsi or Persian language meaning 'hot', masalah meaning article or materials), garam masaleh in Indian and adviyeh in Arabic mean medicine, on account of spices such as saffron, with its medicinal reputation, and cinnamon, for its astringent quality.

Spices vary depending on region to region. Nearer to the south and Bandar Abbas the blend of spices becomes hot, including ginger, cumin and coriander, and their cookery books are based on hotly spiced ingredients. This is due to the passer-by traders from the Indian subcontinent and the influence of the neighbouring Arab country Iraq. In the Caspian region there is more Russian influence and, like the rest of the country, the ingredients become subtle with a blend of fruit and nuts mildly spiced with turmeric, saffron and cinnamon.

POTATO
Sibzamini

Potato picnics began in early autumn. The small potatoes were buried under the hot ash in the garden, with the rising smoke giving the cool autumn air a misty look.

The early evening sun was pale. The garden looked grey and the ground was covered in autumn leaves with winter birds flying overhead sending their sound down, the sign of approaching winter.

Everyone gathered in the corner of the garden away from the cool draught, which blew over patchy snow over Shirkooh, the mountain of milk.

Each waited for their 'Koloogheh', some busy playing chess, my brothers played citar, Memeh was busy knitting. But my vivid memory is baba telling me the history of vegetables. One of which was the potato, a vegetable known to be responsible for causing leprosy and lust.

The religious people of Scotland avoided eating potato, because it was a vegetable not mentioned in the Bible. Although it has been said that potatoes were grown over 6000 years ago not far from Lake Titicaca, it was during the year 1532 that the Spanish arrived in Peru to look for gold, and found the potato, a vegetable precious to the Andes, where it was believed its consumption made labour easy for pregnant women.

Charles Darwin, the English scientist on his travels around the world during the 1830s, made a stop in the south part of Chile, where he discovered the potato plant and thought it to be of the same family as Solanum Tuberosm, a plant thought to be indigenous to Chile.

Peru, where potatoes originate from and where they were cultivated by the Incas for over 2000 years before the arrival of the Spanish in the 16th century, has up to 4000 varieties of potatoes. Many are in root form and different colours, yellow, white, sandy white, yellow purple, which are rather dry, yellow sweet and many others.

I have just returned from the 'capital' of potatoes in Puno and Cuzco in the Andes. There are at least 18 varieties of potatoes grown in the area, at a height of 4600 ft above sea level. After flowering the plant produces small green or purple-green berries which are poisonous. The potatoes also grow wild in the Amazon jungle, and I watched varieties such as Yaca being dug out of the ground. They also produce different flavours by mixing some varieties in the form of mash.

I was astonished and delighted to meet the Amazonians, especially their way of life. I watched as the traditional drink was made from potatoes. First the potatoes are boiled and when soft they are mashed in a large copper, boat-shaped bowl, placed on a high flame. Beside an old lady is sitting and constantly chewing some of the potatoes, pouring them into a bowl with her saliva to fuse with the rest, then the mixture is boiled again to make a traditional drink.

It was during the 17th century, when Charles V, King of Holland, Germany, Austria and Spain ordered potatoes and tomatoes to be imported to Germany. Then the cultivation of potatoes spread rapidly and they became a staple diet especially in Ireland and northern Europe. The crop was taken to north America by the Irish and Scottish in the early part of the 18th century.

There was widespread famine in Ireland during 1845 and 1846, as the European crop suffered from an epidemic of late blight (phytophthora infestans) when an estimated million people died in Ireland due to starvation, and soon after one million emigrated to the United States. The cultivation of potatoes now is widespread in the world, especially in more of the tropical regions, for human and animal consumption.

Potatoes are low in calories – about 20 calories per ounce. Of course by frying the amount of calories increases by at least three times. As the vitamin lies just beneath the skin it is best to bake or boil potatoes. By boiling, the content of vitamin C is reduced by 20 per cent. But when peeled and boiled the vitamin C content is reduced by 50 per cent. If potatoes are kept long, some shoots will appear which must be removed together with any green parts which contain a toxic alkaloid called solanine. As children we were treated with raw potatoes sliced with their crunchy and nutty texture. The juice was drunk to reduce indigestion, also as a soothing remedy for the gastric tract. The vegetable was also a help to those suffering with duodenal and gastric ulcers. My grandmother, who was very health conscious, was anxious we had our share of potato juice to relieve constipation.

TOMATOES
Govjeh Farangi

Tomatoes originate in the Andean region of South America, mainly Ecuador and Peru, and were grown by the Maya and Aztecs before the arrival of the Spanish, as early as 700 AD.

Conquistadors who reached Mexico during the 16th century brought the seeds back with them to Spain, from where the plant spread to Portugal, Italy, and the south of France. Then it slowly found its way to northern Europe. The Spanish also introduced this plant to their colonies, which at the time were the Caribbean, Florida, California, Texas and the American west.

The popularity of tomatoes grew amongst European countries, as the French called it the love apple, the Germans the apple of paradise. But the British were reluctant to adopt this brilliant red-coloured vegetable as a part of their cooking, as they thought it dangerous, being from the family of deadly nightshade. This fear was also prevalent among some American colonists until the year 1812 when tomatoes were eaten in every region of America.

It was not until 1850 when the popularity of the tomato grew in almost every American city. By the 1880s tomatoes grown in the suitable climate of Florida were distributed around the rest of the USA. They have since become one of the most favourite vegetables in the U.S. Now the cultivation of tomatoes is the largest in the world.

In 1893 the supreme court of the USA proved that the tomato should be considered as a vegetable rather than a fruit, as it was eaten cooked with the meal. But more often than not a Persian house wife garnishes the tray or bowl of fruit with tomatoes.

Fresh tomatoes can be kept at room temperature, between 54–70 degrees, if green, and once they are fully ripened they can be refrigerated like other fruit for just a few days, but if kept in the fridge too long they will lose their flavour like other fruit. If tomatoes are harvested green to ripen afterwards the vitamin C content is about 26mg per 100g, whereas if picked ripe there is almost twice the amount: around 44mg per 100g. One average tomato weighing about 3oz produces about one and half times our recommended daily intake of vitamin C and 20 per cent of our vitamin A. The tomato is a good source of fibre, carbohydrate, potassium and iron. It contains very low amounts of fat and sodium.

My research on tomatoes in Peru would not have been completed without trying the most delicious tomato dessert in heavy syrup picked from the tree.

WINE
Sharab

Here with little bread beneath the bough
A flask of wine book of verse and thou
Beside me singing in wilderness
Oh wilderness were paradise enow

Persian poet Hakim Omar-e-Khayam, who wrote about food, wine and love, was born in the third century. His poetry spread into the then civilised world during the 9th century.

Autumn was the end of the season for most fruit. But the time was ripe for grapes of all shapes and sizes with different flavours. Almost everyone in Yazd had a vine orchard, and more often than not guests were invited to spend the day in the bagh (orchard) sitting around the crystal clear stream ready for a picnic eaten with grapes. It was also time for wine making.

The large storage room was prepared with bunches of grapes neatly and separately laid on sofreh (white cloth) spread along the tiled floor, to rest for a week. The grapes were squeezed daily in a large barrel. The whole process took several weeks before producing sweet red wine – an important part of the meal in the Jewish religion at all times, repeated 115 times in the Old Testament. Wine was also important in the Zoroastrian religion, for celebrating happy occasions such as weddings and Novrooz (the Persian new year) and for family dinners and parties.

It all began when Jamshid Shah, the legendary king of Persia, saved a nightingale struggling from a coiling snake. In return the bird scattered seeds into the palace garden, producing delicious sweet berries, and as there were too many to consume all at once, some were turned into juice to be saved for later. But the juice turned bitter and foul-tasting and was declared to be poisonous.

The desperately ill queen could not stand her agony any longer and drank a cup of the poison to put an end to her life peacefully. But instead she woke up refreshed with perfect health.

The legend also says that when the Lord asked Noah to build the ark he was also asked to put animals and birds into the ark so that when the water dried up the earth would become fertile and vegetation would grow. As Noah was a keen gardener he took a couple of roots with him, so he could celebrate after the flood with his friends. The legend says when the flood receded and Noah had his party he had a severe hangover the next day.

It is known that the Egyptians buried wine with their king. It has been said that when the Jews had to leave Egypt during the exodus they were sorry for leaving the wine behind.

But Islam has a different view. The Arab invasion during the 7th century and the spread of Islam throughout Persia led to prohibition. Despite that, Hakim Omar-e-Khayam's poem is full of passion for love, wine and bread. Alcoholic drinks were replaced by Sharbat Drinks made from various fruits (Sharbat in Arabic means drink). Rose water (golab) or water from the rose became popular in the Arab world. Non alcoholic drinkers became creative in every part of Iran, each area having its own speciality, such as the famous punch drunk in the west, a drink from the south (Abadan) which was a mixture of five fruit juices, one of which was grape juice. Soon after, during the 7th century, the Portuguese traders on their way from China back to Europe stopped off for refreshment at the strait of Hormoz or the Persian Gulf. They quenched their thirst with the drink punch, which was made from grape juice, rose water, lemon, sugar, ground cinnamon, lemon juice and crushed ice. The grape juice was replaced by wine, and a new name for Europeans became punch rather than panj (number five in Persian). The drink was also welcomed by English and European travellers during the eighteenth and nineteenth century, as a refreshing drink.

TEA AND COFFEE
Chay va ghahveh

The Arabian conquest of Persia and the consequent and compulsory conversion to Islam led to a sudden decline in Persian culture. Not only did they introduce their religion, but they also brought the prohibition of wines and spirits, an important part of the meal on all occasions for other religions.

When tea arrived from China over 1500 years ago with the early Persian caravans it did not gain popularity as wine was the important drink at the time. It was not until the conquests of Moghol (Mongol), when the country was already under Islamic rule, that tea became more widespread with great popularity as an alternative drink to wine.

The Arab ghahveh (coffee) found its way into Iran in the late part of the 8th and during the 9th century. Mostly drunk for religious ceremony, it also began to be used as an everyday hot drink. Until it was banned in Iran because of its stimulating quality, the use of coffee was dedicated to mourning ceremonies (this also became popular amongst the Zoroastrian community, with the serving of ground dried coffee with sugar on the first, second and third days after someone had died). In recent years granulated coffee is served in restaurants and coffee houses. Also Turkish coffee is served in very small cups, and at mid morning social hen parties where predicting the future is a form of income for some.

Tea is never served in a cup or with milk. Guests are offered black tea in small estekan glasses held by silver holders with a sugar lump and a choice of limes. Tea is always drunk in a see-through glass, or for the family at home in a cup with a sprinkle of cinnamon and served with sugar candies (Nabat).

Most of the supply of tea in Iran is grown in the Caspian littoral in the area of Lahijan, where I watched and helped pick the tea.

Remedy for keeping hair healthy

Beat 2–3 eggs with 2–3 teaspoons of henna powder. Beat in 2–3 teaspoons of ground fresh Turkish coffee and 1 teaspoon of ground coriander seeds. Massage into slightly damp hair and leave for 4–5 hours before washing it off.

PASTA
Reshteh

Pasta, a word which comes from paste, goes back as early as the 4th century, referring to Chinese noodles made with wheat, buckwheat, rice or soy as far back as 3000 BC. Chinese vermicelli (fen), or the Japanese equivalent Barusame, are made like transparent silk threads, from a paste of germinated mung beans which are soaked in water before boiling or frying.

The Koreans insist that pasta was their creation and that the Japanese learned the art of pasta making from them during the 12th century. Soba noodles became a staple of the Japanese diet from the 16th century onwards and are traditionally used as a gift of welcome. The debate goes on that the first Chinese noodle was introduced to Italy by Marco Polo on his return from China in the late 13th century. But the translation of the Italian of Horace's *Satires* and

Martial's *Epigrams*, during the eighteenth century submits the word *pastilla* meaning little pastas, translated before the fourteenth century (during the existence of Marco Polo) describing special round cakes prepared for traditional sacrificial offerings. The erudite 17th century Frenchman De Cange describes *pastillum* – pastry stuffed with meat similar to ravioli or rafiole, a common dish at the time.

In Persia the ancient Zoroastrians began with a very simple method in their healthy diet of adding flour into a soup (shooly). Then a few years later water and flour were mixed together in small balls (omaj) and dropped into the boiling soup. Then during the Sassanian dynasty the flour and water were mixed and made into Reshteh: flour and water made into dough and cut into small strips, used to this day for happy occasions in traditional dishes such as Ash-e-reshteh.

TURMERIC
Zardchoobeh

Turmeric is a very deep yellow root, seen packed in large sacks along the bazaars of different cities in Iran, which then has to be ground for use. It is also available in powder form. A spice indigenous to India, it is the major spice used in Persian cooking.

Because of its colour and pleasant aroma it gives a gentle flavour in all dishes and sometimes can be substituted for saffron in khoresht and ash dishes, but by no means should be substituted for saffron if mixed uncooked, direct with rice dishes as the aroma of turmeric will become obvious, with an unpleasant taste. Turmeric is much cheaper than saffron, and is sold in Persian supermarkets and Indian shops in large quantities.

If too much is used the flavour becomes obvious and rather unpleasant. $\frac{1}{4}$ to $\frac{1}{2}$ a level teaspoon is sufficient for a dish for four people.

An ancient Persian remedy for fractured bones, used even to this day, is 2 beaten eggs with a teaspoonful of turmeric and raw beef or lamb bone marrow as a regular dressing.

BARLEY
Jov

Over 1000 years ago, when the capital of Persia was Persepolice, and the Sassanians were the rulers, barley and wheat were an important crop, and a satisfying diet for all, whereas bread was eaten sparingly by the higher class. The importance of bread is shown in the book by the famous Persian poet Hakim-Omar-E-Khayam, who wrote many verses about bread, wine and love.

Barley is as important today as it was many thousands of years ago, a very satisfying part of the diet and with a special flavour.

PUMPKIN
Kadu zard

An essential part of the diet of the Balkan people for many centuries, pumpkin is used a lot in Persian cooking and contains a good amount of vitamin C. Guests are always welcomed with a bowl of roasted pumpkin seeds, a perfect form of snack what ever the season as it contains 40 per cent of valuable oil, a remedy known to prevent prostate problems in men. Thanks to the Spanish for taking the seeds back to their country from America, the plant then spread to the rest of Europe and parts of Asia. Pumpkin, which is in the same family as melon, courgette and cucumber, produces yellow flowers. Once the fruit and vegetables are picked from their stem they do not ripen any more. These fruit and vegetables have the same effect and are known to be beneficial as anti-helmintic, meaning they aid the removal of worms from the digestive system. Drinking the juice has a gentle effect on the kidneys to reduce water retention.

My vivid memory is as a little girl holding on to Malog (my nanny) as she would take me through to the pumpkin field in the heat of summer. I sat in the shaded thatch wall with a pottery jug full of water as she helped to snip off the pumpkins to be sent to town, mainly for their seeds.

TARRAGON
Tarkhoon

This herb was brought to Spain from where it rapidly spread across Europe via the Arabs during 8th century. Tarragon comes from the word wet, meaning it has to be watered well almost every day. It is usually eaten with salad, and can be dried for flavouring and pickles. Because of its minty flavour it is supposed to be beneficial to the digestive system, like mint.

MARJORAM
Marzeh

Because of its very strong aromatic flavour only a small amount of marjoram leaves are used in a salad bowl. The herb can be obtained in supermarkets in the west.

PISTACHIO
Pisteh

The name pistachio (pisteh) derives from the Persian, where the nut originates from. It is believed the nut was first brought back to Greece by Alexander the Great after his conquest of Persia. Pistachios have always been grown in an arid climate and grew wild in the desert region, almost from when they were first discovered.

The best pistachio comes from the region of Rafsanjan, a city between Yazd and Kerman situated in South East (central) Persia. There are many private pistachio orchards here, but the nut also grows wild.

As a custom, many engaged couples sit under the pistachio tree on a moonlit night to hear the nut crack for good luck. Pistachio now is a widespread nut all over the world and its popularity has grown in the west in the last 50 years. It was first introduced to the USA during the 1880s.

OKRA
Bamya

At the begining of spring and all during the summer one is spoilt for choice of vegetables in Persia. I recall my childhood days in Yazd, waking in the morning to the sound of my nany Malog calling me to get ready to accompany her to the cotton field. I followed her through the deserted back streets of Yazd, where tranquillity filled the atmosphere. We walked along the narrow streets shaded by mulberry trees planted along the water path which carried irrigation water to the nearby orchards. The path was damp from the previous day. 'No one is going to buy water today,' Malog would tell me, as she held on to the large brass key which let us in to the high-walled orchard. On opening the door we were confronted by a bed of thistles, where the water had not reached. I loved looking at the cotton plant. Next to it was the plot of okra, a vegetable which is in the same family as the cotton and hibiscus. There were no men around, and Malog felt free, had already taken off her Chador which covered her clothes. She put it in the corner of the orchard near the dried up water path shaded by the small straw thatch for me to rest on. Wearing her white scarf tied around her head, and humming and singing in a low voice, as she got busy snipping the okra. I also helped to snip off as many okra as possible, as she explained that if okra grow too mature they would grow tough and stringy. We placed them in the straw basket to carry home, where some were reserved to dry for winter use. Okra is originally from west Africa, where it was known as nkruma, and was a part of the diet in the late 1700s. It was first brought to the USA over three hundred years ago, and is now a popular vegetable all over the world, although not many western people are completely adapted to this wonderful delicate vegetable.

THICK BROTH MEAL (*Ash*) & THIN SOUP (*Abgoosht*)

Whatever part of the country or religion, Ash is a very popular substantial meal for celebrations and an important feature in family gatherings. Its importance can be judged from the fact that a cook is called Ashpaz, literally 'the person who cooks Ash' and a kitchen, Ashpaz khaneh, 'the house of Ash'. In a book written during the 16th century by the Safavid Court the number of Ash dishes reaches almost fifty recipes broken into three categories, containing meat, grains such as wheat and barley and some cooked with a tangy flavour.

Ash is a dish with its own category, a mixed thick stew, often cooked with meat, pulses, wheat, barley and vegetables, rich with herbs and mildly spiced with turmeric. Some have a combination of fruit and nuts. Some have pasta (reshteh), and they can be sweet and sour or tangy with lemon.

Ash should not be confused with abgoosht (soup), which has a much thinner consistency.

Ash is typically Persian, warming, economical and nourishing, but is not widely known in the west.

There is no skill involved in cooking Ash. Just measure with your eyes and how large the family is and how big the saucepan. The recommended size saucepan is 2.25 litre/4 pint. The recipes, like all dishes, vary from family to family and by district to district.

It is better and safer to pick over the pulses and grains to remove any grit or other bits that may have got through during packing. Soak them in cold or lukewarm water for several hours, but better still, overnight. Allow at least 2–3 inches space to expand. In all recipes I refer to this as cleaning before soaking. In general beans – in particular red kidney beans and chick peas – absorb water quickly and swell, so it is best to check the level of water and add more during soaking.

Rice contains mucilage, which is a thickening agent, so it is best not to soak it when cooking it in Ash (meal) or abgoosht (soup), but always put them in a sieve and rinse under cold running water, before adding into the pan.

Traditionally pulses are cooked dry without soaking, which means they take much longer to become tender, but is believed to give a better flavour. Never cook or soak pulses with salt. Always add salt at the end of cooking, otherwise they will take much longer to become soft. Cooking time depends on the quality of the meat which can take between 1½–2 hours to become tender. Always choose lean lamb or beef and remove the skin, which contains a high amount of fat, from chicken.

Split yellow lentils take 45 minutes to cook and beans about 1–2 hours.

In most recipes oil is included in the ingredients, but can be eliminated altogether. Onion is the basis for these recipes and should be chopped fine, fried in the oil until golden and or transparent. You can use as little as one teaspoon of oil for frying by covering the pan, lowering the heat to the lowest, and allowing the onion to cook in its own juice.

When cooking red kidney beans after soaking and before adding to the ingredients, pour the water off and boil vigorously for ten minutes before reducing the heat to simmer to become tender.

It is not necessary to soak split yellow lentils before cooking, as this may cause the lentils to disintegrate.

Fruit and vegetables must not be over cooked as they contain vitamins and minerals which will be lost. Cook vegetables and herbs for no more than 5–7 minutes and fruit for no more than 2–3 minutes.

In some dishes tamarind fluid and gooseberries are included in the ingredients. The preparation for these is given under Basic Recipes (Chapter 11).

The initial amount of liquid (water or stock) to cover the ingredients is about 1.2 litres/2 pints. Always check the level of water in the pan and if too dry add a little more at a time. Stir occasionally to prevent it sticking to the bottom of the pan.

Add the spices during the cooking; lemon juice and vinegar five minutes before the end of cooking. Flavouring such as sugar, saffron or cinnamon just before serving. If yoghurt is used, add to the ash while it is still on the stove. To prevent curdling add a little beaten egg white, or beat one teaspoon of flour into the yoghurt before adding to the pan.

If using Persian cheese paste (Kashk), this is obtainable in Persian supermarkets (the names are given at the end of the book). If using dried cheese, soak it in water, then liquidize to a thick paste ready to use. Hot Mint, a mixture of fried dried mint and garlic which is given in Basic Recipes, is often used for garnishing.

At the end of cooking Ash should result in a thick mixture. It can also be prepared in a pressure cooker which saves fuel and reduces the cooking time to about 30–45 minutes. Ash is served as a main course with savoury cakes and with nan.

The ingredients given below are for four servings.

ORANGE MEAL
Ash-e-porteghal

Koofteh, meaning minced meat, and rizeh, meaning small, Koofteh Rizeh is small meat balls added into various dishes or served as starter.

230g/8oz minced lamb, beef or chicken
1 large onion, peeled
1 tablespoon oil
60g/2oz split yellow lentils

230g/8oz spinach leaves, chopped
15g/½oz rice flour
150ml/¼ pint orange juice
salt and pepper
¼ teaspoon saffron

Grate 60g/2oz of the onion over the meat, season with salt and pepper and knead to bind.

Chop the remaining onion and fry in 2 tablespoons of the oil in a large saucepan until golden. Take small balls from the meat as big as a hazelnut, smooth them around in your hands and add to the pan and stir to brown. Add the lentils, cover with cold water and simmer until cooked.

Meanwhile add the spinach, make the rice flour into a paste with a little water and stir in to the pan. Add the orange juice and simmer until thick, season with salt and pepper. Serve hot with nan or savoury cake.

NEVER LOOK BACK

It was the day I left Yazd for Tehran. The house was jam packed with friends and relations coming to say goodbye. I wore a deep lemon dress with black patterns, black shoes and my hair tied in a ponytail. I was the first to leave the house and Memeh, my mother, asked me to wait facing the front door while she held a tray in front of me. On it was the Avesta (the Zoroastrian holy book), a bowl of white fondant (noghl), a mirror and a bowl of water with thyme leaves. First I was asked to open the Avesta and read it, then to eat a fondant and then look into the mirror to see the bright days ahead. Finally I had to dip my fingers in the thyme water and turn my back on the house. Then Memeh, her eyes full of tears and emotion, poured the water mixture behind me, as was the custom and asked me to walk ahead without looking back. All relations and friends followed behind right to the bus depot, from where I was to depart for Tehran.

SARRESHTEH

If someone's husband had got a new job, it was an excuse for the ladies to have a midweek 'hen party'. It was Memeh's favourite to make ash-e-reshteh. The ladies dressed in typical Zoroastrian costume, the scent of joss sticks filled the atmosphere and European classical music was played. The large brass samovar was boiling with the teapot (Ghoori) on top.

To make enough room for the ladies, a large white cloth sofreh was spread on the Persian carpet. After chatting together over cookies and black tea, each lady would sit on a hand-embroidered cushion with an inverted polished copper tray and a rolling pin in front of her. Starting with Memeh they would sprinkle a little flour on each other's foreheads (to bring good luck and for their husbands to have good jobs), then they would all start rolling out the prepared dough 'reshteh'. Aunt Gohar was the best and the eldest, and would teach the others the technique of rolling out; if the dough was too thick she would give a gentle tap on the back of the hand with a rolling pin.

As the reshteh was put into the ash everyone made a wish.

In the early evening all the families would gather in the house to have their share of the ash, and some would be sent to the less well off people.

GOODBYE MEAL IN A BOWL
Ash-e-reshteh

—•—

115g/4oz red kidney beans
90g/3oz chick peas
60g/2oz brown or green lentils
85ml/3floz oil
3 large onions, chopped
1 teaspoon turmeric
115g/4oz each spinach, dill, leek, parsley and
coriander, chopped
175g/6oz noodles or reshteh
salt and pepper

FEW HOURS OF RELAXATION

Esfandiar was a keen farmer, and his wife Azar was very proud of their walled orchard (bagh) just a short walk from their house.

Esfandiar often left the house in the early hours of the morning, returning home on time for his lunch before setting off again. One day he did not return home on time, Azar got concerned and asked the neighbours for help, then a search was organised for him, which lasted for 48 hours. Eventually the search was called off, everyone supporting Azar for the loss of her dear husband. The house was crowded with friends and families making sure she was not left alone. It was not long after when the front door opened and Esfandiar walked in with sleepy eyes, wondering what all the fuss was about. He had fallen asleep under a weeping willow tree on the way home and slept for forty eight hours. He thought he had been asleep for just an hour or two. Azar organised to make ash-e-khirat for everyone, to celebrate her good fortune, and to thank everyone for helping to find Esfandiar.

TO SERVE
225g/8floz plain yoghurt or kashk
1 teaspoon sugar
1/2 teaspoon ground cardamom
3 teaspoons chopped pistachio or any other nuts.

Clean, wash and soak the pulses

Fry the onion in 3 tablespoons of the oil in a large saucepan until golden. Stir in the turmeric. Pour the water off the red kidney beans, add into the pan, cover with cold water. Bring to the boil and boil vigorously for ten minutes. Pour the water off the remaining pulses. Add to the pan and simmer until tender, which takes about 1–2 hours.

Meanwhile add the noodles, with the chopped spinach and the remaining chopped herbs. Simmer until thick, drizzle over with kashk or yoghurt, garnish with the sugar, cardamon and nuts when serving. Serve with savoury cakes.

CHARITY MEAL
Ash-e-khirat

—•—

60g/2oz each red kidney, mung beans,
black eyed beans, chickpeas
1 tablespoon oil
1 large onion, chopped
1/2 teaspoon turmeric
685g/ 1 1/2lb lamb, beef or chicken cut into
1cm/1/2inch pieces
30g/1oz rice, washed
60g/2oz each parsley, coriander and dill, chopped
1 small leek, chopped
salt and pepper to taste

Clean, wash and soak the pulses. Fry the onion and cook the red kidney beans as in the Farewell Meal. Pour the water off the remaining pulses and add to the pan. Add the rice, with the meat, to the pan and cover with cold water. Simmer until tender. Add the vegetables and the herbs. Season with salt and pepper to taste. Simmer until thick. Serve hot with nan.

COMPLETE MEAL
Ash-e-sholeh ghalamkar

❧

60g/2oz each chickpeas, black-eyed and mung beans
30g/1oz each red kidney beans and brown lentils
2 teaspoons each pin barley and cracked wheat
(burghal)
15g/¹⁄₂oz rice
1 tablespoon oil
1 large onion, chopped

455g/1lb lamb, beef or chicken, cut into cubes
1 teaspoon turmeric
115g/4oz spinach, chopped
1 teaspoon each dried mint and tarragon, crushed
60g/2oz each parsley, coriander, dill and leek,
chopped
salt and pepper

TO SERVE
120ml/4floz plain yoghurt
hot mint

Fry the onion in 2 tablespoons oil. Prepare and cook the pulses as in Farewell Meal. Add the rice together with the cracked wheat and the meat. Cover with water and simmer until tender. Stir in the chopped spinach and the remaining vegetables and the herbs. Cook until thick. Drizzle with hot mint and yoghurt. Serve with savoury cake or nan.

TURNIP MEAL
Ash-e-shalgham

❧

115g/4oz mung beans
455g/1lb lean minced lamb, beef or chicken
1 large onion
115g/4oz rice
1 teaspoon cumin seeds
455g/1lb turnips, if too large cut into halves
or quarters
1 tablespoon each dill, parsley and coriander,
chopped
1 small leek, chopped
salt and pepper

Clean and soak the mung beans for one hour. Grate 30g/1oz of the onion over the meat and prepare as in orange meal. Add the rice to a large pan. Chop the remaining onion and add to the pan with the cumin seeds. Pour the water off the mung beans and mix them in. Cover with cold water and simmer. Meanwhile add the meat balls, the chopped leek and the turnips, with the herbs. Serve hot as a meal with nan and sweet chutney or plain yoghurt. For a variation substitute 115g/4oz split yellow lentils for rice, with 455g/1lb kohlrabi peeled and cubed for turnip. Cook in exactly the same way.

MUNG BEAN MEAL
Ash-e-mash

❧

150g/5oz red kidney beans, soaked
115g/4oz mung beans, soaked
1 tablespoon oil
1 large onion, chopped
1 teaspoon turmeric
455g/1lb lamb, beef or chicken
60g/2oz rice
1 small leek, chopped

JUST ADD WATER

The early morning call was from the nightingale, waking us up as we lay on our beds under the vine trellis with the early morning sun flickering through, in the holiday region in Dehbala with its very small community of only a few houses.

The mountains were very nearby, and the stream ran just along the bottom of the deep bank which was only a few feet away from the back door.

Our walk began in the early hours of the morning, up the rocky mountain to reach the mulberry tree in the lower slopes.

Everyone was talented in different ways, and my middle brother Khodabakhsh was good at carving the fresh branches of the tree for us all. It really was a work of art with flowers and birds carved on it. Too precious to dig into the mountain rocks, mine was the smallest and the best. It was carried with me almost wherever I went, but mostly to the orchard where there were many fruit trees interspersed with low growing vegetation, with the delightful scent of herbs. I would shake the unripened fruit trees and was often scolded for knocking off the unripe fruit.

I helped with the cooking, which was served under the vine trellis, in the moonlight under flickering stars.

The life was easygoing. Friends called in at any time, often arriving during the morning and staying on for lunch or even unexpectedly for dinner. My mother always welcomed them warmly, saying 'It is OK. I'll just add water to the pan, so it is enough for everyone.'

60g/2oz each coriander and dill, chopped
230g/8oz young turnips
salt and pepper

Prepare the red kidney beans as in Farewell Meal.

Fry the onion in the oil in a large pan until golden, stir in the turmeric and cook the red kidney beans as in Farewell Meal. Pour the water off the mung beans and add to the pan. Add the meat and the rice, simmer. Meanwhile add the remaining ingredients, season with salt and pepper. Serve hot with plain yoghurt.

AUBERGINE AND MUNG BEAN MEAL
Ash-e-mash va badinjan

685g/1½lb aubergines sliced lengthways
5mm/¼inch thick
salt and pepper
1 tablespoon oil
1 large onion, chopped
1 teaspoon turmeric
685g/1½lb lamb, beef or chicken, cubed
230g/8oz mung beans, soaked

TO SERVE
plain yoghurt or kashk

Put the aubergines on a tray or a plate and sprinkle with about two teaspoons salt on both sides to draw the bitter juices.

Heat the oil in a large pan, add the onion and fry until golden. Stir in the meat, add the turmeric and pour the water off the mung beans, then mix them in. Cover with water and simmer.

Meanwhile rinse the aubergines, add to the pan, simmer until thick. Season with salt and pepper. Mash until smooth. Serve hot or cold with nan and plain yoghurt. For a variation substitute 115g/4oz white kidney or butter beans for mung beans. Cook and serve exactly the same.

JASHN-E-SADEH

The ground was covered with patchy snow, and a cool winter breeze was turning the melted snow to ice, which crushed the dried up winter leaves. It was fifty days before Novrooz, the Zoroastrian New Year. The time the young and the old prepared to celebrate the ancient festival of Jashn-e-Sadeh. The story goes that Hooshang Shah, the legendary king of ancient Persia, was out riding with his soldiers one day when he came across a large boulder with a giant snake curled on top. He threw a stone at the snake, missed it but hit the rock, causing sparks to fly and a fire to blaze which burnt the snake. This event, so the legend goes, marked the festival of Jashn-e-Sadeh and the beginning of cooking. The story was re-enacted in the open, where displays of fireworks were set in a large field, every street had its own bonfire, and everyone danced around the burning flame. As the fire was going out, they would jump over the edge and make a wish. In the late evening the street party began, and lots of potatoes were buried under the hot ash. Everyone contributed home cooking to the colourful display of food. Chestnuts were roasted, and music and dancing continued until the early hours of the morning.

42

TAMARIND MEAL
Ash-e-tambr

90g/3oz green or brown lentils
30g/1oz each chickpeas and pin barley
60g/2oz rice
1 tablespoon oil
1 large onion chopped
½ teaspoon turmeric
455g/1lb lamb/beef/chicken, cubed to 1 cm/½inch
2 medium uncooked beetroots, peeled and
finely chopped or grated
230g/8oz spinach, chopped
60g/2oz each parsley and leek, chopped
1 teaspoon dried and crushed mint
225g/8floz tamarind liquid
4 teaspoons sugar

TO SERVE
hot mint (see index)
¼ teaspoon ground cinnamon
sugar

Clean, wash and soak the chickpeas and brown lentils.

Fry the onion in 2 tablespoons of the oil in a large pan until golden. Add the meat, stir for one minute, then add the turmeric. Drain the water off the pulses and add to the pan, with the meat and the barley. Cover with water and add the rice. Simmer.

Meanwhile add the remaining ingredients. Serve garnished with hot mint, cinnamon and sugar. Serve with nan. For a variation substitute 2 medium cooking apples for the tamarind fluid, 230g/8oz red and white cabbage for spinach.

THE ORCHARD
(*Bagh*)

Almost everyone in Yazd owned a bagh. It is a plot of land surrounded by high walls, with a wooden door entrance.

It was the most popular form of land ownership in Persia, usually handed down from one generation to the next.

Ours was from my grandfather, maybe one of the best. It was built on a terrace and was very large. The 'Bagh season' would start in spring and go on until September or until the first snow was on the ground.

Opening the wooden door to our bagh one passed straight away into an atmosphere of peace and tranquillity. Ripened apricots and mulberries on the ground, panoramic views of fruit and roses, vegetables and pulses growing closely together in rows with brilliantly coloured flowers. With the long narrow channel of running water, which we had to pay for by the minute.

PLUM AND HERB MEAL
Ash-e-alu

1 tabespoon oil
1 large onion, chopped
455g/1lb lamb, beef or chicken, cut into cubes
½ each teaspoon ground saffron or turmeric
and cinnamon
90g/3oz split yellow lentils
115g/4oz rice
90g/3oz coriander, chopped
salt and pepper
30g/1oz each parsley and chives or leek,
and fresh mint, chopped
or 2 teaspoons dried and crushed
455g/1lb fresh plums

Fry the onion in the oil in a large saucepan until golden. Stir in the meat, add the spices and the rice, plus the lentils. Cover with water and simmer, add the remaining ingredients, season with salt and pepper, simmer until cooked and thick. Serve with nan.

BE HAPPY EVEN IF YOU ARE LONELY

There were many stories my mother used to tell me about her childhood days in Yazd. She often used to pass her old school, where I could visualise the scenes of the stories which she told me.

The school building had not changed since her days. We went to the school hall, where the lonely women of the community spent their long winter evenings.

The ladies shared the shopping, buying the ingredients, and cooking was also shared, using the large school copper saucepan. The preparation had to start very early in the evening, because such a large quantity needed to be cooked and the school's paraffin burner was very slow. During the several hours which it took to cook the ash everyone got busy with their knitting, crochet, embroidery and spinning, and the normally long winter evening would pass very quickly with the sound of knitting needles and spinning wheels filling the air. When the ash was served there was much laughter, and afterwards the ladies would entertain themselves with singing, and telling stories and jokes.

SWEET AND SOUR BARLEY MEAL
Ash-e-jo-e-shirin torsh

60g/3oz each brown lentils and chickpeas, soaked
1 tablespoon oil
1 large onion, chopped
455g/1lb lamb, beef or chicken, cut into 1cm/½inch pieces
5 garlic cloves, crushed
1 teaspoon turmeric
60g/2oz pin or pearl barley
115g/4oz chopped spinach
60g/2oz each chopped parsley, chives or leek
½ teaspoon each ground saffron and cinnamon
the juice of 3 large lemons or to taste
salt and pepper
sugar to taste

Fry the onion and the garlic in the oil in a large pan, stir in the meat and add the turmeric. Pour the water off the soaking pulses and add them to the pan with the barley. Cover with cold water and simmer.

Meanwhile add the remaining ingredients. Season with salt and pepper, add the lemon juice and sugar to taste. Serve with nan.

SAVOURY BARLEY MEAL
Ash-e-jo

Follow the recipe as above. Add 60g/2oz black eyed beans, cleaned, soaked and drained into the ingredients, with one tablespoon each of chopped dill and coriander with the herbs. Serve with liquid kashk or plain yoghurt. For variation substitute 230g/8oz broad beans (fresh or frozen) for lentils, substitute flavouring with kashk or 230g/8oz un-ripened grapes or cooked gooseberry juice.

JASHN-E-TIREGAN-VA-TIRMAH

The longest and hottest day of the year is Tiregan, in the month of Tir (Tirmah). Two or three days before Tiregan it was the custom to collect together various items, such as a ring, bracelet, chains in precious metal or articles in wrought iron such as a key or lock. Each one was named after a member of the family and placed in a pottery pot (Koozeh) filled with water, covered with cloth and tied with a string, then placed under a sweet pomegranate or a fruit tree, to rest for several days. On the actual day of Tir, when the temperature reaches over 40 degrees centigrade, everyone will hide bowls, jars and buckets filled with water behind the wall or on their balconies. Any Zoroastrian passers-by – women, children or men leaving for office – are showered. The sound of laughter and giggles fill every corner of the street. Every one has several changes of clothes until late afternoon, when the sun becomes pale. Then the pot was removed from underneath the tree and taken into the house. A young girl who had not reached puberty was chosen, and each person took turns to sing or to say a poem, as each item was pulled out symbolising the future of the owner. The joyful day would end with dinner in the garden starting with a traditional dish of shooly, spinach and beetroot soup. Tambourine music and handkerchief dancing continued into the evening.

SAVE FOR A SNOWY DAY

The midday sun was hot as it shone on the cobbled street in Yazd.

The atmosphere was full of tranquillity, broken only by the odd sound of a summer bird or a bicycle bell.

The area was arid, and everything grown needed irrigated water and was very precious.

Everyone had an afternoon nap, except women, who sat on Doshak (small hand made mattresses) with their front doors left open to make a draught, some busy spinning, knitting and crocheting, others bending over the large and highly polished copper tray, filled with different herbs, cleaning them to be dried for winter use. They were spread on large batik cloths and placed in a warm shaded atmosphere, to be dried and crushed then stored in jars.

WHITE MEAL
Ash-e-sefid

60g/2oz chickpeas soaked
685g/1½lb lamb, beef or chicken, cut into
1cm/½inch cubes
90g/3oz rice
60g/2oz chopped coriander
1 large onion, chopped
½ teaspoon cumin seeds
salt and pepper

Place the meat into a large saucepan, pour the water off the soaking peas and add to the pan, with the rice. Cover with water and simmer. Add the remaining ingredients and continue simmering until tender and thick. Serve hot with nan.

45

A TASTE I NEVER FORGET

My Muslim Nanny Malog took me wherever she went. She had many duties, one of which was to weed the land. I loved sitting under the shaded vine trellis, surrounded by large mulberry and apricot trees, watching her weed.

She always took her chador off when working, she wore long cotton trousers with a short dress over the top and a white scarf.

I looked forward to harvesting time, especially when bunches of chickpeas were pulled out of the ground for me to pop each one and peel and eat them fresh.

My mother use to make her own roasted chickpeas. Soak the chickpeas overnight, drain well and spread them on a clean towel overnight or until the moisture is completely absorbed. Fry them in plenty of salt, shake off the excess salt and when cool serve in small dishes.

Malog always preferred to take them home to share them with her family, cooked in ash.

GRAPE MEAL
Ash-e-angoor

Almost every house has a vine trellis either in the city or in the holiday region. Certain fruit are picked before ripening for cooking and every one waits eagerly to pick the unripened grapes for this dish. To be practical use 8oz of gooseberries

90g/3oz black eyed beans
1 tablespoon oil
1 large onion, peeled
455g/1lb lean lamb, beef or chicken, minced
½ teaspoon each ground saffron, cinnamon
or turmeric
30g/1oz each split yellow lentils and rice,
cleaned and washed
1 small leek, chopped
115g/4oz spinach, chopped
60g/2oz coriander, chopped
the juice of 230g/8oz sour grapes or gooseberries
2 teaspoons dried crushed mint
salt and pepper to taste
sugar to taste

Clean, wash and soak the beans as in Farewell Meal.

Fry half the onion, finely chopped, in the oil in a large pan, until golden and stir in the turmeric. Pour off the water from the beans and add with the lentils and the rice. Cover with water and simmer.

Grate the remaining onion over the meat, about 60g/2oz, and prepare as in Orange Meal. Add to the pan with the spinach, the chopped herbs and the fruit juice. Season with salt and pepper. Stir in the dried mint, saffron and cinnamon, simmer until the mixture becomes thick. Add sugar to taste. Serve hot with nan.

POMEGRANATE MEAL
Ash-e-anar

60g/2oz each rice, chickpeas and brown
or split yellow lentils
1 tablespoon oil
1 large onion, peeled
½ teaspoon turmeric
455g/1lb lamb, beef or chicken, minced
1 small leek, chopped
115g/4oz chopped spinach
60g/2oz parsley and coriander, chopped
salt and pepper
the juice of 5–6 large sour or sweet and sour
pomegranates
½ teaspoon each ground saffron and cinnamon
2 teaspoons dried crushed mint
sugar to taste (optional)

TO SERVE
hot mint (see index)

Clean, wash and soak the chickpeas and brown lentils as in Farewell Meal.

Chop half the onion and fry in oil in a large pan. Stir in the turmeric. Pour the water off the soaking pulses and add them to the pan, with the rice. Cover with cold water and simmer.

Grate the remaining onion over the meat and prepare as in Orange Meal, add to the pan. Add the remaining ingredients, season with salt and pepper and add sugar to taste. Serve hot and garnish with hot mint. For variation substitute tomato juice, or about 3–4 tablespoons tomato purée (dissolved in a little water) for pomegranate, eliminating the sugar.

FRUIT MEAL
Ash-e-miveh
❦

1 large onion, peeled
salt and pepper
1 tablespoon oil
1 teaspoon turmeric
60g/2oz each wheat, red kidney beans
and chickpeas, soaked
30g/1oz rice
230g/8oz minced lamb, beef or chicken
230g/8oz mixed parsley, mint, coriander, beetroot
leaves or spinach and leek, chopped
140g/5oz each fresh or dried cherries, apricots,
red or green plums, if using dry,
soak them over night
¹/₂ teaspoon each ground saffron and cinnamon
sugar to taste (optional)

Chop half the onion and fry in the oil in a large pan until golden. Stir in the turmeric.

Pour the water off the soaking pulses and wheat. Add them to the pan and cook as in Farewell Meal. Add the rice.

Grate the remaining onion over the meat and prepare as in Orange Meal, add to the pan. Add the remaining ingredients, simmer until thick, season with salt and pepper. Add sugar to taste. For variation add 1 large carrot and 1 uncooked beetroot, peeled and grated, with one tablespoon rice flour, to the ingredients. Serve hot with nan.

NOV ROOZ

It was still during harsh winter, weeks before Novrooz, when preparation and excitement began. Wheat and lentils were germinated in traditional earthenware pots (Koozeh) and each day the growing shoots would proclaim the coming of Novrooz.

The warm air gently blew over the snow, melting it to feed the grey sad garden which winter left behind. The blossom on the fruit and almond trees attracted butterflies and bees, and as the snow disappeared, roses and nightingales began to appear. Novrooz – 21st of March, 1st of Farvardeen – was the day the legendary Jamshid shah was crowned, when the first blossom appeared through the snow, signifying the birth of spring. The sunken garden was covered with high-scented Narcissus (nargess) and mauve coloured pansies (banafsheh). Khaneh takani or spring cleaning was undertaken by all members of the house.

Walking through the cobbled street in Yazd at dawn, you could see Zoroastrian ladies sweeping their front doorsteps and sprinkling them with water, with a handful of dried thyme leaves. A few sorb and a piece of fern were placed on each corner of the front door, to signify welcoming Novrooz into their home.

Gifts of sweets and clothing were given to the less well off people known to the family and children at school.

THIRTEEN DAYS OUT
Sisdah be dar

The excitement of Nov Rooz lasted up to the 13th of Farvardeen (April 2nd) the day to be 'seen out'. The custom was to step gently into the green, newly grown wheat during sunset, walk for a short while then sit on the grass and with your hands behind your back knot the green wheat and say this poem.

Sisdah be dar/thirteen days out,
Chahardah be too/fourteen days in
be haghe pir-e-Kotkotoo/trusting Kotkotoo the legendary saint,
Sisdah ra kardim to kado/we put number 13 into a pumpkin
Darash ra bastim ba judoo/and sealed it with glue
Saleh digeh charghat be sar/Next year I wear the scarf [meaning to be married]
Bacheh be baghal/and my baby in my arm.

PUMPKIN MEAL
Ash-e-kadu halvaie

3 tablespoons oil or butter
1 large onion, chopped
90g/3oz brown lentils, soaked
60g/2oz rice
230g/8oz pumpkin flesh, cubed
$1/2$ teaspoon each ground saffron and cinnamon
sugar to taste
lemon juice to taste
salt and pepper

TO SERVE
hot mint (see index)

Fry the onion in the oil in a large pan until transparent.

Pour the water off the soaking lentils and add to the pan with the rice. Cover with 300ml/10floz cold water and simmer.

Meanwhile add the pumpkin and the spices, sugar and lemon juice to taste.

For a variation substitute 230g/8oz plums or any fruit for the lemon. Serve hot, garnished with hot mint, with nan.

YOGHURT MEAL
Ash-e-mast

oil
2 large onions, chopped
3 cloves of garlic, crushed
$1/2$ teaspoon turmeric
455g/1lb lamb, beef or chicken, cut into
1cm/$1/2$inch pieces
90g/3oz each lentils and black eyed beans, soaked
$1/2$ teaspoon turmeric
60g/2oz rice
60g/2oz each leek and coriander, chopped
115g/4oz parsley, chopped
$1/2$ teaspoon each ground saffron and cinnamon
2 tablespoons chopped mint or 1 teaspoon dried and crushed
salt and pepper
300ml/$1/2$ pint plain yoghurt
1 teaspoon flour

TO SERVE
hot mint

Fry one of the onions and the crushed garlic in 1 tablespoon oil in a large saucepan. Add the meat and stir for one minute, then add the turmeric. Pour the water off the soaking pulses and add to the pan with the rice. Cover with cold water, simmer. Add the remaining ingredients except the yoghurt.

Meanwhile fry the remaining onion in deep hot oil until crisp. Mix half the yoghurt with the flour and stir into the pan. Simmer for 3 minutes. Serve with nan garnished with fried onion, hot mint and the remaining yoghurt.

WHEAT AND CINNAMON MEAL
Halim

❧

Halim (harriseh or riseh as it is known amongst the Zoroastrians) was an invention of the 6th century Persian King Khosrov and is a dish with a thick elastic consistency, more like porridge, and falls into the category of Ash rather than soup.

After the Arabs conquered Persia one century later the name and its recipe spread throughout all Arab countries.

The Muslims of Iran regard Halim as the finest winter family breakfast, but the Zoroastrians view it as a dish made for rituals such as Gahanbar or the anniversary of a deceased member of the family. It is garnished with a sprinkle of sugar and ground cinnamon and served with liquid halva for a sad occasion.

To save time and fuel it is best to make Halim in a pressure cooker. The cooking time for meat and wheat is about 30 minutes.

115g/4oz wheat, soaked
230g/8oz lean boneless lamb
2 large onions, chopped
salt and pepper

TO GARNISH
2 teaspoons sugar
1 teaspoon ground cinnamon

Cook the wheat and meat separately with onion in large pans, covered with water until tender, removing any scum. At the end of cooking there should be about 175ml/6floz liquid left in the pan in total.

While still warm, place all the ingredients into a blender, work until smooth, transfer into a saucepan and keep warm over a gentle heat. Season with salt and pepper. Serve as a meal with a sprinkle of sugar and cinnamon.

BORSH MEAL
Ash-e-borsh

❧

455g/1lb lamb or beef with the bone
230g/8oz shredded white cabbage
1 large carrot, grated
1 large potato, diced
1 medium uncooked beetroot, peeled and grated
1 tablespoon tomato purée
salt and pepper
150 ml/¼ pint cream or plain yoghurt

Simmer the meat in a large saucepan, covered with water until tender. When cool remove the bones, leaving the meat in the pan. Add the chopped vegetables and the tomato purée. Season with salt and pepper. Continue simmering until thick, then stir in the cream or yoghurt. Serve with nan.

ANIMAL APPRECIATION
Bahman rooz

Each day in the Zoroastrian calendar is named after a special angel, beginning with the name of the angel of God, called Ormezd. Bahman, Mah, Goosh and Ram are the guardians of 'animals', whose days fall at the beginning of the Zoroastrian month, and on these a true Zoroastrian must not eat meat or kill animals.

In the month of Bahman (January) for one month few Zoroastrians keep to the ancient tradition and for the whole of that month they refrain from eating meat or slaughtering animals. Many choose a special angel, named after each day of the month, on that special day. They put aside the cares and material pursuits of life, and may not allow themselves to eat or taste any wheat product, such as bread, biscuits or cakes. Instead, the time was devoted to helping others or gardening.

PLUM AND EGG MEAL
Ash-e-alu va tokhm-e-morgh

❦

685g/1½lb green plums
2 tablespoons rice flour
140g/5oz chopped coriander
2 tablespoons chopped fresh or 2 teaspoons dried
and crushed mint
salt and pepper
sugar to taste
3–4 eggs, beaten

Cook the plums in a little water, until soft. When cool remove the stones and the skin. Return to the pan.

Dissolve the rice flour in a little water and add in to the pan with the chopped herbs and the eggs. Season with salt and pepper and add sugar to taste. Simmer until thick. Serve with rice.

KOOFTEH

Koofteh means pounded meat, but the word describes many different kinds of meatballs, large and small. Large Koofteh is usually prepared with herbs, sometimes with split yellow lentils and rice, fruit and nuts. It has a very delicate flavour, with no strong spice. It is a typical family dish, both economical and warming, served with plain yoghurt and nan or sweet chutney. The recipes vary from family to family and region to region, as handed down from one generation to the next.

SPICY MEATBALL MEAL
Koofteh-e-berenji

❦

30g/1oz split yellow lentils, soaked
90g/3oz rice, soaked
230g/8oz minced lamb or beef
1 large onion, peeled

1 tablespoon oil
½ teaspoon turmeric
2 teaspoons coriander, chopped
1 teaspoon cumin seeds
salt and pepper
2 teaspoons tomato purée

Simmer the lentils for 15–20 minutes until tender, but not mushy, drain well.

Put the meat in a bowl and add the lentils. Drain the rice and add into the meat mixture, add in the coriander and the cumin seeds. Grate 2oz of the onion over the mixture, season with salt and pepper and knead to bind.

Chop the remaining onion and fry in the oil in a large saucepan until soft. Stir in the turmeric. Add 900ml/1½ pints water, dissolve the tomato purée in 120ml/4floz water and add to the pan. Take balls as big as tangerines from the meat mixture, make them smooth in your hands, and add to the pan. Simmer for about 45 minutes or until cooked. Serve hot with nan. For a variation, add 1 tablespoon chopped coriander, 1 medium potato, diced and 30g/1oz rice in the cooking liquid. Simmer until thick.

MEATBALL SURPRISE
Koofteh-e-tabrizi

❦

455g/1lb minced meat
60g/2oz split yellow lentils, cooked and mashed or
two teaspoons chickpea flour, or bread crumbs
1 large onion, peeled
1 tablespoon oil
salt and pepper
½ teaspoon each ground saffron and cinnamon
1 egg
140g/5oz Alu bokhara (Persian plums), barberries,
sultanas, dried prunes or apricots soaked
and drained
1 hard-boiled egg, diced small
140g/5oz chopped walnuts
2 tablespoons chopped fresh mint or 1 teaspoon
dried and crushed

The juice of 230g/8oz unripened grapes
or gooseberries
sugar to taste

Grate 2oz of the onion over the meat. Add the breadcrumbs, break in the eggs, season with salt and pepper, knead to bind.

Chop the remaining onion and fry in one tablespoon of the oil until golden.

Divide the meat mixture in half and place one portion in a soup bowl. Make a well and place one boiled egg in the centre. Push half of the fruit, nuts and fried onion around the egg. Turn out into your hands and smooth to seal. Repeat with the remaining ingredients and then add to the pan, and stir to brown. Add the saffron and the cinnamon and enough water to cover. Simmer. Add the fruit juice, the mint and sugar to taste. For a variation subsitute 60g/2oz chopped chives or chopped leek, parsley, dill, mint and tarragon for the fruit juice and add 60g/2oz rice, in the pan during simmering. Serve hot. Garnish with nuts. Serve with plain yoghurt, sweet chutney and nan.

THIN SOUP
Abgoosht (shoorva)

Abgoosht or Shoorva is popular amongst all classes and during the harsh winter months it is a meal which sustains rich and poor alike. It is two meals in one. In Persian 'ab' means water and 'goosht' means meat. In Zoroastrian and Persian (farsi) 'shoor' means salty and also in Zoroastrian 'auve' means water. To abbreviate 'shoor' and 'auve' has ended as shoorva. In summer time it is made with the fruits in season; in winter with pulses, herbs and sometimes with dried fruit. It is warming and economical.

Abgoosht is often made when there is a sick person in the home. Then, it will be just meat, a few chickpeas (nokhod) with no spice. The lady of the house often calls door to door to see if neighbours have cooked Nokhod Ab for dinner for her sick child. This was a very common friendly practice amongst Zoroastrians to help one another.

Translation of Abgoosht literally means meat juice, a soup almost like a consommé. The solid ingredients are drained, pounded and eaten as the main course, with rice or nan, and plain yoghurt and sabsi khordan (salad of fresh mint, tarragon, spring onion, radishes, and basil) or with sweet chutney. The pounded meat is often sandwiched cold as a picnic snack. Abgoosht or shoorva has been cooked in Persia for many thousands of years. The recipes vary from family to family from district to district and from town to town.

It can also vary during different seasons depending on the availability of vegetables. Fresh or dried herbs can be used. Ingredients are added according to individual liking and taste. The basic ingredients are meat, pulses and vegetables, to which other ingredients can be added. It can be made without meat and in that case the amount of pulses are increased accordingly. It is always better and safer to pick over the pulses and grains to remove any grit or other bits that may have got through during packing. In all recipes I refer to this as cleaning before washing.

To save fuel and time it is best to soak the pulses for 4–5 hours before cooking, with the exception of red kidney beans which are soaked for at least 8 hours before cooking. When added they should be boiled vigorously for ten minutes before reducing the heat to simmer.

Traditionally the pulses are added without being soaked for the flavour to fuse. To keep the flavour it is cooked on a slow heat. A pressure cooker can also be used to save fuel and time.

If the meat is fatty it is best to cook partially the day before and when cool, skim off the fat before adding other ingredients. This will reduce the calories greatly.

In some recipes oil is included, but can be eliminated altogether, especially where meat is used.

The recommended size saucepan is 2.25 litre/4 pint saucepan, with 1.2 litres/2 pints liquid to cover the ingredients. Check the level of water from time to time, adding a little more if the pan becomes too dry. Cooking time varies with the quality of meat used, usually between 1–2 hours. Always choose lean lamb and beef, remove the chicken skin before cooking as this will reduce the calorific content.

If pulses are not soaked they will need about $1\frac{1}{2}$ to 2 hours to become tender, whereas if they are soaked the cooking time is reduced almost to half.

In some recipes to give a more authentic flavour dried lime (limoo omani) is used, which is obtainable in Persian supermarkets (names are given at the back of this book). It is more convenient to buy in the form of powder, rather than using the whole lime. In that case it is best to remove the seeds, which are bitter, by putting them in a turned off warm oven for about 3–4 minutes. Slit the lime in half and remove the seeds.

Half a teaspoon of turmeric is added in most recipes with the exception of one or two dishes.

Vegetables are always added 5–7 minutes, and fruit 2–3 minutes, before the end of cooking.

I have meticulously measured the recipes given and like Ash there is very little skill one needs as almost everything is measured by eye.

The ingredients are obtainable widely in every supermarket and local shops. Like many dishes the Persians have names for their soup. One very common abgoosht is bosbash bos (meaning nanny goat).

MEAT AND PULSES SOUP
Abgoosht-e-bosbash

— ❦ —

*60g/2oz each red kidney and black eyed beans,
soaked in separate bowls
455g/1lb lean lamb or beef
140g/5oz mixed chives or leek and parsley, chopped
1 large potato diced large
1 tablespoon ground lime or 3 whole with the
seeds removed
1 large onion, chopped
salt and pepper
$1/2$ teaspoon turmeric*

Pour the water off the soaked red kidney beans and place them in a large saucepan. Add cold water to cover. Bring to the boil and boil vigorously for ten minutes. Pour the water off the black eyed beans and add into the pan with the meat, and the chopped onion. Remove any scum and simmer until tender.

Meanwhile add in the remaining ingredients, season with salt and pepper and add the turmeric. Simmer until soft. Serve the liquid as a starter, pound the solid ingredients and serve as a main course with rice or nan garnished with Spanish or spring onion, sprigs of mint and tarragon.

BASIC SOUP
Abgoosht

— ❦ —

*90g/3oz chickpeas
60g/2oz black eyed beans
455g/1lb lamb or beef, cut into portions
1 large onion, chopped or quartered
$1/2$ teaspoon turmeric
1 large or two medium potatoes, quartered
salt and pepper*

Clean and wash the chickpeas and the black eyed beans and cover with water to soak for 5–8 hours before cooking. Drain the water off the pulses and put them in a 2.25 litre/4 pint saucepan. Add the meat and the onion. Cover with cold water, bring to the boil, remove any scum, and add the turmeric. Simmer with the pan covered for about 1–2 hours or until the pulses and the meat are cooked. 15–20 minutes before the end of cooking add the potatoes, season with salt and pepper. When cooked drain the liquid over a bowl or another saucepan, pound or mash the solid ingredients and serve on a flat serving plate. Garnish with spring onion and sprigs of mint and tarragon. Serve hot with rice and nan or cold as a picnic snack.

CHEM AROO

Many primitive beliefs go back hundred of years in the small Zoroastrian communities. One of these is Chem Aroo. A doctor's prescription was taken seriously. But some old people believed it should be combined with an old-fashioned remedy. Chem Aroo had to be a close relation or a friend of the sick person and had to disguise herself with a green silk scarf, leaving only her eyes visible, and her hands had to be gloved.

She would go from house to house knocking on neighbours' doors with a walking stick and gently demanded, with a movement of her head, some small contribution. It had to be something you could eat, such as pulses, vegetables, fruit and nuts, and would be put into the straw basket she was carrying. The food was taken back and made into a meal for the patient.

It was widely believed that someone in the community would have a healing hand and often the patient was cured.

Put the onion, lentils, meat and turmeric into a large pan. Cover with water and simmer until tender.

Meanwhile add the potatoes and the lime. Season with salt and pepper. Serve the liquid as a starter and the solid ingredients with nan or rice. For a variation, slice 455g/1lb aubergines 1mm/½inch thick and sprinkle with salt. Leave for 30 minutes to draw the bitter juices, rinse and add to the soup, with 1 tablespoon tomato purée.

WHEAT SOUP
Abgoosht-e-gandom

❧

60g/2oz each butter or black eyed beans, soaked
1 tablespoon wheat, soaked
455g/1lb lamb or beef
1 large potato, quartered
1 large onion, chopped
½ teaspoon turmeric
1 tablespoon tomato purée
salt and pepper

Drain the pulses and the wheat, put into a large saucepan with the meat, chopped onion and turmeric. Cover with water and simmer until tender. Stir in the tomato purée, season with salt and pepper. Follow the instructions as in Basic Soup. Serve with nan garnished with sprigs of mint and spring onion.

SPLIT YELLOW LENTILS AND LIME SOUP
Abgoosht-e-lapeh va limoo omani

❧

1 large onion, chopped
90g/3oz split yellow lentils
455g/1lb lamb or beef
¼ teaspoon turmeric
230g/8oz quartered potatoes
2 tablespoons lime powder or whole lime with the seeds removed, or the juice of two fresh limes
salt and pepper

MINCE AND CHICKPEA SOUP
Abgoosht-e-koobideh

❧

90g/3oz chickpeas soaked
900g/2lb minced meat
¼ teaspoon cumin seeds
1 large onion, chopped
½ teaspoon turmeric
salt and pepper

1 tablespoon rice
60g/2oz chopped coriander
455g/1lb tomatoes
1 large potato, cut into cubes

Drain the chickpeas well and grind them coarsely in a grinder, put into a bowl, add the meat and the cumin seeds. Knead to bind. Season with salt and pepper.

Add the rice to a large saucepan filled with 900ml/1½ pints boiling water. Take small balls as big as a tangerine from the meat mixture and smooth them in your hands before adding into the pan. Add the coriander and tomatoes. Simmer until thick. Serve the liquid as a starter and the solid meatballs as main course with nan. For variation eliminate tomatoes.

LIME AND BEETROOT SOUP
Abgoosht-e-limoo

115 g/4oz brown or green lentils, soaked
90g/3oz black eyed beans, soaked
900g/2lb lean stewing lamb or beef, cut into portions
½ teaspoon turmeric
1 small onion, quartered
1 medium uncooked beetroot, peeled and cut into 1cm/½inch cubes
455g/1lb spinach leaves, chopped
1 teaspoon dried and crushed mint
salt and pepper
1 tablespoon powered lime or the juice of 4–5 limes

Pour the water off the soaking pulses, put into a large saucepan with the meat and turmeric. Cover with water and simmer until tender. Meanwhile add the vegetables with the mint, season with salt and pepper. Add the lime powder. Serve the liquid as a starter and the solids as a main course with plain rice.

QUICK STARTER
Eshkaneh

Eshkaneh is a typical family dish, and may be one of the dishes every child in the house knows how to make. It is economical, tasty and quick to prepare. The basic ingredients are onion, egg and flour, then vegetables and fruit can be added.

6–7 tablespoons oil
1 large onion, chopped
¼ teaspoon each fresh or dried fenugreek and turmeric
2–3 teaspoons plain flour
salt and pepper
2–3 eggs, beaten

Fry the onion in 2 tablespoons of the oil. Stir in the fenugreek and the turmeric, add a little water with the flour and stir in slowly. Stir in the eggs and season with salt and pepper. Stir until thick. Serve hot as a starter.

For variation substitute 230g/8oz fresh fruit, eg cherries, 1 tablespoon pomegranate purée or plums for the fenugreek

STUFFED SOUP
Doshvareh

The historian Charles Perry admired Persia for its pasta, which has been popular for more than fifteen hundred years. A cookery book written by Shah Abas during the 16th century, when the capital was Esfahan, gave different versions of pasta, some boiled, others steamed and eaten with 'sar gonjeshki' meaning 'sparrow's head', little fried meat balls. The names, like the recipes, vary from region to region. Doshvareh is also called Goosh Barreh which means 'lamb's ears'.

A typical dish from Gilan originated from Ghafghaz, this is a family dish eaten throughout the year.

It is traditionally served with vinegar or tomato sauce and chopped raw garlic. It can also be served to individual taste with pickle, chutney or plain yoghurt.

PASTRY
230g/8oz plain four
1 egg

FILLINGS
115g/4oz minced meat
1 small onion, grated
salt and pepper
900ml–1.2 litres/1½–2 pints stock
2–3 teaspoons dried crushed mint
3 cloves garlic, chopped

TO SERVE
Vinegar and tomato purée

Sift the flour into a large bowl, add the egg and a little cold water to make a pliable dough. Cover and allow to rest for about one hour in a warm place until slightly risen.

Mix the meat with the onion, season with salt and pepper and knead to bind.

Divide the dough into 9 equal balls. Roll out each one on a lightly floured work surface to a 5–6inch/12.5–15cm circle. Brush all around the edges of each circle with water. Place 2 teaspoons of the filling in the centre of each pastry, bringing up the edges to seal. Simmer the stuffed little parcels in stock to which the garlic and mint has been added, for about one hour or until the Doshvareh are cooked.

Serve the soup as a starter, accompanied by the stuffed meat balls on individual serving plates. Serve with vinegar or tomato sauce. I like it with plain yoghurt. For a variation add one tablespoon of rice to the stock during cooking.

THE SABBATH

Dalia was the youngest of Gity's five daughters and my best friend. I spent many days with her during the Jewish high holidays and festivals. She often invited me for the Sabbath (shabat) and explained to me the significance of this important day, which lasts from Friday evening to Saturday evening.

Not only is the Sabbath a day of rest, it is also a time of contemplation and prayers, a day of holiness when man can put aside the cares and material pursuits of life and devote himself to the refreshment of the spirit.

Four different meals were prepared in advance for the Saturday by Dalia's mother, as it was forbidden to work on the Sabbath. Prayers would be said over wine and bread, candles would be lit, followed by the serving of Gondy Shabaty, the traditional Sabbath meal eaten even to this day in Persia.

MIXED CHICKEN BALLS IN LIME SOUP
Gondy shabaty

(Chickpea flour absorbs a lot of liquid so add a little water at the time)
90g/3oz chicken fat, diced small, or two tablespoons oil
1 medium onion, chopped
455g/1lb chicken, cut into quarters
60g/2oz split yellow lentils
90g/3oz each minced beef and chicken
2 level tablespoons roasted chickpea flour or breadcrumbs
¼ teaspoon each ground turmeric and cardamom salt and pepper
1 tablespoon lime powder or 4–5 dried lime with the seeds removed

Some of the many ingredients, including spices and other flavourings, used in Persian cooking

A selection of desserts for all occasions

Aubergine and Yoghurt Starter

Sweet Golden Soup with Zoroastrian Nan

A complete meal, including Stuffed Peppers and Turmeric Nan

Stuffed Courgettes and Hushva Nan, a favourite combination

Stuffed Potato and Stuffed Onion

Persimmon Hors d'Oeuvre and Meatballs in Walnut and Yoghurt Sauce

Aubergine and Tomato Dish (top); Meatball Surprise (bottom)

Chicken Drumsticks with Orange Sauce

Melt the chicken fat over a very slow heat or heat the oil in a saucepan. Add the onion and the chicken pieces and stir. Add the lentils, cover with water to simmer.

Meanwhile put the minced chicken and beef in a bowl and add the chickpea flour, spices and season with salt and pepper. Knead to bind and form into smooth balls the size of tangerines. Add to the pan to simmer for 30–40 minutes. Ten minutes before the end of cooking add the dried limes, or lemon juice.

Gondy Shabaty is served in three parts. The liquid is served as a soup. The pieces of chicken are served separately with rice and the meat balls are eaten with a seasonal salad.

KOHLRABI WITH QUINCE SOUP
Abgoosht-e-beh va kalam

90g/3oz chickpeas, soaked
900g/2lb lamb or beef, cut into large
serving pieces
1 large onion, quartered
1/2 teaspoon turmeric
285g/10oz kohlrabi, peeled and diced into
large 5cm/2inch pieces
175g/6oz quince, peeled, quartered and seeded
salt and pepper

TO GARNISH
fresh coriander leaves

Pour the water off the soaking chickpeas, add to the pan with the meat and turmeric. Cover with water and simmer until tender. Meanwhile add the remaining ingredients, season with salt and pepper. Serve the solid ingredients with the liquid and nan. Garnish with the chopped coriander leaves.

PASSOVER

I helped Elana to dust the kitchen, and with a brush clear all the breadcrumbs which were left around. In Jewish law there should not be any sign of leavened bread in the house during Passover. This festival commemorates the deliverance of the children of Israel from Egyptian bondage. And with the birth of the Hebrew nation, the main meal on the eve of the first day of Passover, is called seder and consists of unleavened bread (matzo), bitter herbs (to symbolise the bitterness of Egyptian bondage), and xoroset, a mixture of nuts, figs, dates, apples, sultanas, cinnamon and wine.

I joined our friend for this special occasion. The Passover meal was always very traditional, beginning with prayers over the wine and matzo, after which passages were read from the Haggada, the Jewish prayer book which is only used at Passover. The glasses for wine were placed in a large bowl of water in the centre of the table and each time they were refilled the water in the bowl was changed. Three pieces of matzo covered with a special cloth were placed in front of Yousof (Elana's father), who was the eldest in the family. Matzo was broken and sandwiched with xoroset, then passed to all around the dinner table, before the main meal began. Unleavened bread is eaten throughout Passover until the eighth day, when it is the tradition for married men to visit their in-laws, taking with them flowers and boxes of sweets. On this occasion ordinary bread is eaten with traditional dishes such as Herb savoury cake (Kuku), Ash and yoghurt.

MUNG WITH POTATO AND BEAN SOUP
Abgoosht-e-mash va lubia

❦

30g/1oz each mung beans and brown or green
lentils, soaked
60g/2oz black eyed or butter beans, soaked
455g/1lb lamb or beef, cut into large cubes
1 large onion and potato, quartered
1/2 teaspoon turmeric
salt and pepper

Pour the water off the soaking pulses, put them
into a large pan with the meat, onion and turmeric.
Cover with water and simmer until tender. Season
with salt and pepper.

Serve the liquid as a starter. Pound or mash the
solid ingredients. Serve with rice and or nan.

OKRA WITH TOMATO AND EGG SOUP
Abgoosht-e-bamya ba tokhm-e-morgh

❦ ❦

3 tablespoons oil
1 large onion, chopped
1/2 teaspoon turmeric
230g/8oz okra, tailed and if too large
cut in half
1 large potato, cut into chip sizes
salt and pepper
230g/8oz tomatoes, halved
4 eggs
salt and pepper

Fry the onion in a large pan in the oil. Stir in the
turmeric, add the remaining ingredients and
600ml/1 pint water. Season with salt and pepper.
Simmer until cooked and thick. Break the eggs on
each corner, simmer until set. Serve with nan.

PLUM AND HERB SOUP
Abgoosht-e-aloo

❦

Plums always look better left whole when served.
If you like to remove the stones, press with a spoon
against the side of the saucepan and you find the
stone will slip out easily. Sugar can be added to
individual taste.

60g/2oz brown or green lentils, soaked
685g/1–1 1/2lb stewing lamb or beef, cut into
serving portions
1 medium onion, chopped
455g/1lb fresh red or green plums or dried prunes,
soaked
115g/4oz mixed chopped mint and parsley
or 4 teaspoons dried and crushed
1/2 teaspoon each ground saffron and cinnamon

Pour the water off the soaking pulses, add to a large
pan with the meat and onion. Cover with water
and simmer until tender. Meanwhile add the
chopped mint, with the spices. Finally, add the
plums. Season with salt and pepper. Serve the liquid
as a starter and the solid ingredients with rice.

SWEET GOLDEN SOUP
Tafteh

❦

White basil seeds are obtainable in Persian supermarkets and Oriental shops (in Persian it is called
tokhmeh-e-sharbati) and if buying in an Indian
shop it is called tukmaria.

30g/1oz butter
1 teaspoon turmeric
1 1/2 teaspoons ground or rice flour
1 teaspoon white basil seeds, soaked
2 teaspoons sugar to taste

Fry the turmeric in butter for 1–2 minutes.
Dissolve the rice flour in 900ml/1 1/2 pints water.

Stir into the pan and simmer. Add in the seeds with their soaking water with the sugar to taste. Serve hot with nan (also delicious cold).

SPINACH WITH VINEGAR AND LENTIL SOUP
Shooly

A very ancient Zoroastrian recipe, going back centuries. First flour was added to the soup, then later it was made into small balls with a little water. Later still, it was made into reshteh (noodles).

90g/3oz brown or green lentils, soaked
1 large onion, peeled
685g/1½lb minced lamb or beef
3 tablespoons oil
salt and pepper
½ teaspoon turmeric
230g/8oz raw beetroot, grated

SENNE BOLOOGH
(*Coming of age*)

For a Zoroastrian girl, the onset of puberty was an important occasion. I recall arriving at my aunt Paris's house from school, as a girl of only nine, to find her house was packed with young ladies and their mothers. It was a surprise party for my cousin Banoo, with non-stop music and hot bowls of golden soup. Everyone showered my cousin with presents as she sat there, in her frilly, girlish pink dress with white patent shoes, looking so shy. At that moment I made a decision that when my time came, Memeh should give me just one big present rather than announcing the news far and wide.

---

2 teaspoons rice or plain flour
230g/8oz spinach, chopped
85–120ml/3–4floz vinegar or according to taste

Grate 60g/2oz of the onion over the meat, season with salt and pepper and knead to bind.

Chop the remaining onion and fry in the oil in a large saucepan until brown. Take a little of the meat mixture as big as a hazelnut, smooth it around in your hands and fry with the onion until brown. Stir in the turmeric, pour the water off the soaking lentils and add to the pan with the beetroot.

Dissolve the rice flour with a little water and add to the pan. Stir in the spinach, season with salt and pepper and add the vinegar. Simmer for 5–7 minutes. Serve with savoury cake and nan

NOODLE AND BEAN SOUP
Abgoosht-e-reshteh

1 tablespoon oil
1 large onion, chopped
685g/1½lb chicken, cut into quarters
½ teaspoon turmeric
2 garlic cloves, crushed
½ teaspoon each dried and crushed mint and tarragon
1 tablespoon tomato purée
1 large potato, cut into 5mm/¼inch cubes
230g/8oz runner beans, topped, tailed and cut into 5mm/¼inch pieces
60g/2oz reshteh or noodles

Fry the onion in the oil until transparent, add the chicken and fry for 1–2 minutes. Stir in the turmeric and add the prepared vegetables. Cover with water, simmer until tender. Meanwhile add the noodles and tomato purée dissolved in a little water. Season with salt and pepper. Serve with nan.

SAVOURIES (*Mazzeh*)

Mazzeh, meaning taste in the Persian language and more familiarly known in the west as Messeh, is the most delightful feature of the table, whether it is a family gathering or a dinner party. The table is set with a tantalising selection of starters depending on the season. During spring and summer the traditional salads consist of diced feta cheese (panir), tomatoes with spring or Spanish onions, seasoned with salt and freshly ground pepper; garnished with fresh mint, tarragon and basil. Lettuces are left whole or cut into half as each person can eat more than one or two each, usually treated as a mid morning snack. Each leaf is separated then dipped into a mixture of syrup and vinegar or syrup and lemon juice or as a starter for lunch or dinner dipped in plain yoghurt mixed with finely grated cucumber, crushed garlic, fresh or chopped mint and tarragon, chopped nuts and sultanas, all eaten with nan.

Autumn and winter breakfasts start with boiled baby turnips dipped in a little salt.

For lunch or dinner an appetising starter is shiny red sweet and sour pomegranates which are set on plates arranged along the table.

Fresh dates from the south with bowls of nuts and a selection of pickles complete the basic range of dishes in the traditional Persian home.

This chapter includes recipes for one of the most traditional Persian dishes, Kuku (Savoury Cake). Kuku in Persia are classified as cakes rather than omelettes. These nutritious savouries, which are 2–3 inches thick with a firm texture, mildly spiced with cinnamon, turmeric or saffron, are golden yellow filled with carrots and pumpkins or light green with herbs or vegetables, crunchy with nuts and in some cases filled with sultanas or currants. They make the most popular hot or cold snacks.

The cake can be cut into small squares and served with alternative green and yellow colours at dinner parties, also served as an hors d'oeuvre or a side dish or sandwiched between nan to make a perfect picnic snack.

The ingredients used are fresh, but frozen or dried vegetables can also be used. The basic ingredients can be prepared a day in advance to save time. One of the major ingredients is onion, which is finely chopped.

Cooking Kuku in the oven is more satisfactory than cooking it on the top of the stove, as it cooks more evenly and there is less danger of burning. If it is prepared for the oven, choose a square ovenproof dish about 20cm/8inches square 5m/2inch deep. Put 2oz of oil or melted butter in the dish and swirl it around, place in the preheated oven for about 7 minutes or until hot. Pour in the mixture, cover the dish to begin with and only about 10 minutes before the end of cooking uncover to brown. The time of cooking depends on the quantity and texture. It varies between 30–60 minutes, until the centre is well cooked and firm. Usually when the texture is loose the cakes take a little longer to cook than when mixed with more solids. If cooking on the stove choose a large, deep frying pan with a well fitting lid, preferably non stick or heavy aluminium.

Pour in the same amount of oil or butter and heat before adding the mixture. Cook slowly on a gentle heat for about 15–20 minutes until risen, then turn over to cook the underside.

Generally Kuku can be frozen – unless it contains vegetables such as courgettes as they may become soggy and watery after defrosting, but they can be refrigerated for 1–2 days before serving.

Kuku sabzi or seasonal herb cake, with the basic finely chopped herbs plays an important role during Persian New Year (Nov Rooz). They are placed on a specially laid table with other items for good luck and a prosperous year ahead.

Traditionally walnuts are used in some recipes in this chapter, but substitute any nuts, coarsely chopped. Dried fruit such as dates can be substituted for sultanas. Substitute the finely chopped green part of spring onions for chives. For garnishing use hot mint (see index for recipe), and Persian dried cheese kashk can be added (see Chapter 11).

The ingredients are measured for 4 servings, with the exception of savoury cakes, which are sufficient for at least 8 people.

MELON SURPRISE
Pishghaza-ye-kharbozeh

2 ogen melons
60g/2oz each long grain rice and brown or green lentils, cooked and drained
1 tablespoon sultanas
1 teaspoon each fresh mint and tarragon, chopped or one teaspoon dried and crushed
2 teaspoons chopped chives
$\frac{1}{4}$ teaspoon each ground cinnamon and saffron
2 tablespoons lemon juice
1 small potato, boiled and diced
3 heaped tablespoons plain thick yoghurt
90g/3oz chopped walnuts
salt and pepper

Cut the melons in half, remove and discard the seeds. Scoop out the flesh for use in fruit salad.

Reserve 4 teaspoons of the nuts, mix the rest with the remaining ingredients and toss well to combine. Season with salt and pepper.

Fill the melon halves with the resulting mixture, sprinkle on the reserved nuts. Serve as a starter.

WISH ME LUCK

In my teenage days in Tehran, I learned a lot about the different customs of different religions.

One day during mid summer, I was sitting in the garden shaded by the large persimmon tree laden with fruit. The air was cool and fresh as the water was sprayed over the roses and the low growing shrubs.

The brass samovar was bubbling in the corner, with cookies piled high on plates, as family and friends would call unexpectedly, for an afternoon visit. Amongst them was an unknown lady, with a dress over her arm. She was smiling gracefully, but rather shy. She pulled my mother into the corner where they had a private discussion in whispers. Then she handed the dress (belonging to her daughter) to my mother and went away. When all the family and friends had left, my mother spread the dress over the persimmon tree, as the lady believed the fruit tree would bring her daughter good luck to find a husband. This was an old Jewish custom, and they were somehow right; it was only a few weeks later that we heard that the lady's daughter had found a fiancé, and was soon to be married!

PERSIMMONS HORS D'OEUVRE
Pishghza-ye-khormaloo

~

4 large ripe persimmons
3 tablespoons soft cheese (curd)
1 teaspoon each ground cinnamon and icing sugar
1 tablespoon plain yogurt
1 tablespoon pine nuts

TO SERVE
a few flaked roasted almonds
4 lettuce leaves

Cut off a thin slice from the top of each fruit and scoop out the middle. Reserve the pulps and the caps.

Put all ingredients and some of the pulps into a mixing bowl, toss well to combine.

Fill the persimmon cases with the resulting mixture. Serve on lettuce leaves, garnish with almond flakes.

GHERKIN

As summer approached, gherkin was the first vegetable in the shops or picked from the garden. It was eaten almost with every meal – as a morning snack with nan, feta cheese, honey and walnuts; for lunch and dinner as a starter with yoghurt, in salad and garnished on fruit trays and bowls.

It was a custom for the host to peel a gherkin lengthways, leaving about an inch at the end to hold on to, then sprinkle the flesh with a little salt and pepper. The skin was then put back over the flesh so that it would not be touched by the fingers and placed on a side plate in front of the guest. This would break the ice and the guest would then feel free to help himself. But my father's hospitality was different: he would ask his male friends for a drink, choose the largest of the gherkins, scoop out the middle, eat the flesh then fill the cases with Vodka (aragh) and drink to each other's health. But my sweet memory of my childhood is a surprise from my brother Firooz, showing a small bottle containing a very large gherkin. It puzzled me, until I realised that he had actually grown it in the bottle by placing the bottle on the ground beside the plant with the barely formed shoot inside. When the cucumber was fully grown he cut it free and filled the bottle with alcohol to preserve it.

CRUNCHY MIX GHERKIN
Pish ghaza-ye-khiyar

—◆—

4 fat gherkins or two small fat cucumbers
2 teaspoons chopped spring or sweet Spanish onion
or chives
2 teaspoons each finely chopped mint and tarragon
or $1/4$ teaspoon each dried and crushed
1 tablespoon oil
175g/6oz hard cheese, diced small
(preferably feta)
2 teaspoons chopped walnuts
30g/1oz sultanas or 2 teaspoons golden syrup
or honey
salt and pepper

TO SERVE
radishes sliced into thin rings

Slice the gherkins in half lengthways and scoop out the middle.

Put all ingredients into a bowl and toss well. Fill the gherkin cases with the mixture. If using syrup, trickle a little on each. Garnish with radish rings. Serve with nan.

ROASTED CHEESE WITH EGGS
Panir-e-bereshteh ba tokhm-e-morgh

—◆—

30–60g/$1/2$oz butter
230g/8oz grated panir (feta cheese)
4 eggs, beaten

Fry the cheese in butter until lightly melted. Pour over the egg. When set cut into portions. For variation add one tablespoon chopped dill with the beaten egg, before pouring it into the pan. Serve with rice or nan.

BREAK THE EVIL WITH AN EGG

As long as there was an egg in the house, there was not really fear if someone was sick. A traditional belief amongst the Zoroastrian ladies was that a person with a cold or cough can be cured with a raw egg. First hold an egg in your hand and with the other, using a thick black felt pen, draw circles (representing the eyes) repeating the names of people you know starting with your own, then close family and relations, then friends, and then even people you don't know, whom you see in the street and at work. The circles are drawn until there is no more space on the egg.

Once the egg is covered, fill a bowl about a quarter full with cold water, and hold it over the patient's head, then with force vigorously break the egg into the bowl of water, thus breaking the evil eye. Soon after throw the egg and the water into the street, or outside the house.

Another custom is to boil the egg and draw the eyes, then place it in the middle of a small fire, lit away from the house, such as in the garden. The louder the sound when it bursts the more effective the cure.

AUBERGINE AND EGG DELIGHT
Mirza ghasemi

—◆—

4 medium aubergines
90g/3oz butter or 7 tablespoons oil
5 cloves of garlic, crushed
$1/2$ teaspoon turmeric
230g/8oz tomatoes, peeled and quartered
salt and pepper
4 eggs

Make four small slits on the sides of each aubergine. Place them under the grill or in a hot oven turning them every five minutes until soft. Remove the skin and mash, fry them in half the butter. Remove into a dish, add more butter, fry the garlic with the turmeric. Add the aubergines and the tomatoes, season with salt and pepper, simmer until all the liquid is absorbed, spread the mixture evenly in the pan. Add the remaining butter and break the eggs in each corner and allow to set before serving.

For variation substitute courgettes for aubergines. Slice the courgettes thinly and fry in a little oil until soft. Mash, then follow the recipe as above.

CHICKEN AND ALMOND HORS D'OEUVRE
Pishghaza-ye-morgh

685g/1¹/₂lb lean chicken, cooked and minced
115g/4oz ground almonds
150ml/¹/₄ pint plain yoghurt or soft cheese
2 teaspoon chopped dill
2 teaspoons sultanas
salt and pepper

TO GARNISH
¹/₄ teaspoon ground saffron (optional)
roasted almond flakes

Mix all the ingredients and toss well. Serve garnished with almond flakes.

SPINACH WITH YOGHURT AND CINNAMON
Borani-e-esfenaj

Borani was a favourite dish during the Sassanian period (of the Zoroastrian rulers) in AD 624, especially for the Queen Azarmindokht and Queen Poorandokht (who were the rulers at the time). It is still a popular dish in a Persian home today.

Use only plain yoghurt with a smooth texture.

60g/2oz butter or margarine
4 cloves of garlic, crushed
455g/1lb chopped spinach
salt and pepper
150ml/¹/₄ pint plain yoghurt

TO SERVE
¹/₄ teaspoon ground cinnamon
1 tablespoon roasted flaked almonds

Fry the garlic in butter. Add the spinach, season with salt and pepper. Cover the pan to cook in its own juice, until the liquid is absorbed. Serve mixed with the yoghurt, sprinkle on the cinnamon and almond flakes. For variation add cooked mortedela sausages, diced small.

AUBERGINE WITH YOGHURT AND MINT
Borani-e-badinjan

455g/1lb aubergines, sliced 5mm/¹/₄inch thick
salt and pepper
oil
230g/8oz minced lamb or beef
1 large onion, peeled

TO SERVE
hot mint (see index)
175ml/6floz plain yoghurt
1 teaspoon ground saffron

Put the aubergines on a tray or plate, sprinkle with salt on both sides to extract the dark bitter juices. Rinse, dab dry and fry in shallow oil until golden.

Grate 2oz of the onion over the meat. Season with salt and pepper, knead to bind.

Chop the remaining onion and fry in two tablespoons of oil.

Take small balls as big as hazelnuts from the meat, make them smooth in your hands and fry with the onion until brown.

Arrange the aubergines neatly over the meat. Mix the saffron with 3–4 tablespoons water and add to the pan. Simmer until the liquid has been absorbed. Drizzle with yoghurt and hot mint when serving.

TOMATO AND EGG STARTER
Pamador chegher tameh

60g/2oz butter
1 large onion, chopped
salt and pepper
455g/1lb tomatoes, skinned and quartered
4 eggs

Fry the onion in butter, add the tomatoes, season with salt and pepper, simmer until thick. Break in the egg. When set serve with nan.

MEATBALLS IN YOGHURT AND NUT SAUCE
Kaleh joosh

230g/8oz minced lamb or beef
1 large onion, peeled
oil

1 teaspoon each turmeric and dried crushed mint
salt and pepper

TO SERVE
175ml/6floz plain yoghurt
60g/2oz chopped walnuts

Prepare the meat as in the recipe Aubergine with yoghurt and mint.

Chop the remaining onion and fry in 2 tablespoons of oil with the turmeric and the mint. Add the meat, stir to brown, add 3–4 tablespoons water, simmer until the liquid has been absorbed. Before serving, garnish with fried aubergines, drizzle with yoghurt, sprinkle with the nuts and serve with nan.

AUBERGINE AND YOGHURT STARTER
Kashk-o-badinjan

455g/1lb aubergines sliced 5mm/¼inch thick
salt and pepper
oil
1 large onion, chopped
½ teaspoon turmeric

TO SERVE
150ml/¼ pint kashk or plain yoghurt
For a sweet taste: 2 teaspoons sugar, teaspoon ground cardamom, pinch of cinnamon and one tablespoon coarsely chopped nuts
For a savoury: hot mint (see index for preparation)

Prepare the aubergines as in the recipe Aubergine with Yoghurt and Mint.

Fry the onion in 2 tablespoons of oil until soft. Add the turmeric. Spread some of the kashk or yoghurt into a serving dish. Arrange the aubergine slices on top, add the fried onions, drizzle with more yoghurt, garnish with sugar and cardamom. Sprinkle on the nuts. For savoury drizzle on hot mint. Serve with nan. For a variation slice courgettes and fry in butter or oil and follow the instructions as above.

SHAHNAMEH
(The Epic of Kings)

During hot summer days the cellar was the favourite sitting room, with its marble floor laid with Persian carpets, with bolsters all the way around the octagonal pond, filled with crystal clear water. There was the scent of freshly cut roses, and along the shelves you could see many bottles filled with home-made drinks. There were also book shelves, where Baba often read, and played a game of chess with uncle Shari. I often dozed in the early hours of the afternoon in the relaxing atmosphere with Baba reading the famous book of Shahnameh (The Epic of Kings) to me with his soft musical voice.

Many of the stories written by Ferdowsi were about Zoroastrian religion and history.

It was much later in life, when visiting Mashhad the holy city of Muslims, that I made the journey by bus to Tus to see Ferdowsi's tomb. I stood under the shaded tree in a cool breeze, and almost drifted back to my childhood days in the cool cellar with Baba reading the book of Shahnameh to me all over again.

PICNIC IN THE WASH ROOM

In the early hours of the morning the distinctive smell of steam from Hammam, the traditional bathing building (which goes back to the Romans' time) spreads along the streets of every city or village in the country.

The building has a flat roof and numerous domes, built with frosted glass in green and blue for the sun or light to reflect to the heated rooms.

If public, two or three males or females would spend several hours to wash and relax in the steamy atmosphere, and be rubbed down by kisehkesh. The private Hammam had two rooms: an entry or changing room and a steam room. The entry room was often made into a picnic room, where everyone joined in between the wash to have their drink and mid morning snack. During snack time everyone shared each other's food. It was a place for gossip, while they waited to be rubbed down by the kisehkesh.

This was a weekly treat, as everyday showers at home were not considered clean enough, as hygiene played a big part in everyone's life.

SAVOURY HERB CAKE
Kuku-ye-sabsi

5–6 tablespoons oil
1 medium onion, chopped
140g/5oz chopped spinach
90g/3oz chopped chives
30g/1oz each parsley, dill and coriander, chopped
2/3 lettuce leaves, chopped
1/4 teaspoon each turmeric and ground cinnamon
4 large eggs
1 teaspoon self-raising flour
60g/2oz chopped nuts
salt and pepper

Fry the onion in 3–4 tablespoons of oil until golden, add the chopped herbs and turmeric, and stir for 1 minute.

Preheat the oven to 350°F/180°C/Gas mark 4.

Pour the remaining oil into a 5cm/2inch deep, 20cm/8inch wide square baking dish. Place in the oven until hot.

Beat the eggs, season with salt and pepper, and add the cinnamon. Mix with the cooked and cooled onion and herb mixture. Remove the dish from the oven and add the egg mixture. Return to the oven and bake for about 15 minutes. Serve hot or cold with rice or sandwiched between nan.

POTATO WITH FRUIT AND NUT CAKE
Kuku-ye-sibzamini

—◆—

5–7 tablespoons oil
1 large onion, chopped
1–2 cloves of garlic, crushed
4 large eggs
1 teaspoon baking powder
230g/8oz potatoes, cooked and grated
2 tablespoons plain yoghurt
salt and pepper
1/4 teaspoon each ground saffron and cinnamon
115g/4oz chopped nuts
2 teaspoons sultanas

Fry the onion in 2–3 tablespoon oil, stir in the garlic.

Beat the eggs with the baking powder with the remaining ingredients and cook as savoury herb cake. Serve hot or cold.

SAVOURY CARROT CAKE WITH DATES AND NUTS
Kuku-ye-havij

—◆—

5–6 tablespoons oil
1 large onion, chopped
230g/8oz carrots, grated
4 large eggs, beaten
1 heaped teaspoon self-raising flour
2 tablespoons plain yoghurt
90g/3oz each chopped dates and nuts
1/4 teaspoon each ground saffron and cinnamon
salt and pepper

Fry the onion in oil until soft. Add the carrots, cook for 2–3 minutes longer.

Mix all ingredients with beaten eggs and cook in the same way as the Herb Savoury Cake.

Serve hot or cold.

COURGETTE AND LENTIL SAVOURY CAKE
Kuku-ye-kadoo

—◆—

6–7 tablespoons oil
1 large onion, chopped
2 cloves of garlic, crushed
90g/3oz split yellow lentils, cooked and mashed
4 large eggs, beaten
1/4 teaspoon each ground saffron and cinnamon
1 teaspoon baking powder
salt and pepper
2 tablespoons plain yoghurt

Fry the onion in 2–3 tablespoons of oil, stir in the garlic and the courgettes. Add 85ml/3floz water and simmer until the liquid has been absorbed, then mash. Mix with the beaten eggs, add all the other ingredients, and cook in the same way as the Herb Savoury Cake. Serve hot with nan or rice.

CHICKEN AND LIME CAKE
Kuku-ye-morgh

—◆—

5–6 tablespoons oil
1 large onion, chopped
5 large beaten eggs
455g/1lb chicken, cooked and minced
1 teaspoon ground saffron
1 teaspoon self-raising flour
1 teaspoon baking powder
1–2 tablespoon lime or lemon juice
salt and pepper

Fry the onion in 2 tablespoons of oil and stir in the garlic. Add all the ingredients into a mixing bowl with the eggs, season with salt and pepper and cook in the same way as the Herb Savoury Cake. Serve hot or cold.

SLICED AUBERGINE
Varagheh

❦

685g/1½lb aubergines
salt and pepper
oil
½ teaspoon each turmeric and ground cinnamon
4/5 large eggs

Prepare the aubergines as in the recipe Aubergines with Yoghurt and Mint. Put two tablespoons of oil in an ovenproof dish and heat in the oven. Arrange the aubergine slices neatly in the dish.

Beat the eggs with the spices and pour over the top. Bake in the same way as the Herb Savoury Cake. Serve hot with nan, plain rice and plain yoghurt. For variation add the eggs whole.

AUBERGINE CAKE WITH FRUIT AND NUT CAKE
Kuku-ye-badinjan

❦

285g/10oz aubergines
salt and pepper
oil
1 large onion, chopped
2–3 cloves of garlic, crushed
4 large eggs, beaten
1 teaspoon self raising flour
115g/4oz chopped nuts
2 teaspoons sultanas
1 teaspoon ground saffron
½ teaspoon ground cinnamon
1 teaspoon dried crushed mint

Prepare the aubergines as in the recipe Aubergine with Yoghurt and Mint, then mash.

Fry the onion and garlic in 2 tablespoons oil, remove to cool. Add all the ingredients with the beaten egg in a mixing bowl and cook in the same way as the Herb Savoury Cake.

Serve hot or cold, with rice or nan.

BROAD BEAN SAVOURY CAKE
Kuku-ye-baghla

❦

230g/8oz podded broad beans, cooked and drained
5–6 tablespoons oil
1 large onion, chopped
4 cloves of garlic, crushed
1 tablespoon finely chopped dill
¼ teaspoon turmeric
4 large eggs, beaten
1 teaspoon self raising flour
salt and pepper

Fry the onion and garlic in two tablespoons of the oil until soft. Stir in the turmeric.

In a large bowl mix the beaten eggs with all the other ingredients. Add the cooled beans. Cook as in the recipe for Herb Savoury Cake. Serve with rice and sweet chutney.

PUMPKIN WITH FRUIT AND SAFFRON CAKE
Kuku-ye-kadu halvaie

❦

5–6 tablespoons oil
1 large onion, chopped
260g/9oz pumpkin flesh, grated
4 large eggs, beaten
1 teaspoon self raising flour
1 teaspoon each ground saffron and cinnamon
2 teaspoons sultanas or chopped dates
sugar to taste (optional)
salt and pepper

Fry the onion in 2 tablespoons of the oil until soft. Add the pumpkins and stir. Cover the pan and allow to cook slowly for 3–5 minutes until tender. Mash, mix with beaten eggs and all the other ingredients. Cook as in recipe herb savoury cake. Serve hot with rice.

SHIRAZ

We drove along the eight kilometre motorway which linked the airport to the outskirts of the town. The journey was uninterrupted rose-gardens, truly announcing Shiraz the 'city of roses, wine and poets'. It was during early afternoon in June and the parks, one of the town's attractions, were looking magnificent.

The long and wide avenues led from one side of the city to the other. They were an incitement to students strolling holding on to their books, studying for the last term, or some leisurely wandering during siesta time.

The inhabitants of Shiraz attach great importance to their reputation as intellectuals and artists. Cultural events took place throughout the year. The interesting feature of many villas is peristyles supported by delicate wood columns, opening onto beautiful small flowered gardens. The populated quarters in the city centre are a busy trading area. The picturesque quality of the Persian Bazaar is enhanced here, where one sees the nomads or semi-nomads, elements from southern Persian tribes, which includes the Ghashghaie, whose woman are easily recognised by their brightly coloured dresses.

The Bazaar and several mosques were built during the Zand dynasty (1758–1799), during which Shiraz was the capital of the Kingdom.

The town is separated into sectors of uneven size by the very wide bed of Roodkhaneh Khoshk, meaning dry river, which is generally dry. To the north up to the foot of the mountains there are large gardens, which includes the beautiful Bagh-e-Eram. To the east is the tomb of two great poets, Hafez and Saadi, surrounded by parkland.

Hafez lived in Shiraz from 1300 to 1389. Even seven centuries later his verses are well known to all Persians and valued as aphorisms. His book is found in every Persian home and often used for serious prediction. One of his best poems is the 'Ghazal' engraved on his tomb:

> Sit near my tomb, and bring wine and music – feeling thy presence I shall come out of my
> sepulchre – rise softly moving creature, and let me contemplate thy beauty.

Saadi died in 1291 at the age of 100. The inscription on his tomb reads:

> From the tomb of Saadi, son of Shiraz
> The perfume of love escapes – thou shalt smell it.

Still one thousand years after his death, I visited these gardens and, as was the custom, placed two fingers on the flagstone of both poets, as a gesture of tribute.

Shiraz lies at an altitude of 1500 metres in a fertile valley, always known for its vineyards. The Shiraz grape is still known to winegrowers throughout the world.

The climate is pleasant during winter and summer – never too cold or too hot.

The settlement of Shiraz occurred as early as the Achaemenian period, when it was already an important regional centre under the Sassanians. It became the provincial capital until around AD 693. Shiraz became important and grew in size after the Arab conquest, and during the 12th century became an important artistic centre.

It grew further under the Atabaks of Fars. In 1382 Atabak and Tamoor Lang saved the city from destruction. This was because Shah Shoja the local monarch agreed to give up his Army and even offered the hand of his grand daughter in marriage to a grandson of Tamerlan (taymoor-E-lange).

During the Timurid and Mongol (mughol) periods Shiraz was at its peak, with the presence of Hafez and Saadi with many other brilliant artists.

Shiraz became one of the greatest cities in the Islamic world throughout the 13th and 14th centuries – a centre of calligraphy, painting, literature and architecture.

Many artists contributed their talent, beautifying many cities both inside and outside the country. The most famous was Ostad Isa, who lived during the 17th century. He was the architect who provided the design for the Taj Mahal in India, under Shah Abbas 1. Emam Gholi Khan, at the time the governor of Fars, constructed a large number of palaces and other ornate buildings on the line of the Royal capital at Esfahan.

Shiraz declined for one century, due to many earthquakes, the Afghan raids of the 18th century, and an uprising led by its governor in 1744, which was put down after a siege by Nader Shah.

During the year 1747, when Nader Shah was assassinated, most of Shiraz's historical buildings were damaged or ruined, but soon Karim Khan, first of the short-lived rulers of the Zand Dynasty, returned Shiraz to prosperity and was determined to raise the city into a prosperous capital the same as Esfahan.

Under Shah Abbas 1 many fine buildings were constructed, including the finest Bazaar in the country.

Karim Khan's heirs were unable to fulfil his gain. When Agha Mohammad Khan, the cruel founder of the Ghajar dynasty, came to power killing Ali Khan, the last of the Zand Dynasty, Shiraz's city fortifications were destroyed. In 1789 the national capital was moved to Tehran, but Shiraz kept its level of prosperity as a result of the continuing importance of the trade route through Bushehr, until before the revolution.

Shiraz was known to be a good administrative centre and, because many people prefer life in big cities, its population has grown considerably since the revolution.

OKRA AND CUMIN SAVOURY CAKE
Kuku-ye-bamya

▬◆▬

550g/1¼lb okra, topped and tailed,
sliced into thin rings
oil
1 large onion, chopped
½ teaspoon turmeric
¼ teaspoon cumin seeds
4 large eggs, beaten
1 teaspoon self raising flour
salt and pepper

Fry the okra in hot oil until golden. Remove with a slotted spoon.

Fry the onion in 2 tablespoons of the oil in the same pan until golden. Stir in the cumin seeds with the turmeric.

In a large bowl mix the beaten egg with all the remaining ingredients. Season with salt and pepper then mix in the cooked and cooled okra and cook in the same way as the Herb Savoury Cake. Serve hot with rice and yoghurt or cold as a picnic snack.

FISH ROE SAVOURY CAKE
Kuku-ye-tokhm-e-mahi

▬◆▬

6–7 tablespoons oil
1 large onion, chopped
2 cloves of garlic, crushed

275g/10oz fish roe, with the skin removed
and chopped fine
115g/4oz chopped parsley
4 large eggs, beaten
salt and pepper

TO GARNISH
lemon or orange rings, sprigs of parsley

Fry the onion and garlic in 2 tablespoons of oil.
Add the fish roe and fry for another two minutes.
Add the beaten egg with the remaining ingredients.

Cook in the same way as the Herb Savoury
Cake. Serve hot or cold with rice and nan. Garnish
with lemon or orange rings and sprigs of parsley.

CAULIFLOWER
SAVOURY CAKE
Kuku-ye-gol-e-kalam

230g/8oz head of cauliflower
salt and pepper
85ml/3floz oil
1 medium onion, chopped
3 cloves of garlic, crushed
4 large eggs, beaten
1 teaspoon ground saffron
$1/2$ teaspoon ground cinnamon
1 teaspoon baking powder

Simmer the cauliflower for about 7 minutes until
semi-cooked. Drain well and mash coarsely.

Fry the onion and garlic in 1 tablespoon of oil
until soft. Mix the cooked and cooled cauliflower
and the remaining ingredients into the beaten eggs.
Add all the other ingredients and season with salt
and pepper.

Bake as for Herb Savoury Cake. Serve hot with
rice.

SHIRAZI SWEET
CINNAMON CAKE
Khagineh-e-shirazi

3 tablespoons oil or butter
4 large eggs, beaten
1 teaspoon self raising flour
a pinch of salt
sugar to taste

Heat the oil in a frying pan. Mix all ingredients
and pour into the pan. When set turn the cake
over to cook the other side. Serve hot with nan.

AZARBAYEJAN SWEET
SAVOURY CAKE
Khagineh-e-azarbayejani

A variation from the above recipe. A speciality in
the Caspian region where it is treated as a dessert.

Mix 3–4 dessertspoons milk or water with one
dessertspoon self raising flour. Add to the egg
mixture and cook as above.

Make the syrup.

Mix 115g/4oz sugar with 85ml/3oz water and
teaspoon ground saffron. Simmer for about 4
minutes until semi-thick. Pour over the cake when
serving.

SPICED MEAT CAKE
Shami ba sibsamini

230g/8oz cooked and mashed potatoes
salt and pepper
345g/12oz lean minced lamb or beef
1 medium onion, grated
1 large egg
1 teaspoon ground cinnamon
2 cloves of garlic, crushed
175ml/6floz oil

Put all ingredients except the oil in a large mixing bowl and knead to bind.

Take a little of the dough slightly larger than a walnut. Make it smooth, then press it in the palm of your hand to about 1cm/½inch thick. With your finger make a little hole in the middle and smooth out. Fry a few at the time in moderately hot shallow oil until golden. Drain on kitchen paper.

Serve hot or cold with salad and or rice.

For variation substitute 115g/4oz cooked and mashed split yellow lentils for potatoes and simmer the cooked meat cakes for 10–15 minutes in 175ml/6floz tomato purée dissolved in a little water with the juice of one large lemon.

STUFFED MASHED POTATOES
Kotlet-e-sibzamini

400g/14oz mashed potatoes
2 eggs
½ teaspoon each ground saffron and cinnamon
salt and pepper
1 tablespoon sesame seeds
oil
tomato slices for garnishing

FILLING
2 tablespoons oil
1 small onion, chopped
4 cloves of garlic, crushed
2 teaspoons sunflower seeds
2 teaspoons sultanas

Beat one of the eggs in a bowl and add the mashed potato with the spices. Mix with your hand.

Fry the onion and garlic in 2 tablespoons of oil.

Beat the second egg in a bowl. Dampen your hands with the beaten egg and roll the potato mixture into a small ball the size of a tangerine. Make a well in the centre of each ball with your index finger and fill with a little of the seed, fruit and onion mixture. Cover the filling with potato

UNFORGETTABLE PICNIC

The holiday region of Manshad had many rocky mountains. Many with springs gushing down from underneath, which sparked with brilliant pieces of gold and some with semi precious stones. My father loved to search for the rare small pieces of mountain quartz, which could be found in almost inaccessible places. Nothing was 'impossible' for him, and he responded to the challenge.

On one occasion he hired a pair of asses to go in search of stones and my sister and I insisted on accompanying him. As we would have to be on foot for part of the way we deliberately avoided the hottest part of the day and set off in the late afternoon.

It was all very exhilarating, especially when we reached our destination. I felt I was riding the wings of imagination. I stroked the precious quartz with my little hands, imagining that I could pick out a piece of the sparkling treasure, but sadly we made our return journey empty-handed.

I sat on the front of one of the asses with my sister, who was tightly hugging the snack-box of Kuku which my mother had packed in anticipation of our feeling peckish.

It was getting dark – darker than we had reckoned. There was no light, save from millions of stars shining overhead, as we trotted down the mountain path far away from any sign of civilisation. With the hypnotic movement of the asses my sister and I began to doze off. I gently slid over the ass's head onto the rocky mountainside and only woke when my sister shouted to alert my father.

The atmosphere was tranquil, with the smell of vegetation. We sat beside the running stream in the dark, enjoying the delicious taste of my mother's cooking. We were soon back on the mule on the way home.

so that it does not ooze out during cooking. Roll in the beaten egg, coat with sesame seeds and fry in shallow oil until golden. Drain on kitchen paper. Serve garnished with tomato slices.

SAVOURY PASTRIES
Pirashki (sambuseh)

Despite the invasion of the Arabs, Zoroastrians kept their traditions and rituals, such as Gahanbar, or the anniversary of a deceased member of the family, when traditional recipes were and still are used.

The founder of Sambuseh, known today as Sambooseh or Sambusik, was King Khosrov (a Zoroastrian ruler), who lived and reigned during the 7th century. The popularity of this pastry dish was so great that many years later the Royal Safavid Court (Safavieh) wrote a book of recipes in one volume which included sweet and savoury pastry made in different shapes and sizes.

The original recipe is made as in soorog (fried nan). Two flat pieces of dough are stuffed with fried spiced meat and onion and fried in oil. The name and recipes with slight variations spread through different countries such as India, where the name became Samosa, and in the Middle East where it is known as Sambusak.

The more modern version, slightly varied in shape and recipe, is known as Pirashki.

PASTRY
200g/7oz plain white flour
1/2 teaspoon baking powder
pinch of salt
60g/3oz butter or margarine, softened
1 teaspoon sugar
1 large egg, beaten
1 tablespoon plain yoghurt

FILLINGS
2 tablespoon oil
1 small onion, chopped

115g/4oz minced lamb, beef or chicken
1 medium potato, diced
1/2 teaspoon ground saffron or turmeric
1/2 teaspoon ground cinnamon
salt and pepper

Sift the flour and baking powder and salt.

Beat the butter or margarine with the sugar until white, beat in the egg, yoghurt and flour. Gather together with your hands to make it smooth.

Chill for 30 minutes.

Fry the onion in 2 tablespoons of oil until golden. Add the meat, stir until brown. Add the potato, spices, salt and pepper to taste. Cook gently until soft.

Divide the pastry into 9 equal balls and roll each on a well floured worktop to about 12.5–15cm/5–6 inches circle. Brush all around the edges of each circle with water.

Place 2 teaspoons of the cooked and cooled mixture in the centre of each pastry, bring the edges up and twist or crimp them. Fry in deep, moderately hot oil for 4 minutes until golden. Remove with a slotted spoon and drain on kitchen paper. Serve hot or cold with sweet chutney. For vegetarian Pirashki, substitute 115g/4oz chopped nuts for meat and add 60g/2oz cooked grated carrots, 30g/1oz feta or other hard cheese and 60g/2oz mixed chopped chives or green part of spring onion, dill and parsley. Follow the recipe as above and cook in the same way.

COURGETTE NARCISSUS
Narges-e-kadu sabz

685g/1 1/2lb courgettes, cut into rings 5mm/
1/4inch thick
oil
1 large onion, chopped
1 medium potato, diced or grated coarsely
1 heaped tablespoon chopped dill

2 cloves of garlic, crushed
salt and pepper
½ teaspoon each ground saffron or turmeric
and cinnamon
4 eggs

Fry the courgettes until lightly golden. Remove with a slotted spoon.

Fry the onion and garlic in 2 tablespoons of the oil from the pan until soft and transparent. Stir in the dill with the spices and add the potatoes. Cook until soft, then add another 2 tablespoons of oil. Smooth with the back of a spoon and arrange the courgette slices over the top.

Break an egg in each corner. Cover the pan and allow to set. Serve with rice or nan, plain yoghurt and sweet chutney garnished with tomato slices.

RUNNER BEAN NARCISSUS
Narges-e-lubia sabz

685g/1½lb runner or French beans, cut into
1 cm/½inch pieces and cooked
90g/3oz oil
1 large onion, chopped
2 cloves of garlic, crushed
½ teaspoon each turmeric and ground cinnamon
salt and pepper
4 medium tomatoes, skinned and quartered
90g/3oz panir (feta) or hard cheese, grated
1 tablespoon chopped parsley
1 tablespoon chopped nuts
4 eggs

Fry the onion and garlic as in the recipe for Courgette Narcissus. Add the tomatoes, simmer until all liquid is absorbed. Add the cooked beans, cheese, parsley and nuts.

Break the eggs in each corner and allow to set.

Serve hot with nan and sprinkle with parsley. For a variation eliminate the nuts and the tomatoes and cook in the same way.

CARROT NARCISSUS
Narges-e-havij

115g/4oz butter or oil
1 large onion, chopped
275g/10oz carrots, grated
1 medium potato, grated coarsely
1 tablespoon chopped parsley
½ teaspoon each ground saffron and cinnamon
salt and pepper
4 eggs
115g/4oz chopped pistachios

Fry the onion in half the fat, add the potato and carrots and cook until soft. Stir in the spices and parsley, with the nuts. Make it smooth with the back of a spoon. Add the remaining oil. Break the eggs in each corner. Allow to set and serve hot with rice.

SPINACH NARCISSUS
Narges-e-esfenaj

90g/3oz butter or oil
1 large onion, chopped
2 cloves of garlic, crushed
455g/1lb spinach, chopped
pinch of nutmeg
salt and pepper
4 eggs
4 pinches of paprika for garnishing

Fry the onion and garlic as in the recipe for Courgette Narcissus. Add the spinach and spices, simmer in its own juice until the leaves are wilted and all the liquid is absorbed. Smooth out with the back of a spoon. Cook the eggs as in the recipe Courgette Narcissus. Serve with nan and plain yoghurt, garnish with paprika.

OKRA NARCISSUS
Narges-e-bamya

❧

685g/1¹/₂lb okra, tailed and sliced into rings
oil for shallow frying
1 large onion, chopped.
2 cloves of garlic crushed
¹/₄ teaspoon cumin seeds
¹/₂ teaspoon turmeric
salt and pepper
2 heaped tablespoons chopped coriander leaves
4 eggs

Fry the okra rings in 5 tablespoons of oil until brown and crisp. Fry the onion and garlic in the same oil until golden. Stir in the spices and cumin seeds. Add the cooked okra with a little more oil and smooth the surface. Break the eggs on each corner. Allow to set. Serve hot or cold with nan and or rice.

AUBERGINE NARCISSUS
Narges-e-badinjan

❧

455g/1lb aubergines, sliced lengthways to
5mm/¹/₄inch thick
salt and pepper
oil
1 large onion, chopped
2 cloves of garlic, crushed
¹/₂ teaspoon each ground saffron and cinnamon
115g/4oz chopped nuts
2 teaspoons sultanas
4 eggs

Prepare the aubergines as in the recipe for Aubergine with Yoghurt and Mint.

Fry the onion and garlic as in the recipe for Courgette Narcissus, then stir in the spices. Remove half the onion mixture and arrange half the fried aubergines over the remaining onion in the pan. Top up with sultanas, nuts and the onion mixture,

ending with a layer of aubergine. Add 2 more tablespoons of oil if necessary. Break the eggs on each corner. Allow to set. Serve hot with nan and rice.

YOGHURT AND SHALLOT MIX
Mast-o-moosir

❧

A favourite dish throughout Persia, this speciality is served with chelov kabab in a restaurant rather than at a buffet table.

Soak, drain and finely chop 7–8 shallots. Mix with 225 ml/8floz yoghurt. Chill before serving.

CUCUMBER AND POMEGRANATE MIX
Salad-e-khiyar va anar

❧

One of the places I visited as a teenager was Dezful, 125km north of Ahvaz in the south east of Kermanshah. Staying with friends we ate home cooking and local specialities. This delicious salad is eaten as a starter.

Pomegranates are available in Persian shops during autumn. Use sweet and sour with reddish skin rather than just sweet.

To seed the pomegranate, full instructions are given in the recipe Tribute to a Lady (page 84).

the seeds of 3 large sweet and sour pomegranates
1 large cucumber or 4 gherkins, chopped
2 teaspoons chopped parsley, a few mint leaves and
one small Spanish onion, finely chopped

Mix all the ingredients together and serve with plain yoghurt.

DO NOT MAKE THE SAME MISTAKE AGAIN

I watched Memeh closely when she cooked. But sometimes simple things were made in a matter of minutes, and mostly when I was at school.

I have a vivid memory of a harsh winter's day, when there was a rapid snow fall towards evening, and the atmosphere inside became cosy. Memeh already had prepared the dinner before leaving to visit one of her friends.

I was a little girl of only eight, lifting the lid of every saucepan and any dish to see what was there for dinner. One dish was prepared with red ruby beetroot and plain yoghurt, as a starter. I thought I would give Memeh a surprise and turned the mixture into a saucepan to make it hot, for such a cold winter evening. But it turned into a curdled mess.

Memeh was understanding, and explained that yoghurt and beetroot starter is eaten cold. Then she explained that if I ever wanted to make yoghurt hot just add a little beaten egg white or a teaspoon of flour to stop it curdling.

YOHGURT AND BEETROOT
Mast-o-laboo

As the autumn approached, so did the seasonal vegetables. Walking up the steep hill of Shemiran, north of Tehran, the hot, steaming, red ruby beetroot spread their aroma in the atmosphere, as the men standing in rows served from their large wooden trolleys along the hill side, with every one standing eating, holding on to the side plate and a fork.

Use only freshly cooked beetroot, not pickled in vinegar.

To crush the mint rub between your hands.

225ml/8floz plain yoghurt
2 medium beetroot, cooked and diced

TO GARNISH
A little fresh or dried and crushed mint

Mix all the ingredients and sprinkle with mint. Serve at room temperature in winter and chilled during the summer season.

YOGHURT AND CUCUMBER
Mast-o-khiar

To give a more authentic flavour use dried mint. Fresh mint can be used also.

225ml/8floz plain yoghurt
½ medium cucumber, peeled and grated
2 teaspoon sultanas
60g/2oz chopped nuts
2 cloves garlic, crushed
½ teaspoon each fresh crushed or finely chopped mint and tarragon

Mix all ingredients together. Serve chilled with nan.

TRADITIONAL MEAL (*Khoresht*)

The word khoresh, or khoresht, derives from the Zoroastrian (Sassanian) language commonly used before the Arab invasion in the 7th century (as it always has been amongst the Zoroastrians of Iran). The Arab influence spread rapidly through the country, and their alphabet was moulded into Persian script. Khoresht became gholyeh, meaning stew, derived from Arabic, and it appears in the cookery book written in 1547. But in the last 400 years, with the influence of different monarchs, and respect for old traditions and language, the word khoresht has once again become more commonly known in the country, except for those nearer to the Persian Gulf with Arab neighbours, where the name gholyeh still remains.

Khoresht is a very popular family dish which is eaten almost every day, served over polov or chelov rice, or eaten with nan. The thick sauce is a combination of meat or poultry, pulses, vegetables, fruit, nuts and herbs, with a most subtle taste. It is never over-powering, never hot, peppery or strong. It is sometimes flavoured sweet and sour reddish pink with quince, lemon and rhubarb; deep red with pomegranate purée or juice; bright red with tomatoes; green with spinach and herbs; or golden yellow with carrots, pumpkin and plums, spiced with turmeric, saffron and cinnamon. Khoresht is a popular dish throughout the year, especially during late spring and early summer when most vegetables, herbs and fruit are in season. During winter it is more popular made with pulses, herbs and dried plums.

Before freezers were introduced it was a common practice amongst some Persian families to dry certain vegetables such as aubergines, okra, and tomatoes to be used during winter, when fresh vegetables were not in season. It is best to freeze the basic ingredients, which are: finely chopped onion and crushed garlic, sautéed in oil or butter, rather than freeze the whole dish when cooked with the vegetables, as some such as courgettes, carrots, potatoes and okra will become soggy and unpleasant when thawed because of their water content.

As most vegetables and fruit contain vitamins and minerals it is best not to overcook them.

Always add the vegetables 4–5 minutes and fruit 2–3 minutes before the end of cooking.

The amount of fat used in Persian cooking is individual: you can use as little oil or butter as you like – 4 teaspoons of oil is enough for ingredients cooked for four people. Fry over a low heat with the pan covered for the onion to become transparent in its own juice. When using turmeric, this is stirred with the onion for one or two minutes, but saffron and cinnamon are added during or at the end of cooking.

It is always best to choose lean lamb and beef with no fat. Chicken or poultry should also be lean, with the skin removed.

Choose a 2.25 litre/4 pint non-stick or heavy aluminium saucepan with a well-fitting lid. The initial amount of water to cover is about 225–300ml/8–10floz. Always simmer with the pan covered, on a slow heat, for the flavour and juice to blend and fuse. Once the vegetables are added, stir as little as possible to retain their shape.

Check the level of liquid from time to time, adding more gradually, so the pan does not become too dry or too runny. At the end of cooking uncover the pan and boil vigorously to reduce to a thick mixture, but it should remain juicy.

Cooking time for chicken is about 45 minutes and for meat, depending on the quality, $1\frac{1}{2}$ to 2 hours.

Always pick over the pulses, remove any grit which may have got through during packing, and wash under cold running water until the water runs clear. Beans such as red kidney beans in particular and black eyed beans should be soaked for at least 5 hours or overnight. Using split yellow lentils soaking is not necessary, as this may cause the lentils to become mushy at the end of cooking. The cooking time for pulses is about 45 minutes to one hour.

Unripened grape juice is used in Persian cooking, but to be more practical substitute gooseberry (look under basic recipes for preparation). Also the preparation for tamarind and orange rind can be found in the same chapter.

Ground saffron is used in almost every dish – full instructions are given under Saffron.

Dried lime (Limoo Omani) is used abundantly, and is obtainable in Persian supermarkets. Using common lemon does not give the authentic flavour. It is best to buy powdered lime. If whole lime is required, see Dried Lime for preparation.

Fruit such as Alu bokhara is obtainable in Persian supermarkets, but you can use plums or prunes instead.

Although it is a matter of taste and choice, most khoresht are cooked with fruit and sometimes with nuts so very little salt is required, which is a benefit to health.

Each region has their own speciality and flavour. In the northern part, the Caspian littoral, the ingredients are herb based, which are chopped fine. Whereas Abadan, the Persian Gulf, is influenced by neighbouring countries such as Iraq with a more spicy flavour. But in the more central provinces the combination is fruit and nuts.

A Persian housewife makes the best of vegetables and fruit in season, from sour unripe grapes to sour unripe plums, until the time when they are fully ripened.

You can buy most ingredients in the supermarket near you but I have also given full names and addresses of all Persian supermarkets in the UK at the back of this book.

Onion, which is the basic ingredient, gives a strong, pungent and pleasant flavour to the dish. Onion is indigenous to Iran, also western Pakistan, and has been traced back to 3200 BC when it was an important food crop for the Egyptians. Onion production dates back to 600 BC and there are records of the crop used by Greeks and Romans about 400–300 BC. By the early Middle Ages, the onion was cultivated in northern Europe. Most tropical parts of the world have large scale onion cultivation.

The ingredients given in all recipes below are for four servings.

SPINACH AND PLUM KHORESHT
Khoresht-e-alu va esfenaj

—❧—

When the plum and prune seasons begin in Iran they are first used for cooking then for eating. The plums are picked when green and firm, with a very sharp flavour, added to the fruit bowl when in season, for family or guests, and dipped in salt before eating.

Spinach and plum Khoresht is an elegant dish often cooked for lunch or dinner and for more informal and special occasions such as weddings and festivals.

The plums today derive from a number of species grown over thousands of years in Europe including Britain, which includes cherries. But the origin of plums is the southwest part of Russia bordering the Caspian Sea. There are many varieties in Britain in many forms (shapes and colours) and these have spread over the years in to Europe. For cooking, greengages or Victoria plums or any other type in season can be used, but for this recipe it is worth using Alu Bokhara, which are small dried plums packed in small bags and obtainable in Persian supermarkets in the west.

If fresh plums are not in season use 115g/4oz dried prunes soaked overnight. Cook them for the same length of time as the fresh (do not use tinned as they are in syrup and rather sweet).

1–2 tablespoons oil
l large onion, chopped
455g/1lb lamb, beef or chicken, cut into
1cm/¹/₂ inch pieces
¹/₄ teaspoon ground saffron or turmeric
¹/₄ teaspoon ground cinnamon
455g/1lb plums
230g/8oz spinach, chopped
1 level tablespoon lime powder
salt and pepper

Heat the oil in a large, heavy saucepan, add the onion and fry gently until golden. Add the meat and stir for 3–4 minutes until browned on all sides. Add the turmeric and stir for one minute. Add 225–300ml/8–10fl oz water and bring to the boil. Reduce the heat to the lowest possible simmer with the pan covered and cook for 1–2 hours until the meat is tender.

Add the plums, spinach, salt, pepper, cinnamon and saffron with lime powder if using. Simmer until thick. Serve with plain rice.

AUBERGINE WITH PLUM KHORESHT
Khoresht-e-badinjan ba alu

—❧—

Potatoes, tomatoes, peppers and petunias are members of the deadly nightshade family – so is aubergine. The old English called it 'mad apple', due to lack of experience.

Opinions on its origins are mixed. It was cultivated at a very early time in India and was mentioned in a 5th century book in China. The British colonists call it Brinjal (an Arabic word). The Arab invasion of Persia during the 7th century spread Arabic culture and influence thoughout Iran, most significantly replacing Mohammed for Zoroastrianism. The Arab alphabets were moulded into the Persian scripts between 637 and 642. During the year 711 the Arabs invaded Spain through north Africa, when the Persian 'Badinjan' became 'Al Badinjan' (in Arabic Al meaning the) and in Spain Berenjana (here the letter J pronounces as KH). It was not until the 13th century when the aubergine spread to northern Europe, imported by the Italian trading state. People were very curious about this vegetable at first, but it became more widely known by the 16th century. Eventually introduced into France during the 18th century, it was not until the 20th century when it found its way into England. The most popular dish in Greece prepared with aubergine is Moussaka. In France and all over Europe another favourite dish using aubergine is ratatouille. But the biggest variety of dishes cooked with aubergine is in a Persian kitchen.

A MARRIAGE FOR EVER

(That is what Zaratrostra said, believing in one God and that there should be only one wife.)

During the seven days of a Zoroastrian wedding the second was the most colourful, the day I always looked forward to, when the bride and the groom received all their presents.

It was a spring day, the scent of newly bloomed roses in the open style house in Yazd spread as far as the front door. I was only a little girl of seven, dressed in a lime floral dress and wearing black patent shoes.

The sound of joy and laughter was loud. The house was jam packed with family and friends, many of whom had taken their seats in the large drawing room where the ceremony was to begin. I pushed my way through, and stood beside Meme's chair. There were several trays covered with green silk cloth which had gold tassels all around, placed on low coffee tables, sprinkled with thyme leaves, white fondant and silver coins.

The bride and the groom sat beside each other on a low chair. Every one waited eagerly for the colourful ceremony to begin. Kety, the bride's mother, who wore a crushed velvet suit in pale green, removed the embroidered green silk cover from one of the trays, as she pointed to her daughter Mahvash and her husband Manoochehr with a smile. Then she placed a small silver tray under their feet, containing a type of grass called movr, symbolising everlasting vegetation (to symbolise everlasting marriage). The atmosphere was filled with happiness and joy and shouts of 'hurrah' as Manoochehr gently removed the stocking from one of his wife's feet. Mahvash reciprocated by removing one of his socks, then the two feet were put on top of one another in the tray on the grass. Kety then handed the groom a china jug containing cold milk. The cheering continued, as the groom poured the milk on his bride's foot, stroking it gently with his other hand as he began to wash it. The bride repeated the ritual, which symbolises strength. The groom then offered a rose water drink to his bride to sip (holding it to her lips) and the bride repeated this for her husband. Finally the tray was moved away and the spilt milk was poured in to the nearest running stream. At this moment the priest and bridegroom recited prayers from the Avesta (the Zoroastrian holy book) wishing the couple a healthy and happy life. The ceremony continued, as Kety removed the cover from the remaining trays, lifting each gift and announcing the name of the person who presented it to the bride and groom, placing them on to the bride's skirt. Then everyone took their places for dinner.

230g/8oz aubergines sliced 5mm/¹/₄ inch thick
salt and pepper
oil
1 large onion, chopped
685g/1¹/₂lb lamb, beef or chicken, cut into cubes
230g/8oz Alu bokhara or fresh plums or prunes
¹/₄ teaspoon each ground saffron and cinnamon
1 level teaspoon dried crushed mint

Put the aubergine slices on a tray or large plate. Sprinkle both sides with salt and leave for 1 hour to extract the dark and bitter juices. Rinse under cold running water and pat dry with a clean tea towel.

Heat some oil gently in a frying pan, add the aubergine slices in batches and fry over a gentle heat for 2 minutes on each side. Transfer to a colander or kitchen paper towel to drain while frying the remainder, then set aside.

Fry the onion in one tablespoon of oil, stir in the meat and spices and cook as in the recipe for spinach and plum khoresht. Add the plums, sprinkle on the dried mint, stir in the cinnamon and saffron, and season with salt and pepper. Add the aubergine

83

PRESENT FROM THE MOTHER

On the third day of the wedding the groom's house was pleasantly untidy, with thyme leaves, pieces of fern and silver coins sprinkled on the highly patterned Persian carpet from the day before. Estekan glasses with their silver holders were placed beside the bubbling samovar and sweets were piled high on large plates. The kitchen was busy with ladies close to the groom, making the Ash-e-Reshteh (the traditional dish made on that day). In early afternoon a cheer went up as the bride's family procession approached the house with a tray of presents covered with a green cloth and gold tassels all the way around. On entering the front door they were showered with thyme leaves, white fondant and silver coins, and the tray was carried into the reception room, to be placed beside other trays next to where the bride sat with her new husband, welcoming her family into her new home.

The joyful atmosphere was filled with the scent of joss-sticks. Tea (chay) and rose water drink (Sharba-te-golab) were offered as everyone gathered round to see the present, as Kety the bride's mother removed the bright cover from the tray to reveal the gift, presenting to her daughter and the groom a set of jewellery. There was a loud cheer of 'Hurrah' as the bride and the groom were the first to help themselves to Ash-e-Reshteh.

slices neatly on top. Baste with some of the juice from the pan. Allow to simmer until thick. DO NOT STIR. Serve with Saffron Rice with orange and almonds. For variation substitute 225ml/8floz tamarind fluid for plums or sour grape juice for tamarind (see Basics chapter for preparation).

AUBERGINE IN SWEET GRAPE JUICE
Badinjan ba ab-e-angoor-e-shirin

I have to dedicate this recipe to my mother for creating this most mouth watering dish by substituting 225–300ml/8floz fresh white grape juice, for plums. Cook the same way. Serve with plain or crispy potato rice sprinkled with roasted almond flakes.

NAZ-E-KHATOON
Tribute to a lady

Pomegranates are a native of Persia. The best grow in Saveh, an agricultural town near Tehran, and Taft in the province of Yazd. They are in season during autumn, the ones with yellowish skin being sweet and only for eating. For cooking choose only the sweet and sour which have very dark red skin. The fruit is now obtainable in the west but the best quality and selection are seen in Persian supermarkets. The sweet and sour pomegranates are delicious to eat as fruit, their seeds piled high on a plate which is often sprinkled with a little salt and eaten with a spoon. But I loved eating them straight from the tree, squeezing the fruit by holding it with both hands then making a hole and sucking the juice out. To eat the seeds or to extract the juice, take a thin slice off the stalk end and cut the fruit in half with a sharp knife and then into quarters. Remove the thin yellow membrane and the pith, which are extremely bitter, then the seeds will release easily. Before modern equipment was introduced into my mother's kitchen she used a hand grinder to extract the juice. The seeds can be placed in a sieve and pressed with the back of a spoon to extract the juice (rather a difficult task). Personally I much prefer an electric juice extractor.

Naze Khatoon is a recipe which goes back many hundreds of years. Traditionally sour pomegranate juice is used in this recipe but to be more practical use 230g/8oz gooseberries (for preparation look under Basics chapter).

685g/1½lb aubergines
225g/8oz tomatoes
225–300ml/8–10floz pomegranate or
gooseberry juice (if using gooseberry
add 1–2 teaspoons sugar or to taste)
1 teaspoon dried mint
salt and pepper
4 heaped tablespoons parsley

Place the aubergines in the oven or under the grill until soft enough to remove the skin, chop and place them into a saucepan. Place the tomatoes into a bowl and cover with boiling water to remove their skin, chop and add into the pan with the parsley, cover with the fruit juice and simmer. Stir in the mint, season with salt and pepper, and simmer until thick. Serve with rice and nan.

RHUBARB KHORESHT
Khoresht-e-rivas

Rhubarb is seasonal, as in the west, and rather an inexpensive fruit which has been used in this recipe for a few hundred years. Rhubarb khoresht, cooked with chicken or lamb, is a family dish, tasty and pretty.

2–3 tablespoons oil
1 large onion, chopped
455g/1lb chicken or lamb, cubed
¼ teaspoon each ground cinnamon, saffron
or turmeric
salt and pepper
1 tablespoon fresh or 1 teaspoon dried and
crushed mint
455g/1lb rhubarb, trimmed and cut into cubes
2 teaspoons sugar
the juice of one lemon

TO GARNISH
roasted flaked almonds

Fry the onion and the chicken, stir in the mint with the spices, then cook as in the recipe for Spinach and Plum Khoresht. Cover with water and simmer until tender. Add the rhubarb, with the sugar and lemon juice, season with salt and pepper, and simmer for an additional 2–3 minutes until the rhubarb is cooked but not mushy. Serve with plain rice and garnish with almond flakes.

CELERY KHORESHT
Khoresht-e-karafs

Celery in a Persian home is used in a cooking pot as well as in a salad bowl.

When it is in season, celery khoresht is cooked at least twice a week as a family dish for lunch or dinner; it is rarely served in a restaurant or at a buffet table.

2 tablespoons oil
1 large onion, chopped
455g/1lb chicken, lamb or beef, cut into portions
½ teaspoon ground saffron or turmeric
230g/8oz celery, trimmed and cut into cubes
and the leaves chopped
2 heaped tablespoons chopped parsley
salt and pepper
1 tablespoon fresh chopped or 1 level teaspoon
dried and crushed mint.
1 level tablespoon dried lime powder or the juice of
one large or lemon to taste

Prepare the meat, onion and spices as in the recipe for Spinach and Plum Khoresht. Cover with 175–225ml/6–8floz water and simmer until tender.

Add the celery with its chopped leaves, season with salt and pepper and simmer until cooked.

Meanwhile add the parsley, mint and lime powder or lemon juice. Serve with rice or nan.

GREEN PLUM KHORESHT
Khoresht-e-govjeh sabz

Follow the recipe for Celery Khoresht but substitute 455g/1lb green sour plums for celery, add 1 tablespoon chopped tarragon or mint and cook in the same way.

GREEN BEAN KHORESHT
Khoresht-e-lubia sabz

Haricot beans, or French beans, are the most popular of all for making this elegant khoresht. The species is thought to have originated in central America, but varieties also come from Peru and Mexico. It was not until the 16th century when it was first introduced to Europe, and soon after to tropical Africa. Now haricot beans are a major crop which grows all over the world. I have a vivid memory of the man calling aloud in the street with his mule to sell his vegetables to the locals, the colourful display of the vegetables were as good as any shop's, and so freshly picked from the nearby farm.

2 tablespoons oil
1 large onion, chopped
455g/1lb chicken, lamb or beef, cut into cubes
455g/1lb green beans, cut into 1cm/¹/₂inch pieces
¹/₂ teaspoon turmeric or saffron
¹/₄ teaspoon ground cinnamon
2 teaspoons tomato purée
1 tablespoon ground lime powder
salt and pepper

Fry the onion and cook the chicken as in the recipe for Spinach and Plum Khoresht. Cover with water and simmer until tender. Add the beans, dissolve the tomato purée in a little liquid from the pan and stir in. Season with salt and pepper, stir in the lime powder, and cook until the mixture is thick. Serve with plain rice.

COURGETTE KHORESHT
Khoresht-e-kadu

Marrow, courgette or zucchini, is a bushy, trailing annual producing large, cylindrical, edible fruits. Immature marrows of some cultivars are called courgettes or zucchini. Their centre of origin is considered to be northern Mexico and the southern United States.

Courgettes are seen in every greengrocers all over Persia. From the beginning of spring and during the summer it is a family favourite. Courgettes are often recommended as a soothing remedy made into soup with lamb for a patient suffering with a bad chest, and they are also extremely laxative.

275g/10oz courgettes, cut into 1cm/¹/₂inch
thick rings
oil
1 large onion, chopped
¹/₄ teaspoon each turmeric and
ground cinnamon
455g/1lb chicken, lamb or beef, cut into cubes
90g/3oz split yellow lentils, cleaned and washed
1 tablespoon tomato purée
salt and pepper

TO GARNISH
chopped parsley

Fry the onion with the chicken and spices as in the recipe for Spinach and Plum Khoresht. Add the split yellow lentils, cover with water and simmer until tender. Season with salt and pepper.

Meanwhile fry the courgettes in shallow oil until golden. Dissolve the tomato purée in 4–5 tablespoons of cold water and stir in. Add the courgette rings neatly in the pan over the meat mixture, sprinkle on the cinnamon, and baste with some of the gravy from the pan without stirring. Garnish with chopped parsley. Serve with rice or nan. The courgette can also be added without being fried.

POTATO AND PLUM KHORESHT
Khoresht-e-sibzamini ba alu

Potatoes are annual vegetables. After cultivation the plant produces small red flowers, which we were warned as children are poisonous. The origin of potatoes is in the Andean highlands of Peru, Colombia, Ecuador and Bolivia, where they had been cultivated for more than 2000 years, before the first arrival of the Spanish during the 16th century.

Despite the belief that it was first brought to the west by Sir Walter Raleigh, it was brought in first by Sir Thomas Harriot, in 1587 and then it became a widespread crop all over northern Europe. The first crop of potatoes to arrive in north America was taken by the Scottish emigrants. Potato cultivation now is world wide and it is grown as a major crop.

Potato and Plum Khoresht is a popular dish, especially during Zoroastrian weddings. I have a vivid memory of watching the men cooking in large saucepans enough for the guests plus enough for the many people who could not attend the wedding, which volunteers took to them on a tray either on foot or by transport. A very simple dish, and yet so delicious.

2 tablespoons oil
685g/1¹/₂lb lamb, beef or chicken, cut into portions
1 large onion, chopped
¹/₂ teaspoon each ground cinnamon and saffron or turmeric
685g/1¹/₂lb potatoes, diced large
455g/1lb alu bokhara, or plums (preferably red)

Fry the onion and the meat with the spices as in the recipe for Spinach and Plum Khoresht, cover with water and simmer until tender. Meanwhile, add the potatoes and the plums. Cook until the mixture becomes thick. Serve hot with nan or rice.

For a variation substitute 90g/3oz split yellow lentils for potatoes, and add three cloves of crushed garlic, fried with the onion, and substitute skinned and chopped tomatoes for plums.

SPLIT YELLOW LENTILS AND LIME KHORESHT
Khoresht-e-ghimeh

A dish cooked for all occasions, especially during weddings and, for the Muslims of Iran, cooked for a sad occasion. Only very recently I visited Iran, and I was in Tehran when my sister-in-law advised me that, because it was tasoa va ashoora, almost every street was contributing charity food for the public as this was the anniversary of Ali's death. The Muslims' first Imam and leader of a Shiite sect, Emam Ali was attacked by his enemy Yazid a Khalifeh and died on the second day of Ashoora. I followed my sister-in-law and we saw men and woman queuing up in the street, the numbers reached over a hundred in each direction. But it was worth waiting to take part in this very sad occasion. Eventually there was a seat in the garden, and the aroma of this dish wafted throughout the large and magnificent surroundings. Many people took their family share of food home with them after this great charitable occasion.

oil
l large onion, chopped
455g/1lb lamb, cubed large
1 teaspoon turmeric
¹/₄ teaspoon ground cinnamon
salt and pepper
90g/3oz split yellow lentils

87

ALI REZA THE EIGHTH IMAM

When I was seven years old my Muslim Nanny Malog dressed me up to go to the local mosque where she prayed. She promised that one day she would take me to Mashhad to see the tomb of Ali Reza the eighth Imam (the holy man) but it was much later in life when I finally did travel to the holy city, some 540 miles east of Tehran. I remember seeing the golden dome of the 200-metre high mosque glistening at a distance, as the plane was banking to land.

I was met by my friend Shahnaz, who took me to her home in the suburbs. Soon after arriving she suggested a visit to the shrine during midday, as many would prefer the cooler part of the day and there would be fewer pilgrims about.

Shahnaz gave me the choice of several chadors, the long cloth worn by Muslim women, to cover their clothes. I recalled the colour of Malog's chador and chose brown with white spots, remembering how she taught me to wear it as a little girl. I wrapped the long shawl over my clothes, making sure that my hair and face were completely covered with only one eye showing.

It was exciting, arriving on the wide avenues of the city centre, with bustling people and heavy traffic, but as we approached the mosque, I felt quite relaxed. On entering the ante-chamber in the forecourt of the mosque, we were asked to remove our shoes, as it is the custom to enter the mosque in bare feet.

The mosque was made up of several high-ceilinged rooms, some of which were highly ornate with mirror-mosaic patterns set into plaster or woodwork. Gold leaf was much in evidence, decorating walls and ceilings, and numerous chandeliers hung from the ceilings, giving the place an almost fairy-tale atmosphere.

There were several thousand pilgrims, and hardly enough room for anyone to move about, but I was determined to touch the famous Zary near the tomb and make a wish. I found my way amongst the thousands. Some who had already reached the tomb held on to their gold jewellery – bangles, rings, chains and necklaces – as they thronged through the decorative iron lattice work which covered the actual tomb. Some cried out to Imam-Reza, urging him to make their wishes come true. The atmosphere was highly charged with emotion and every moment more pilgrims arrived.

Back at home Shahnaz served chilled rose water drink and showed me around her modern house. Dinner was served in the garden, after which my hosts allowed me to sleep on the flat roof of the house so that I could enjoy the spectacular scenery of this holy city under the stars.

1 level tablespoon tomato purée
l tablespoon dried lime powder or 4–5 dried limes,
cut in half with their seeds removed,
or lemon juice
4 medium potatoes, cut into chip
(French fry) shapes

TO GARNISH
a few red plums or prunes with a tablespoon
of garden peas

Fry the onion with the chicken and spices as in the recipe for Spinach and Plum Khoresht, cover with water, add in the split yellow lentils and simmer until tender.

Meanwhile fry the potatoes and set aside. Add the tomato purée with the lime powder, season with salt and pepper and simmer until thick.

Serve in a round platter, garnished with potato chips and plums/prunes and a few garden peas. Serve with rice.

SPLIT PEA AND AUBERGINE KHORESHT
Ghimeh-e-badenjan

—◆—

Follow the recipe as above, substituting 2 large aubergines for the potatoes, prepared and fried as in the recipe for Aubergine Khoresht.

KHORESHT-E-GOL DAR CHAMAN
Flower in the lawn

—◆—

Garlic, like onion, gives a strong aromatic flavour to food and is a favourite flavouring in Persia. Garlic has been cultivated for many thousands of years and is a species of onion. It is believed that it may have originated in Iran. It was also cultivated in Egypt before 2000 BC. It is now widely grown throughout the world. Garlic is good for asthmatic patients, is known to prevent some rheumatic problems, and is also known to increase temperature. The green leaves can be chopped and used in salads. Traditionally this dish is vegetarian but if you like to add meat use 455g/1lb lamb or chicken, cubed, add to the saucepan with the fried onion, cover with water and simmer until tender. Add in the remaining ingredients, following the recipe.

4–5 tablespoons oil
1 large onion, chopped
1–2 cloves of garlic, chopped fine
455g/1lb podded broad beans
60g/2oz chopped dill
salt and pepper
4 eggs

Fry the onion in two tablespoon of the oil until golden, add the garlic, and stir for a minute. Add the beans and the dill, cover with 225ml/8fl oz water and simmer for 5–7 minutes until the beans are cooked. Season with salt and pepper. Add the remaining oil, break the eggs in each corner of the pan and allow to set. Serve with nan or rice.

CARROT KHORESHT
Khoresht-e-havij

—◆—

The Zoroastrian called the carrot 'Gezer', which was the term used for this vegetable in ancient Persia. Carrots grown in Iran are usually red and large. The juice is extracted during the summer season in every grocers, and on the way to work one glass makes a delicious morning drink. It is believed to come originally from southwest Asia and the Mediterranean.

2 tablespoons oil
1 large onion, chopped
685g/1$^1/_2$lb chicken, lamb or beef,
cut into cubes
$^1/_4$ teaspoon each ground cinnamon, saffron
or turmeric
salt and pepper
275g/10oz carrots, diced large
230g/8oz Alu bokhara, or fresh plums,
or 115g/4oz dried prunes

TO GARNISH
a few almond flakes

Fry the onion and the chicken with the spices as in the recipe for Spinach and Plum Khoresht. Cover with water and simmer until tender. Meanwhile stir in the saffron, cinnamon and the carrots with the plums or prunes, and season with salt and pepper. Simmer until the mixture becomes thick. Serve with rice, garnished with flaked almonds.

DILL AND CORIANDER KHORESHT
Khoresht-e-bosmocheh
◆

The herb season in Persia lasts from early spring to late autumn, when you can see the housewives queuing patiently to buy their share of herbs as their fragrance permeates throughout the busy bazaar. Herbs are bought almost every day, or at least four times a week, not just to eat them fresh, but to dry for winter use. Usually they are sold in bundles tied with a string to make them easy to carry.

I have vivid memories of my childhood days in Yazd in mid-summer when the tranquillity filled the cobbled narrow streets in the residential area of Yazd, with the odd bicycle bell breaking the silence warning the occasional pedestrian out at that time of the day. The wooden doors to people's houses were left open, with ladies dressed in typical colourful Zoroastrian costume. There was the soft sound of a spinning wheel, some busy embroidery, crocheting or knitting, and others sitting on small, hand-made mattresses (doshak) with large copper trays were sorting out the herbs to wash and dry on large batik cloth to store for winter use. The small open-style garden was cultivated with individual herbs such as mint, tarragon, Persian basil, costmary, used for flavour and decoration, and eaten with nan and panir (feta cheese), accompanied with dates and walnuts as an appetiser. Other herbs such as coriander, dill, chives, parsley, spinach and fenugreek, were all used in the family khoresht.

2 tablespoons oil
1 large onion, chopped
1 clove of garlic, crushed
115g/4oz black eyed beans, soaked
455g/1lb chicken, lamb or beef, cut into cubes
1 teaspoon turmeric
salt and pepper
115g/4oz each dill and coriander leaves, chopped
1 large potato, diced small

TO SERVE
lemon juice

Fry the onion, garlic and chicken with the spices as in the recipe for Spinach and Plum Khoresht.

Pour the water off the soaking beans and add them to the pan. Cover with water and simmer until the meat and the beans are cooked. Meanwhile add the potatoes with the chopped dill and the coriander. Season with salt and pepper. Serve lemon juice at the table. Serve with nan or plain rice.

LOUNGE WITH A STREAM

Visiting family and friends was always unexpected, and there was never a formal invitation; food was prepared in only a matter of minutes, even if it was a large gathering. Almost everything was from the garden. Everyone liked to visit my cousin Banoo's home, which was built on a green and fertile piece of land, just on the outskirts of Yazd, with fruit trees overlapping the high walls. Friends and family were always welcomed warmly.

The main entrance to the house was from the orchard.

The narrow bricked path led into the main building, where everyone loved the unusual sitting room, as a crystal clear stream ran through the middle under the floor!

On either side of the stream there was a decorative tiled floor, with full-size Persian carpets laid on top. The room was cool and fresh, decorated with Persian ornaments. Lunch was served on low furniture. And herbs (sabsi khordan) such as mint, tarragon, basil were washed in the stream which was pure enough to drink.

QUINCE KHORESHT
Khoresht-e-beh

The quince is indigenous to Persia and commonly grown both in the garden and in large orchards, mostly in the mountainous region. This vegetable, which also counts as a fruit, is used for sweet and savoury dishes. As an old remedy the seeds are supposed to reduce coughs: place a few seeds under your tongue to soothe the throat.

2 tablespoons oil
1 large onion, chopped
685g/1¹/₂lb chicken or lamb, diced large
¹/₄ teaspoon each ground cinnamon, saffron
or turmeric
455g/1lb quince, peeled and cubed
8oz Alu bokhara or fresh plums or dried prunes
the juice of one lemon
1 teaspoon sugar or to taste
salt and pepper
1 teaspoon dried crushed mint

Fry the onion and the chicken with the spices as in the recipe for Spinach with Plum Khoresht, cover with water and simmer until tender. Meanwhile add the quince with the plums, season with salt and pepper, add the crushed mint, stir in the sugar with the lemon juice, and simmer until the quince is soft.

For a variation, add 60g/2oz split yellow lentils to the pan with the chicken, and simmer, following the recipe as above. Serve with plain rice.

OKRA KHORESHT
Khoresht-e-bamya

This is a favourite dish for every one, during the okra season, and was often cooked at least twice a week. During my childhood days in Yazd this dish was eaten in mid-summer under the vine trellis, with the scent of vegetation in the air, the vegetable iself having been freshly picked from the garden.

2 tablespoons oil
1 large onion, chopped
2 cloves of garlic, crushed
455g/1lb lamb or chicken, cubed
¹/₂ teaspoon turmeric
¹/₄ teaspoon cumin seeds (optional)
salt and pepper
2 teaspoons tomato purée
230g/8oz okra, tail removed and cut into half
if too large

TO GARNISH
chopped fresh parsley

Fry the onion, the garlic and the chicken with the spices as in the recipe for Spinach and Plum Khoresht. Cover with water and simmer until tender. Season with salt and pepper and add the okra. Meanwhile dissolve the tomato purée in some of the juice from the pan and stir in. Simmer for another 7–10 minutes or until the okra is cooked but not too soft (do not stir). Serve with plain rice garnished with parsley.

For a variation substitute 455g/1lb podded peas for okra, and cook in exactly the same way.

For a vegetarian dish substitute one large diced potato for the chicken.

CAULIFLOWER KHORESHT
Khoresht-e-gol-e-kalam

2 tablespoons oil
1 large onion, chopped
2 cloves of garlic, crushed
900g/2lb chicken, lamb or beef, cubed
¹/₂ teaspoon ground cinnamon
¹/₄ teaspoon turmeric
90g/3oz split yellow lentils
345g/12oz cauliflower florets
salt and pepper
2 tablespoons each chopped parsley and mint
1 tablespoons tomato purée
the juice of one lemon

Fry the onion, garlic, chicken and the spices as in the recipe for Spinach and Plum Khoresht. Cover with water, add the lentils and simmer until tender. Season with salt and pepper, stir in the tomato purée, lemon juice and chopped parsley. Add the cauliflower and simmer until cooked but not too soft. Serve with rice.

APPLE KHORESHT WITH CHESTNUT AND MINT
Khoresht-e-sib ba balut va naana

Apples are a widespread fruit in southwest Asia, especially in the Caucasus. They are also extensively grown in western Europe, including Britain. The growing of apples can be traced back to the Middle East, Egypt and from there to Greece and eventually Rome, then across Europe and to Britain. From there, the colonists introduced the fruit to other parts of the world. This highly versatile food was recognised long ago. A fruit which was not known during ancient times, the plant is believed to have been introduced into Britain in about 1568.

Fresh chestnuts may be used when in season and for this recipe you will need 345g/12oz. Prepare and cook them as in the introduction for Grey Mullet with Chestnuts, Grapes and Herbs (page 128).

140g/5oz dried chestnuts
2–3 tablespoons oil
1 medium onion, chopped
¼ teaspoon saffron or turmeric
salt and pepper
285g/10oz lamb or beef, cubed
2 medium uncooked beetroot, peeled and cubed
1–2 teaspoon dried mint
1 teaspoon sugar or to taste
4 large eating apples (not cooking apples as they may disintegrate), peeled, cored and cubed large
the juice of one small lemon

TO GARNISH
a few almond flakes

Wash the chestnuts, place in a bowl and cover with water. Leave to soak overnight.

The next day, place the chestnuts in a small saucepan and cover with 325ml/11floz cold water. Bring to the boil, reduce the heat and cover tightly. Simmer for 45 minutes until soft, then drain.

Fry the onion, the chicken and spices as in the recipe for Spinach and Plum Khoresht. Add the beetroot, chestnuts and saffron, cover with 750ml/1–1¼ pint of water and simmer until tender. Meanwhile add the apples, mint, sugar and lemon juice, season with salt and pepper. Serve with plain rice, garnished with almond flakes.

ROOF PARTY

During hot summer days when the sun sank behind Shirkooh, the mountain of milk, the air over the cobbled stones around the garden was still hot. There was a cool breeze on the flat roof of the house where cousins gathered watching the dusk approach. The moon shone through the broken clouds, constantly changing shapes, and we children pointed out as they formed new pictures. Sometimes they would completely disappear leaving the night sky visible and we would study the starlit heavens.

Even as a little girl I knew the star constellations. They often seemed near enough to touch and I felt they were almost joining in our conversation. Dinner was served sofreh style, prepared by aunt Pari and Memeh. They both made dishes to compliment each other, for every one to taste different dishes. Sometimes after the meal neighbours came to play cards, my brothers played citar and my cousin would play his violin. Some joined in handkerchief dancing until gone midnight.

MINCE AND POTATO KHORESHT
Khoresht-e-kimeh ba sibzamini

This family dish is popular in every city and every home, a quick and easy meal to prepare, and one which is economical and tasty. It is eaten during harsh winter evenings, sitting around the Korsi (traditional fire) or during hot summer days in the cool cellar.

3 tablespoons oil
1 large onion, chopped
685g/1¹/₂lb minced lamb, beef or chicken
1 teaspoon turmeric
¹/₄ teaspoon ground cinnamon
salt and pepper
455g/1lb potatoes, diced large
2 teaspoons tomato purée

Fry the onion in the oil, add the meat, and stir to brown, add the spices, season with salt and pepper add the potatoes, cover with water, simmer for 20 minutes or until the potatoes are tender.

Meanwhile dissolve the tomato purée in a little water add to the pan, simmer until thick.

Serve with rice or Nan.

LAMB IN HERB SAUCE
Khoresht-e-ghormeh sabsi

Chives are grown for their leaves, which are used in flavouring many dishes in Iran (the kind that grows in Iran is called tareh, a much larger leaf). It is widely grown in the wild, especially in countries such as China, India and Iran.

Khoresht-e-Ghormeh sabsi is a popular, traditional, dish for all occasions. A table is never complete without it; there is the aroma of Ghormeh sabsi in every Persian kitchen.

Chives are traditionally used in this recipe for their flavour, but to be more practical leek is used instead.

BRINGING THE BRIDE

Bringing the bride – or Arooskeshan – is an old Zoroastrian custom. The colourful procession from the bride's to the groom's house started in the early hours of the afternoon. Close members of the family followed the shy bride who held on to her father's waist as he stopped along the street, demanding the bride's welcoming fee from the groom's family.

Old and young stood at the entrance of their front door, lighting a small fire of soft wood and singing poems of good luck while showering the bride with dried thyme leaves and white fondant. It took several hours to cover the short distance.

The wooden door to the groom's house was left open, and there was a display of red roses, with the scent of burning sandalwood and joss sticks filling the cobbled entrance. Family and friends gathered around the octagonal pond in the open style house handing each other pieces of fern, thyme leaves with white fondant and silver coins.

Plates were piled high with various sweets, and some people were helping themselves to tea (chay) from the brass samovar.

Tambourine music filled the air and many of the guests would take part in the handkerchief dance.

The bride was welcomed with the loud cheer of Hurrah, as she entered her husband's house. The priest led the young couple round a small fire in the garden which was lit to signify warmth and sincerity. The shouts of Hurrah continued and they were showered with thyme leaves, sugar plums and silver coins. Then they were led through to the lounge for dinner, where the husband announced he was to give her property and jewellery.

115g/4 oz red kidney beans, cleaned and soaked
2 tablespoons oil
1 large onion, chopped
455g/1lb lean lamb, cubed
1 teaspoon mixed cinnamon, cardamon, ginger,
turmeric and paprika or ½ teaspoon turmeric
salt and pepper
1 medium leek, chopped.
275g/10oz chopped parsley
1 teaspoon chopped fenugreek
2 tablespoon lime powder, or fresh lime
but it will lack flavour
salt and pepper

Fry the onion with the chicken and spices as in the recipe for Spinach and Plum Khoresht.

Remove the chicken into a dish, with a slotted spoon. Pour the water off the red kidney beans and add them to the pan. Cover with water, bring to the boil and boil vigorously for 10 minutes, then reduce the heat to simmer until they are tender. 45 minutes before the end of cooking add the chicken, with the chopped herbs, and the leek. Add the lime powder and continue simmering until the mixture becomes thick. Serve with plain rice. The beans can be cooked in a pressure cooker separately, which will take about 30 minutes to become tender.

For a variation make this northern (Gilani) dish:

MEAT WITH BEAN AND HERB KHORESHT
Khoresht-e-goosht-e-torsh

Substitute 230ml/8floz orange or sour grape or gooseberry juice and 230g/8oz tomatoes for the lime powder, adding a few sprigs of finely chopped dill in with the herbs. Also for both recipes substitute soaked and drained black eyed beans for red kidney beans, which can be simmered with the other ingredients.

TRADITIONAL WEDDING CEREMONY

A large copper tray containing various nuts, sugar plums, dried fruit such as apricots, peaches, sultanas, figs, sweets, fondant and crystallised sugar (Nabat) was placed on the walnut table in the hall of the fire temple in Tehran. Beside it was a display of flowers and a lit candle.

My sister Sarvar wore a long white gown, with lace covering her hair and forehead, and she sat beside Khosrov, her husband to be.

Every seat was taken and the atmosphere was filled with joy. Sarvar smiled at the family and friends as Rostam, a close family friend, held a green silk cloth over the groom's head. In the cloth was a pomegranate (sign of fertility), boiled egg (meaning past sin), a needle and cotton (for future occupation), scissors (symbolising compatibility) and some thyme leaves and sugar plums.

The ceremony began by Moobed Ardeshir (the priest) reciting from the Avesta in a musical voice. The marriage bond was said and the benediction announced, asking Sarvar to devote one day in the Zoroastrian calendar for charity, to help the poor and disabled. At the end of the service the couple placed a sweet in each other's mouths, to loud cheers from the congregation.

My mother got hold of the boiled egg and wrapped it up, to throw away the past sin as soon as possible.

Everyone waited behind as the priest accompanied Sarvar and Khosrov to the fire temple. According to Zoroastrian history the fire has burned in the brazen vessel for the past 3000 years. The priest blessed the couple and recited again from the holy Avesta, while walking three times in a circle around the vessel. A nut and sweet mixture was distributed amongst the congregation, and then everyone took their seats in a large hall in the temple grounds for a dinner to celebrate the big occasion.

CHICKEN IN POMEGRANATE PURÉE
Khoresht-e-fesenjan

The large walnut trees grew everywhere in the mountain region of Yazd, in every back street, on the slopes of the mountains or in the cultivated lands of Manshad. The trees were very high. My grandfather estimated that some reached 18–30m (60–100ft). The nuts are indigenous to Persia, and they have been cultivated extensively for thousands of years. Their timber is used for the best quality furniture which can be seen in every Persian home.

Nuts are a form of food that prehistoric people survived on. It is believed that the first walnut tree was taken to Greece in the year 490 BC, then on to Rome. It was not until the 16th century when it was introduced to England, and in the 1930s found its way to North America.

The leaves have a very pleasant and strong smell when they are crushed (my father often used it for brewing wine). The oil has a very delicate flavour when added to salad, and it can also be used for frying. But it tends to go rancid quickly. I remember as a child reaching the thick branches of the tree as it overlapped the flat roof of our country home in Manshad and enjoying the sap which trickled down into my dress.

Research has shown that some parts of the tree have medicinal uses. The leaves are a laxative, and are also the best cure for someone with fungal disease.

During autumn when the family had the fun of sharing and picking the leaves then we would spread them on a large batik cloth in the empty room in the house where it was sheltered and warm allowing them to dry. Some were given to family and friends, and later were made into a form of broth used for the treatment of coughs and vertigo. The nuts were eaten by young and old as it is strongly believed they help prevent kidney stones.

Some part of the leaf was believed to be a treatment for cancer, as research shows that it contains anti-cancer qualities. One of the traditional remedies for sore throats was to boil the green kashk, mix it with fresh honey and gargle it. If someone had a skin problem, walnut oil was used. The husk was often used for cleaning teeth.

The leaves were always kept handy, as an instant treatment for an insect bite. My vivid memory of my childhood days in Manshad is walking up the steep path picking the nuts from the lower branches of the trees and with a knife splitting them in the middle, covering my hands in their dark paint. The nuts are released from their shells whole and neatly. The shelled nuts were sold along the steep hills of Shemiran north of Tehran.

The dried fresh nuts are used for confectionery and cakes, and of course just eaten as nuts. For full flavour as fresh nuts, place them in a bowl and cover with cold water. Change the water several times during soaking. Then drain them about 15 minutes before eating. Buying walnuts in large supermarkets gives rather a bad impression as they are usually stale with a very bitter taste. The best quality are those regularly imported from Persia and available in Persian supermarkets in the west, and some reputable Indian grocers. Eat one or two when you are still in the shop, to make sure of their quality.

Walnuts are eaten on all occasions during every season: in autumn fresh from their shells; in winter with nan, feta cheese (panir) and dates, and sometimes figs; in spring as nuts on their own; and in summer as hors d'oeuvre with nan, panir and dates. They are also pickled when they are very young with their shells. Walnuts can be ground to give a delicate flavouring to cooking, such as Fesenjan, a traditional and aristocratic dish of ancient Persia popular to this day, prepared for honoured guests.

The main ingredient to give the dish a special texture and colour with the most delicate taste of sweet and savoury is the mixture of walnuts and pomegranate purée. The added meat can be minced lamb, veal or any type of poultry. It can also be prepared with duck, game or pheasant. The most popular meat is chicken or mince. Pomegranate purée is obtainable in Persian supermarkets. It is far better to buy the purée rather than use the juice. Never use sugar or lemon juice as this will take away the natural flavour.

1–2 tablespoons oil
1 large onion, chopped
900g/2lb boneless chicken, cut into portions
115g/4oz ground walnuts
¼ teaspoon ground saffron
salt and pepper
1 teaspoon ground cinnamon
230–275g/8–10oz pomegranate purée
according to taste

Fry the onion with the chicken as in the recipe for Spinach and Plum Khoresht. Add the walnuts and cover with water, simmer until the chicken is tender. Meanwhile add the cinnamon and the saffron and season with salt and pepper. Dissolve the pomegranate purée with a little water and add it to the pan. Cook until the mixture thickens. Serve with rice.

For a variation grate 60g/2oz onion over 230g/8oz minced chicken or meat, take balls a little larger than hazelnuts, smooth in your hands and fry them with the onion. You could also substitute cubed fish for meat, cooking the fish for only 10–15 minutes.

CHICKEN IN ORANGE, SAFFRON AND NUT SAUCE
Khoresht-e-morgh ba ab-e-porteghal

➤

The following two recipes are also dedicated to my mother for her wonderful creation.

Orange is a name which derives from ancient Persia. In today's Zoroastrian dialect it is called norang, showing only a slight variation from orange in English and orange in French. These noranges, which grew in the Caspian region for more than two thousand years, were sour. After the Arab invasion during the 7th century and the conquest of Spain in 711, the plant found its way into Spain through north Africa. But the oranges which grew in China were sweet and wild, and were brought in by the Portuguese explorer Vasco Da Gama during the 16th century on his way back to Europe, replacing the sour oranges in the Caspian and Persian Gulf for sweet ones. Out of respect for the explorer, the Persians named the orange porteghal, after the country of his birth. It was at this time that sweet oranges became known in Europe and across the Atlantic to the USA.

ZOROASTRIAN WEDDING INVITATION

One of the most vivid memories of my childhood days, was the old tradition for wedding invitations amongst the small Zoroastrian community in Yazd. Wedding cards were sent for those living far away, but for those living within walking distance, the invitation came from two ladies, a relation from each side of the boy and girl. They dressed in traditional colourful Zoroastrian costume with their wedding guest list, and walked gracefully through the narrow cobbled street area of Yazd, calling un-expectedly at individual houses to offer invitations.

As a little girl on the way home from school, I used to watch the direction of the ladies, hoping they were heading for our street and our house. I used to run really fast to tell Memeh the invitation ladies were heading for our house, so that she could put the samovar on for tea (chay). I would sit there anxiously, hoping it was not a false alarm, as they might be heading for the next-door-neighbour and not for us.

Lemons are known to have originated from India where they grew wild, and also in Burma and China. Again it was the Arabs who replanted them into Persia and from there they spread to north Africa. It has been said that the first lemon was taken by Christopher Columbus from Spain to Haiti in the year 1493.

There are two different types of lime in Persia: the sweet limes are the most well known with extremely delicious sweet juice; I have not seen them in any other part of the world. The green skinned limes are very popular and during the season shopkeepers extract the juice, which is then bottled and sold. It is believed the sharp limes are originally from the East Indies, then the Arabs introduced them to India and Iran.

2 tablespoons oil
1 large onion, chopped
900g/2lb chicken, cut into portions
4 medium carrots, diced
3 large oranges
1 teaspoon sugar
2 teaspoons rice flour
$\frac{1}{2}$ teaspoon each ground saffron and cinnamon
salt and pepper
about 30 shelled pistachio nuts

TO GARNISH
a few almond flakes

Fry the onion in the oil, add the chicken and toss to brown. Cover with water and simmer until tender. Add the carrots. Prepare the orange rinds as shown in the basic recipes chapter (orange rinds p. 188), squeeze their juice, and reserve. Mix the juice with the flour, the saffron and the cinnamon, stir the flour mixture into the chicken with the orange rind and liquid and the nuts and cook until the sauce thickens. Serve with plain rice, garnished with almond flakes.

THE FIRST DAY OF NOVROOZ

The mild spring air blew over the pink and white blossoms on the almond and fruit trees, scattering their petals over the newly bloomed garden. Numerous different roses and highly scented Narcissus gave out spectacular colours. Some, freshly cut, were displayed in every room, their fragrance permeating throughout the house. It is still the custom for a traditional Zoroastrian home to have a table set with haftsheen, seven items starting with the letter 'sh' symbolising prosperity and plenty in the New Year.

A small table covered with a hand-embroidered white tablecloth was placed on a highly patterned Persian carpet, and reflected in a full-sized mirror. Fully grown cress in an earthenware pot (koozeh) is placed in the centre of the table and surrounded with wine (sharab), milk (shir), jujub (shilooneh), sweets (shirini), a drink made from rose water, sugar and basil seeds (sharbat), fenugreek (shanbelileh) and greenery (sheshah). These seven things symbolise the making of a wish to our lord, asking for food and nourishment in the coming year. The three candles (shaam) placed in front of the display symbolise good thought, good word and good deed – the words Zaratrostra taught his people. Other items also placed on the table included a hand mirror, a rose water pourer containing rose water and an apple studded with silver coins in a bowl of water and thyme (the sign of wealth), the holy Zoroastrian book (Avesta), a picture of Zaratrostra, a bowl of fruit, some bread (nan) and cheese (panir).

Following this Zoroastrian custom of Novrooz, in a Muslim home a table is also set with seven things, but these are different and all begin with the letter 's' so as to eliminate the wine (sharab) from their table. It is set with greenery (sabsi), an apple (sib), vinegar (serkeh), garlic (seer), sumac (sumagh), hyacinth (sonbol) and sweet drink (sharbat).

CHICKEN DRUMSTICKS WITH ORANGE SAUCE
Ran-e-morgh ba ab-e-porteghal

1 small onion, grated
½ teaspoon ground cinnamon, cardamom,
turmeric and paprika, mixed
6 large or 12 small chicken drumsticks, skinned
(total weight 900g–1kg/2–2½lb)
60g/2oz margarine or butter
3 large oranges
2 teaspoons sugar
1 teaspoon riceflour or cornflour
salt and pepper

TO GARNISH
a few almond flakes

Preheat the oven to 180°C/350°F/Gas mark 4.

Rub the onion and the spices over the chicken drumsticks. Melt the margarine or the butter in a large casserole, add the drumsticks and toss to coat. Cover and cook in the oven for about 1 hour until tender.

Prepare the orange rinds as in the basic recipes chapter (orange rinds p. 188). Remove the drumsticks from the casserole with a slotted spoon, cover and keep warm. Pour the cooking liquid into a clean saucepan, leaving behind any fat. Halve the oranges and squeeze the juice.

Mix the flour and the orange juice together, stir into the cooking liquid and simmer gently until thick. Season with salt and pepper.

Arrange the chicken on dinner plates and coat with the sauce. Serve with crispy potato rice. Sprinkle with the glazed orange rind and the toasted almonds.

PUMPKIN KHORESHT
Khoresht-e-kadu halvaie

3 tablespoons oil
1 large onion, chopped
900g/2lb lamb or chicken, cubed
230g/8oz pumpkin, peeled and cut into cubes
115g/4oz dried Persian plums or any fresh plums,
or 4oz prunes, soaked
the juice of one large lemon or to taste
2 teaspoons sugar or to taste
½ teaspoon ground saffron
salt and pepper

Fry the onion and the chicken in two tablespoon of the oil, as in the recipe for Spinach and Plum Khoresht. Cover with water and simmer until tender, then add the plums. Fry the pumpkin in the remaining oil until golden. Stir the saffron and sugar into the pan containing the meat, add the pumpkins and simmer gently, adding the lemon juice to taste. Baste the vegetables with some of the juice from the pan. Do not stir as the pumpkins will go mushy. Lift the pumpkin onto a serving dish, then pour over the remaining ingredients. Serve with plain rice.

SOUR CHICKEN KHORESHT
Khoreshte morg-e-torsh

2 tablespoons oil
1 medium onion, chopped
2 cloves of garlic, crushed
455g/1lb chicken, cut into portions
½ teaspoon turmeric
30g/1oz split yellow lentils
230g/8oz mixed leek, parsley, coriander and mint,
chopped
2 eggs, beaten a little
150ml/¼ pint sour orange, or sour grape juice
or the juice of 8oz cooked gooseberries
salt and pepper

Fry the onion with the garlic and the chicken in the oil, as in the recipe for Spinach and Plum Khoresht. Stir in the turmeric, add the lentils, cover with water and simmer until tender. Add the fruit juice and the herbs, season with salt and pepper, stir in the eggs. Serve with rice or nan.

SOUR CHICKEN KEBAB KHORESHT
Khoresht-e-torsheh kabab

oil
1 medium onion, chopped
685g/1½lb chicken, cut into portions
½ teaspoon each ground cinnamon and turmeric
salt and pepper
2 medium potatoes, sliced into rings

about 6 small tomatoes
230ml/8floz sour orange or unripe grape juice, or gooseberry juice, or lemon juice to taste (for a sweet dish add the same amount of fresh grape juice or the juice of any fruit)

Fry the onion in two tablespoons of the oil, add the chicken with the spices, and cook as in the recipe for Spinach with Plum Khoresht.

Meanwhile fry the potatoes in oil until brown on both sides, fry the tomato in the oil in the same pan, and place over the chicken mixture. Add the fruit juice and simmer until the mixture thickens. Serve with rice, garnished with the potato and tomato mixture. For a variation prepare two medium aubergines as in the recipe for Aubergine and Plum Khoresht and add to the garnish.

THE FOOD OF THE CASPIAN

After travelling through many parts of Iran where people live at altitudes of up to 2,000 metres, we arrived at the Caspian coast where the level is only 20 metres. In contrast to many parts of the country – in particular in Yazd where the clouds are rare and appear as mere decoration and the air is dry and limpid – we arrived at the more humid Caspian. Our skin and lungs recaptured a forgotten flexibility, and the thick clouds burst on to the neighbouring mountains. There is no sign of ghanat in Rasht as the annual rainfall is between 1 and 30 metres.

We drove along the land where rice, cotton, wheat, barley, sugar cane and tea were grown.

I have vivid memories of my childhood days walking through some of the fields. There was no access to the thick forest covering the abrupt slopes of the Alborz mountain.

The mountains were very close to the coast – some only just over a kilometre away.

The sound of torrents was angry in deep ravines where only hunters dared to reach.

The torrents became calmer as the river became wider, forming large estuaries where the fishermen were catching the sturgeon, which could be between 2–3 metres long and weigh between 80 and 100kg. It has been recorded that animals over 800kg have been caught. We watched them removing the caviar and the flesh was to be stored. The fishermen explained that the caviar is usually about one tenth of their weight.

We drove along the beach, a really long beach with pure sand. It was a pleasing and relaxing atmosphere to stroll along the sea shore in the evening as the aroma of cooking fish such as carp, perch, pike, mullet or grilled sturgeon mixed with many other dishes.

Our daytime walk was along the coast road of the channel linking Pahlavi lake to the sea, where we sat on wooden stools drinking hot tea with a snack of pistachio nuts.

We drove through by far the most beautiful site of the whole coast: wooded hills spread rolling down to the beach, with the impressive backdrop of the Alborz mountain. The coast line was a continuous bed of flowers, palm and orange trees.

We continued driving the 65km from Bandar-E-Pahlavi beyond Hashtpar very close to the mountain and very near the sea. We had to cross several jungles (the word jungle is originally from the Persian language). It was almost impossible to penetrate any of these jungles which give cover to a wide range of wild animals such as leopards, jackals, boars and tigers. In recent years a Persian lion has been spotted.

The rainy Caspian plateau is the most suitable area in the country for growing rice, which is the main agricultural crop of the region. Fruit have become increasingly important in Mazandaran, in particular oranges and citrus fruit.

The most attractive part of the region, Gilan which is the centre of Gilan province, which has an area of 14,000 sq km and a population of more than 3 million, was independent until the 16th century and still has its own distinctive dialect and traditional dress. As the city developed late it has less archaeological interest than Mazandaran.

The most important river is sefid rud (the white river) which runs from Sadd-e-sefid rud (the white river dam) on the border with Zanjan province to the Caspian Sea. This area is the wettest part of Iran and it produces rice, silk and tea which is the major agricultural speciality of Gilan.

Mazandaran has an area of 500 sq metres and its population is more than 5 million.

Mazandaran province stretches from the eastern border of Gilan to the frontier of Khorasan province and the former Soviet republic of Turkemenistan.

In Zanjan and Semnan, there are two distinctive geographical regions in the province. One, the coastal strip, stretches from the western border with Gilan to the khalij of Gorgan (Bay of Gorgan). To the far east of the southern Caspian littoral is terrain with thick forest, which continues towards the northern slopes of the Alborz, rolling almost to the sea.

Dasht-e-gorgan (gorgan plain) is more fertile, situated between the Turkaman Desert and the mountains. This area is prone to harsh blizzards and snow falls with frequent avalanches, and the population is limited.

Sari is the provincial capital, with a smaller population than Rasht province. In Gilan the origin of Sari (in ancient Persian Sariya) is known to have been the first capital of the province from perhaps as early as the Sassanian era until the 8th and 9th century, a part which was the last to fall into the hand of Islam. Some of the Sassanian treasures of gold and silver from Sari were displayed in Tehran Museum. Mazandaran has one of the most agricultural areas of Iran, where rice and corn are the main crops, with orange groves visible along much of the coast.

The Gillanies, like the people of other parts of the country, have their own special recipes.

SEARCH IN THE DARK

Our holiday home in Manshad was built in the slope of the mountain, and about three miles from the nearest shop. There were many reservoirs down the slope, where the mountain stream was stored for irrigation, and walnut and almond trees grew. The walnut trees were really large, which shaded us from the midday sun, and made them a favourite meeting place for us girls and boys. We used to swap stories and brag about who was the bravest in the group.

I was only ten at the time, and decided to show my bravery. So I picked several walnuts, and marked them with a knife, and asked my friends to take them to the nearest reservoir about one mile away, and place them under a tree near to it, and that I would fetch them in the dead of the night.

I was excited about my forthcoming adventure. The day was arranged. Approaching evening I became rather anxious but kept a brave face. The sound of wolves was loud in the surrounding mountains, and often they searched around our house for food. I remember distinctly hoping that the nearby farmer would not leave left over food outside the house tonight. The evening was fresh with the sound of crickets and croaking frogs. The area was totally uninhabited. The night was dark, except for millions of stars flickering above. I wore my favourite dress in deep lime with black patterns, and wore giveh on my feet (hand knitted shoes). I opened the small wooden gate and stepped down into the lower terrace which led directly into the open. I held a small cloth bag tight with one or two sweets in it and began to walk. The road was rough, covered in pebbles, and rather slippery. I tripped a few times, but managed to keep control by singing my favourite song, which seemed to echo around the mountain. There was the sound of howling wolves in the mountain nearby. I began to walk briskly, down the valley towards the reservoir. Then I stopped, and looked around me, I could no longer see the dim light of our house, and was in total darkness, but continued walking. It was nearly one hour since I had left the house. There were the sounds of many streams pouring into the reservoirs. I stopped a few times, but could not judge the distance I had come. I noticed the dim light of other houses from the other end of the valley, about a mile away. I had given up hope when, suddenly in the dark, the area seemed familiar. I walked towards the walnut tree and began to search. I was in despair – there was nothing. I walked around further for a while, then stepped into the cultivated land where there were slow growing vegetables. I began to sing again, trying to keep calm. I had walked only a few steps when I felt a small bundle, picked it up and there were the walnuts. I placed them under my arms and began to walk briskly, as the sound of wolves was getting nearer. I stood still among this wilderness of rocks and thorns, and heard an odd sound. I tucked myself into a comfortable position and hid behind a small rock; it was a moment of terror. A storm was blowing up the valley, the air was getting colder and I could feel the cold sweat running down my back. But at all costs I had to be out of sight, and back with my family. The revealing sound was an old man following his mule. I waited a while. The road begun to climb again, and I began to run up the slope, I was becoming breathless with the climb. At a turning I noticed the dim light from our house. How far had I come? It seemed more than two hours since I left the house. I fell into Memeh's arms and I was admired for my bravery and achievement.

CHICKEN KHORESHT WITH EGG AND FRUIT
Khoresht-e-chaghartameh

❦

This khoresht is a speciality of the nomadic people of Gilan (northern Persia).

455g/1lb chicken, cut into portions
3 tablespoons oil
1 medium onion, chopped
1/2 teaspoon each ground cinnamon and saffron
salt and pepper
4 eggs
230ml/8oz sour orange or lemon juice to taste

Place the chicken into a saucepan with a little water – just enough to cook the meat.

Fry the onion in the oil. Beat the egg with the spices and add it to the pan with the fried onion and mix. When set, stir it into the simmering chicken. Add the fruit juice and simmer until the mixture thickens. Serve with rice.

WALNUT WITH MEAT AND HERB KHORESHT
Khoresht-e-anar bij

❦

Traditionally this dish is prepared with pomegranate juice, but to be practical we can use orange juice instead.

230g/8oz mixed leek, parsley, coriander and mint, chopped
115g/8oz ground walnuts
90g/3oz minced lamb, beef or chicken
1 medium onion, grated
1/2 teaspoon ground saffron
salt and pepper
230ml/8floz pomegranate or orange juice

Put all ingredients except the meat and the onion

into a saucepan, cover with water and simmer. Meanwhile mix the meat with the onion and the saffron and season with salt and pepper. Take small balls as big as hazelnuts and roll them in the palm of the hand before adding to the pan. Add the fruit juice and simmer until the meat balls are cooked and the liquid has thickened. Serve with rice.

CHICKEN WITH POMEGRANATE SEED KHORESHT
Khoresht-e-anar daneh mosama

❦

685g/1 1/2lb chicken, cut into portions
2 tablespoons oil
1 large onion, chopped.
the seeds of one large sharp or sweet and sour pomegranate
2 tablespoons chopped fresh mint or one teaspoon dried and crushed
1/2 teaspoon ground saffron.
salt and pepper
1 teaspoon sugar or to taste

Place the chicken in a large saucepan with a little water and simmer until tender.

Meanwhile fry the onion with 2 tablespoons of the oil until soft. Stir in the pomegranate seeds, add the mint, then transfer the mixture into the pan with the chicken. Add the saffron and simmer until the mixture becomes thick. Serve with rice.

TURKEY IN PEACH, WALNUT AND CINNAMON SAUCE
Khoresht-e-motenjen

❦

Peaches and nectarines are originally from China, and it was via the silk road that they were brought through Kashmir and Afghanistan into Persia. Then from Persia their distribution gradually proceeded through the Middle East, into Spain during 711 and gradually reaching into Europe and central America. Peaches have been cultivated since at least 2000 BC.

In this recipe use dried or fresh peaches, but traditionally dried are used (obtainable in health shops). Cook both in the same way.

685g/1¹/₂lb turkey or chicken, cut into portions
115g/4 oz ground walnuts
2 tablespoons oil
90g/3oz dried apricots or 4 fresh with their
stones removed
1 tablespoon sultanas
2 tablespoons pomegranate purée or the juice
of two large pomegranates
(first seed them then extract the juice)
If not available, use 115ml/4floz or a little
more tamarind fluid
¹/₂ teaspoon each ground cinnamon and saffron
salt and pepper

Place the turkey into a saucepan with the walnuts, cover with water and simmer until tender.

Meanwhile stir the apricots and the sultanas in 2 tablespoon of the oil and add to the pan with the turkey. Add the fruit juice, the ground saffron and the cinnamon and season with salt and pepper. Simmer until the gravy is thick. Serve with plain rice.

PHEASANT IN GARLIC AND FRUIT JUICE KHORESHT
Khoresht-e-sir gholyeh

Traditionally this recipe is prepared with garlic leaves, but to be more practical we use garlic cloves instead.

2 tablespoons oil
115g/4 oz garlic leaves or 6 garlic cloves, crushed

685g/1¹/₂lb pheasant or chicken cut into portions
¹/₂ teaspoon ground saffron or turmeric
90g/3oz split yellow lentils
230ml/8floz sour orange juice
(I also use sweet orange juice)
or unripe grape, or gooseberry juice
salt and pepper
4 eggs, lightly beaten

Fry the garlic or the leaves with the pheasant as in the recipe for Spinach and Plum Khoresht. Stir in the saffron, add the lentils and the fruit juice and enough water to cover, then simmer until tender. Season with salt and pepper, stir in the beaten egg, and allow to set. Serve with plain rice.

PUMPKIN WITH WALNUTS AND POMEGRANATE
Khoresht-e-kooie tareh

Pumpkins are native to central and south America, now grown widely throughout the tropical countries.

¹/₂ tablespoon oil
1 large onion, chopped
¹/₂ teaspoon each ground saffron and cinnamon
90g/3oz ground walnuts
230g/8oz pumpkins, peeled and cubed small
2 tablespoons pomegranate purée dissolved in a
little water, or tamarind liquid

Fry the onion in the oil until transparent, add the ground walnuts and the pumpkins with the fruit juice. Season with salt and pepper, simmer until cooked but not mushy. Serve with nan or plain rice.

HERB WITH FRUIT AND EGG KHORESHT
Khoresht-e-torsheh tareh

—◆—

230g/8oz mixed parsley, leek, coriander, mint
and spinach, finely chopped
2 tablespoons rice, cleaned and washed
3 tablespoons oil
4 cloves of garlic, crushed
salt and pepper
$\frac{1}{2}$ teaspoon turmeric
230ml/8floz sour or unripe grape
or gooseberry juice.
4 eggs, lightly beaten

Place the herbs and rice into a saucepan, add the fruit juice and enough water to cover. Simmer for 20 minutes or until the rice is cooked.

Meanwhile fry the garlic in 1 tablespoon of the oil and stir in the turmeric. Remove half of this mixture into the pan with the rice mixture. Add the remaining oil to the pan, add the eggs and season with salt and pepper. When set add to the saucepan with the herb and rice mixture and simmer until thick. Serve with nan.

Spinach and Rice Mould; Carrot Savoury Cake and Okra Savoury Cake (top)

Courgette Khoresht, Lentil & Crispy Potato Rice & Spicy Meatballs (main dish); with Spiced Meat Cakes, Date Chutney & Pickled Grapes

Baklava and Pistachio Baklava (left); Cardamom, Rosewater and Nut Pasties (top right); Rice Crumbles and Rosewater Fondants (bottom right)

Khoresht-e-bamya (Okra Khoresht) served with Pumpkin and Plums as part of a dinner party

RICE *(Berenj)*

Throughout the centuries rice has provided one of the basic elements of man's diet. It can be cooked according to the different customs of Persian, Chinese, Indian and other cuisines. It is perhaps one of the most versatile basic foods to which vegetables, meat, fruit, nuts and other ingredients can be added.

The most popular of the rices in the west are Patna, originally from north-east India and now from America, and risoto from Italy. There is long grain processed rice, which retains its shape but lacks in aroma. The most popular rice – obtainable mostly in Indian and Persian supermarkets – is basmati from Pakistan which is nearest in texture and flavour to sadri (the species introduced to Persian soil just before the 20th century). Domsiyah (black tail), Ambar-boo, and darbari (royalty) are grown in the north of Persia in the Caspian region and are not obtainable in the west. Champa is a short grain rice, used in thick soup, Ash and Shoorva or thin soup (abgoosht) as it contains mucilage which gives special flavour to the gravy. The seed was cultivated by the Egyptians, the Persians and Babylonians, and eventually was traded to the rest of the East. Rice was cultivated in Greece around 300 years BC, and it was from there that it eventually found its way to Italy.

The Persians have always been admired for the art of their cooking, especially rice.

The Persian housewife, who is a perfectionist in her kitchen, always looks for the best grade of rice which she then cooks in various ways, such as chelou, which is plain rice, or polov, which is rice mixed with ingredients such as vegetables, meat, fruit and nuts. Kateh is cooked with one part rice and two parts water with a little butter or oil, and often made as a quick meal or for a sick person to be eaten with plain yoghurt if the patient is suffering from an upset stomach.

Dampokht is a mixture of rice and pulses to which other ingredients such as potatoes and herbs can be added and served as a main family meal for lunch or dinner.

Traditionally rice was bought monthly in a large sack, and its cleaning was shared by the women in the family. A few handfuls of the grain were placed on a large and highly polished copper tray to see the bits, then stored in a barrel, and placed in a cool place such as the cellar. There was always a measuring cup beside the container, one cup for each person.

Although the amount of rice eaten depends on the appetite of the person, the normal amount used is about 345g/12oz for four people.

The Persian way to cook rice is unique: first the rice is parboiled then it is drained of all the water. Cooking is finished off over a dry heat in a heavy saucepan with a well-fitting lid, with very little oil or butter.

To measure the rice for cooking is not that important as long as the saucepan is large enough for the rice to expand during daming (steaming). The length of cooking depends on the amount of rice being used. Cook on a very low heat for between half an hour and one hour. This method is called daming ('brewing') or steaming, and it allows the rice to cook in its own steam, producing separate grains with a fluffy texture.

When Persian rice is served it is turned out on to a serving plate so that the crisp layer is uppermost. This is called Tahdig (Tah meaning 'bottom' and dig meaning 'pan') and is considered the best part of the rice.

TO COOK RICE THE PERSIAN WAY

Rice is an important part of the meal in a Persian home, a dish which is served every day or sometimes twice in one day, for lunch and dinner, served with Khoresht and savoury dishes, plain yoghurt, or even with nan.

Although the rice which we buy in supermarkets today may seem clean, it is best to place it on a white plate or tray, to check that there are no odd pieces of grit or other bits which may have got through while packing. In all recipes in this book I refer to this as cleaning before washing. After cleaning, place the rice either in a large bowl or a sieve and rinse with cold water to remove any dust which may have got through during packing. Soak the rice in a large bowl in cold or lukewarm water for about 5–6 hours before cooking or over night, to ensure that each grain cooks evenly, as when soaking pulses. Rice can also be soaked for half an hour in hot water. If rice is cooked dry, without soaking, it needs a little more simmering – about 2–3 minutes longer.

The amount of oil I have given in most recipes is about 2 tablespoons best vegetable oil (unless stated otherwise), sufficient for 4 people, although just 1–2 teaspoons is enough for steaming the rice. If using butter, melt and pour over the rice in the pan evenly. It is always best to add one tablespoon of the oil in the pan and swirl it around so it greases the inside well, to prevent the rice sticking to the bottom of the pan and this reduces the danger of burning during steaming (daming). This I refer to in all recipes as greasing the pan.

To serve with a main course, 345g/12oz long grain basmati rice is enough for four people. For this quantity of rice you need a 2.25 litre/4 pint heavy based saucepan with a well-fitting lid (it is best to use a non-stick or heavy aluminium pan). Fill the saucepan about one-third to one-half full with water (no more or it will boil over), add two teaspoons of salt (optional) and bring to the boil. Drain the soaked rice, add it to the water and bring back to the boil. Immediately lower the heat to simmer gently and parboil for 4 minutes (this is called zendeh, meaning alive). It is a common practice to remove a few grains from the pan and test them between the fingers to make sure they are ready and only half cooked. Do not stir during simmering as this could break the grains of rice. Do not be tempted to add any form of citrus during cooking as this may ruin the texture, and flavour. Drain the rice in a sieve to remove the excess salt (not in a colander as you may lose half in the kitchen sink). Wash the pan well to remove any scum.

For people who are weight conscious the Persian way of cooking rice is ideal, as by parboiling and draining the extra starch, and therefore calorie content, is greatly reduced.

Always use a large saucepan during steaming (daming) so that the grains are not packed tightly together, but allowed to move freely to produce separate grains with a fluffy result.

It is best to use your hands to add the rice into the pan by sprinkling – this will allow the air to get between the grains during steaming. If the rice has been standing in the sieve too long to drain, add two or three tablespoons of water to the pan. Put the lid on tight (no need to use the traditional cloth as it has been instructed in my previous book) and place the pan on a high heat for about one minute, to allow the steam to rise. Lower the heat to the lowest possible and allow the rice to cook in its own steam. The longer the rice is cooked the crispier it becomes. Never increase the heat during steaming as this will cause the rice to over cook and burn. Usually 30 minutes is sufficient for a saucepan of 2.25 litres/4 pints unless it is mixed with other ingredients, such as meat or vegetables, which may take about 10–15 minutes longer.

The initial amount of liquid (water or stock) needed to cover the ingredients, such as chicken or meat, is about 225ml/8floz. The cooking time will vary according to the type, cut and quality of meat used: for chicken about 45 minutes and for meat 1–2 hours. Always choose lean fillet of lamb, beef or boneless chicken with the skin removed.

If the pan becomes too dry during cooking add water a little at a time, and if there is too much liquid in the pan, boil vigorously to produce a thick but still juicy mixture.

Onion and herbs should be chopped fine. The green part of spring onions can be substituted for chives if mixed uncooked with rice. If cooked, substitute the young part of a leek as well.

Orange rinds are given as part of the ingredients in some dishes, and the instructions for their preparation is given in the Basic chapter. Persian dried lime (limoo omani) is obtainable in Persian supermarkets. Do not substitute common lemon for lime as it will not give the authentic taste.

Instructions for ground saffron are also in the Basic chapter, substitute turmeric for saffron if it is part of the recipe to be fried with onion, meat or other ingredients. But NOT if it is mixed with rice without being fried as this will give rather a strong, bitter and unpleasant taste, in Persian terms this is called raw or kham.

I suggest buying walnuts from Persian supermarkets because of their quality and freshness, although you can substitute any nuts coarsely chopped.

During serving it is best to scoop out the rice first into a large flat serving platter with the crispy base (tahdig) over the top as a garnish.

PRODUCE OF THE CASPIAN

We drove the 400 miles from Tehran through groves where the oranges looked like gleaming light bulbs. We were very close to the border of Russia at the time, which was a very exciting thought. The tour was personal and by private car as my brother-in-law drove us everywhere. We saw the sturgeon being caught and watched the extraction of caviar. Most of our visit centred around the cultivated lands. It was rice harvesting time, which was like a dream come true. To visit the actual sight was only allowed by permit, and fortunately we were allowed in to see the mountain of rice, to see how they thrashed it to remove the husks, and also to watch the planting of the seed below inches of water. On the way back at the end of the holiday we stopped at various restaurants in the open air, enjoying the cool breeze from the mountain and the sea as we sat beneath the trees with millions of stars shining through. The smell of Jujeh Kabab (barbecued chicken) sprinkled liberally with fresh lime juice, fish dishes and rice, all filled the air in that province. It is an area to be avoided during harsh winter months, when often those who trusted the mountains were killed by fatal avalanches.

AN INVITATION FOR THE BRIDE
TO HER OLD HOME

Following the old Zoroastrian custom, my sister Sarvar had to wait for an 'official' invitation from our parents to visit them at the home she had left before getting married. Without this invitation she would not be able to visit them freely in the future! On the arranged date some soft wood was lit in the barbecue (manghal) and sprinkled with sandalwood and wild rue. There were displays of freshly cut roses in all rooms. The mist from the burning joss-stick perfumed the atmosphere.

Sarvar and her husband Khosrov stretched their arms over the low flame and stroked their faces to signify warmth and sincerity. Then Memeh presented them each with a gold sovereign placed on a piece of green silk, with some thyme leaves, sweets and a piece of fern, together with sugar loaf, wrapped in shiny green paper for Sarvar. Rose water drink was offered to the couple on entering the house, then the special drink was offered to the remaining guests. Over the buffet-style lunch every one issued lunch or dinner invitations to the newly married couple.

PLAIN RICE
Berenj-e-sadeh

455g/1lb long grain basmati rice
a little salt (optional)
2 tablespoons oil

First clean, wash and soak the rice as in the general instructions above. Fill the saucepan about one-third to one-half full with cold water (no more or it will boil over), add 2 teaspoons of salt and bring to the boil. Drain the soaked rice, add it to the water and bring back to the boil. Immediately lower the heat to simmer gently and parboil for 4 minutes. Drain in a sieve and rinse under cold running water to remove any scum. Thoroughly wash the pan to remove all scum then add one tablespoon of the oil and swirl it around. Then, using both hands, sprinkle the rice into the clean pan (this allows air to get between the grains). If the pan has been standing over the kitchen sink to drain add only 2–3 tablespoons water. Pour the remaining oil over the rice, fit the lid on tightly, and place the pan over a high heat for 1 minute (this will allow the steam to rise ready for steaming/brewing (daming). Then reduce the heat to very low and steam for 20–30 minutes, without lifting the lid, until the rice is cooked and the base crisp. To release the crispy rice base (tahdig) from the pan, press a wet kitchen towel lightly on the base or simply place the pan in the kitchen sink filled with a little cold water (although this is not always necessary). Serve garnished with the tahdig (crispy base).

For a variation try the following:

CRISPY POTATO RICE
Polov-e-sadeh ba sib zamini

Peel and slice one small potato, arrange neatly in the pan then add the rice and steam (dam) as above. Serve garnished with the crispy potatoes.

REMEMBERING ON THE WEDDING DAY

There was always someone who was unable to attend the wedding, and on such a happy occasion the less well off were always remembered too.

Large numbers of dishes filled with wedding food were placed on highly polished copper trays, and carried to various local houses by volunteers. According to Zoroastrian tradition, the recipient would wash and dry the empty dishes after eating, then place a handful of thyme leaves, mixed with sweets and cookies in them to return to the sender.

CRISPY FISH AND DILL RICE
Berenje ba mahi va shevid

Fry 4 fillets of white fish in 3–4 tablespoons of oil until lightly golden, and substitute for the potatoes in the above recipe. Mix 2 tablespoons of chopped dill with the parboiled rice and follow the instructions for plain rice. Serve with plain yoghurt.

MUNG BEAN RICE
Mash-o-berenj

4 tablespoons oil
1 medium onion, chopped
¹/₄ teaspoon each cumin seeds and ground saffron
¹/₂ teaspoon turmeric
90g/3oz mung beans, cleaned and soaked
115g/4oz rice, cleaned and soaked
1 tablespoon tomato purée
1 medium potato, cut into chip (French fry) shapes
salt and pepper

TO GARNISH
sprigs of fresh mint or parsley

Fry the onion in 1 tablespoon of oil until golden, then stir in the spices. Pour the water off the mung beans and add them to the pan with 600ml/1 pint water. Simmer for 45 minutes until cooked. Meanwhile pour the water off the soaking rice and stir in the tomato purée, the remaining oil and the potatoes. If necessary, add 375ml/12floz water. Simmer with the pan covered for 30–40 minutes until all the liquid is absorbed. Serve with plain yoghurt and salad garnished with mint and parsley.

For variations try the following recipes:

RICE IN MEAT AND TOMATO
Eslamboli polov

Substitute 60g/2oz red kidney beans for mung beans. Soak the beans for 6–8 hours, drain then put them in a pan covered with water and boil vigorously for ten minutes and simmer until tender. Drain and follow the cooking instructions as above.

BROADBEAN AND SULTANA RICE
Dami-e-baghla

Substitute 455g/1lb podded broad beans for mung beans, mixed with one tablespoon of sultanas and 2 tablespoons of chopped dill.

ZOROASTRIAN PROPOSAL IN YAZD

Mahin, my cousin who was much older than me, told me with a shy voice that she and Iraj liked each other, and a day had been arranged for proposal.

It was a hot summer's day, the low coffee tables were set with different cookies and sweets piled high on silver plates. The large silver tray was filled with different fruit and the large brass samovar was lit. There were displays of fresh cut flowers in all rooms.

Mahin was dressed in a creamy-coloured chiffon dress with pale green and pink flowers. She wore delicate thin gold jewellery, as she sat gracefully in a low chair by the picture window of her drawing room in Yazd. A small cut glass antique dish in green was filled with white fondant and placed beside the display of flowers in front of her on the low coffee table.

In the early hours of the afternoon, two ladies colourfully dressed arrived, one carrying a green silk handkerchief containing white fondant sweets, sugar plums and thyme leaves. On entering the house they were warmly welcomed by aunt Gohar and her husband Rosi, who they asked for the hand of Mahin for Iraj. The answer was yes (as it was expected) then they placed a white fondant into Mahin's mouth to signify her acceptance of the proposal. The ladies were offered home made wine, sweets and fruit and the celebration continued well into the night.

111

SAFFRON RICE WITH ORANGE AND ALMOND
Shirin polov

❧

315g/11oz rice
salt
2 large oranges
2 teaspoons sugar
90g/3oz each unsalted, unroasted pistachio and
blanched almonds, shredded
$\frac{1}{4}$ teaspoon ground saffron
2 tablespoons oil

Clean and soak the rice according to the general instructions, then parboil, drain and rinse as in the recipe for plain rice.

Prepare the orange rinds as in the Basics chapter.

Swirl one tablespoon of oil over the inside of a large saucepan. Put half of the semi-cooked rice in the pan and cover with the orange and nut mixture. Sprinkle the ground saffron over the top, add the remaining rice and the oil. Cook as in the recipe for plain rice. Serve with any kind of khoresht.

For variations try the following recipes:

STAR RICE
Marseh polov

❧

Add 1 heaped tablespoon of sultanas, barberries, or a mixture of barberries and sultanas to cook with the orange rinds (if using sultanas use one tablespoon lemon juice).

Fry one small onion chopped fine with 455g/1lb chicken or meat, diced with $\frac{1}{2}$ teaspoon turmeric, cover with water and simmer until tender, cooking until the mixture becomes thick, but still juicy. Follow the recipe as above, put the cooked and cooled meat mixture over the orange and nut mixture in the pan, top up with the remaining rice, and add the remaining oil. Serve with plain yoghurt or khoresht.

CARROT RICE
Havij polov

Follow the recipe for jewelled rice, using the same amount of chicken or meat.

Cook 230g/8oz carrots, made into strips, in with the orange rinds. Follow the cooking and preparation instructions for Saffron rice with orange and almonds.

GREETINGS AT EQUINOX (*Salgardesh*)

Whatever time of the equinox, a family gathering was important. Everyone got very excited and emotional as the time approached. We all wore new clothes, Memeh wore a green dress in raw silk to signify good luck. My favourite was a frilly pink dress in silk with small white flowers.

We all gathered together in the lounge, where the low coffee table was already set with various sweets laid on large silver plates. The family stood near the haftsheen table covered with a hand-embroidered white table cloth. On it was also a small cut glass dish containing white fondant, a small silver tray lined with silk cloth in green containing strands of fern, thyme, sorb and a few white fondant sweets (noghl). The candle was lit and placed beside Zaratrostra's picture, and a hand mirror with a rose water pourer.

At the exact time of the equinox (salgardesh) my parents would greet each other, then embrace their children, making a present of a silver coin to each member of the family. My mother would pour a little rose water in our cupped hands, to stroke our hair with the perfumed water, which spread a special fragrance throughout the room. Everyone handed each other a small piece of fern, and finally Memeh offered us a fondant sweet (noghl) for us to eat to make a new year wish.

VERMICELLI PILAF
Reshteh polov

Substitute 60g/2oz vermicelli for nuts, and simmer in a little water for 4–5 minutes. Drain well. Substitute 115g/4oz chopped dates and one teaspoon cinnamon for orange rinds. Use the same amount of meat and follow the cooking instructions for jewelled rice. Follow the steaming and cooking instruction for the rice as in the recipe for saffron rice with orange and almonds.

HERB AND LIME PILAF
Polov-e-ghormeh sabsi

315g/11oz rice
2 tablespoons oil
1 medium onion, chopped
685g/1½lb chicken, lamb or beef, diced
½ teaspoon each ground cinnamon, saffron and turmeric
2 tablespoons ground lime or the juice of one large lemon
1 tablespoon chives, chopped
2 tablespoons parsley, chopped
salt and pepper

Clean, wash and soak the rice as in the general instructions, parboil, drain and rinse, as in the recipe for plain rice.

Fry the onion in 1 tablespoon of oil until soft and transparent. Stir in the meat to brown, then stir in the turmeric, and season with salt and pepper. Cover with water, simmer until tender, add lime powder and the cinnamon. Simmer until thick.

Grease the pan with one tablespoon of oil. Add half the semi-cooked rice, top up with the cooked and cooled mixture, and cover with the remaining parboiled rice and the remaining oil. Steam as in the recipe for plain rice.

Remove one ladle of the cooked rice and mix in with the saffron.

Serve the rice with plain yoghurt and salad, garnish around with the saffron rice.

For a variation make:

ORTHODOX MUSLIM WEDDING IN YAZD

As a girl of only six I looked forward to going to a Muslim wedding, especially when my Muslim nanny would dress me up, wearing a chador to cover my clothes, 'Make sure one hand is always by your chin,' she would say. Hold the chador tight to show only one eye. It was an exciting moment. After a short bus ride, we reached the bride's house, the front door to the cobbled entrance was left open. On entering, the paved area around the octagonal pond in the open style house was packed with ladies wearing chador, some in black and others dark brown with a small pattern. They were helping themselves to tea (chay) from the large brass samovar, and trays piled with various sweets were offered to the guests.

Malog took my hand, pushing through the crowd of women, to see the bride, who wore a black chador and sat in the corner of the paved area, on a doshak (a hand-made mattress). Malog pointed out the bride's bright red hands and nails, and told me as a custom they had to be painted with henna the night before.

Sakineh the bride, who sat beside Hassan her husband to be, held the chador tight over her face with one hand and in the other she held a small mirror. Hassan wore a dark suit with a white open-necked shirt.

The ceremony began with the Mola (Muslim priest) reciting passages from the Qu'ran, and pronouncing the couple man and wife. Then Sakineh slowly unveiled her face for her husband to see for the first time reflected in the glass which she held in front of her. There was a sound of joy and cheering amongst the guests as the groom found her very attractive and was very pleased with his mother's choice.

LIME PILAF
Ghimeh polov

Cook 60g/2oz split yellow lentils for 30–40 minutes until soft. Add into the meat mixture to simmer with 25ml/1floz tomato purée. Leave out the herbs and cook in the same way as Herb and Lime Pilaf.

RAMAZAN

Ramazan is one of the most important Muslim festivals and based on the lunar calendar. It is a whole month of fasting and prayer when no music or entertainment is allowed, an exercise in self-denial, because their holy book, the Qu'ran was revealed to their prophet in this month.

Muslims fast from sunrise to sunset, during which time not only are eating and drinking prohibited, but smoking and any form of physical pleasure.

For Muslims who fast the days are dull and slow, until after sunset when activities begin again and shops and stores stay open until well after midnight.

After sunset in Yazd, Muslim families would gather to break their fast, continuing their social life until the early hours of the next morning, right up to sunrise when you could hear the sound of Azan calling the faithful to pray.

It was a month to look forward to as a child, with its appetising specialities such as soft syrup fingers (bamya) and sweet syrup circles (Zolubia). Piled high on large copper trays in their golden rose water syrup, at the entrances to the shops so that their syrup would sparkle and glint in the lamplight.

HERB PILAF
Sabsi polov

If this is to be served with a fish dish leave out the meat and use 90g/3oz extra rice.

250g/10oz rice
230g/8oz lamb
3 tablespoons oil
2 cloves of garlic, crushed
2 tablespoons each chopped parsley, coriander,
chives, and one tablespoon chopped dill
$^1/_2$ teaspoon ground saffron

Clean, wash and soak the rice as in the general instructions, parboil, drain and rinse as in the recipe for plain rice.

Cook the meat as in the recipe for Herb and lime pilaf.

Mix the semi-cooked rice with the herbs.

Swirl one tablespoon of oil into a large pan, add half the rice, top up with the meat mixture, add the remaining rice and the oil. Cook as in the recipe for plain rice. Serve with plain yoghurt.

For a variation make:

BROAD BEAN PILAF
Baghla polov

Substitute 2 tablespoons of chopped dill for parsley and coriander and cook 230g/8oz podded broad beans with the meat. Follow the recipe for herb and lime pilaf.

LENTIL WITH FRUIT PILAF
Adas polov

The ancient Persians followed their prophet Zaratrostra's word as he said that a healthy mind is part of having a healthy body.

Lentils were known at that time to give strength and confidence of body and mind. They are a food which is most popular in Iran even to this day, and is still one of the major crops. Lentils are inexpensive and tasty and are eaten at any time of the year. When I was a little girl in Yazd I remember vividly my mother adding a handful of lentils into the soup to give thickness and to calm the nerves.

315g/11oz rice
115g/4oz green or brown lentils
salt and pepper
3 tablespoons oil
1 large onion, peeled
230g/8oz minced lamb or beef
1 teaspoon ground cinnamon
60g/2oz each sultanas and chopped dates
$^1/_2$ teaspoon ground saffron

Clean, wash and soak the rice as in the general instructions, parboil, rinse and drain as in the recipe for plain rice.

Grate 2oz of the onion over the meat, season with salt and pepper and knead to bind.

Chop the remaining onion and fry in 1 tablespoon of the oil until soft and transparent. Take a small ball as big as a hazelnut, make it smooth in your hand, add it to the onion and stir to brown.

Stir in the mixed fruit, remove the pan from the heat.

Grease the pan with one tablespoon of oil. Add half the semi-cooked rice, top up with the meat and fruit mixture, sprinkle on the cinnamon, then top up with the remaining rice and oil. Steam for 45 minutes as in the recipe for plain rice, remove one ladle of the cooked rice and mix with saffron. Serve with yoghurt and salad, garnished with the saffron rice.

BARBERRY PILAF
Zereshk polov
❦

315g/11oz rice
60g/2oz barberries
2 teaspoons sugar
685g/1½lb chicken, cut into portions
(or cooked chicken)
3 tablespoons oil
¼ teaspoon each cumin seeds, turmeric,
ground cinnamon and saffron

Clean, wash and soak the rice as in the general instructions; parboil, rinse and drain as in the recipe for plain rice.

Fry the chicken in one tablespoon of the oil until lightly coloured, stir in the turmeric, add three tablespoons of water and, with the pan covered, simmer until tender.

Cook the barberries with the sugar and 75ml/3floz water for 5–7 minutes until soft.

Grease the pan with one tablespoon oil, arrange half of the chicken neatly in the pan. Add quarter of the parboiled rice, then the remaining chicken, sprinkle on the cinnamon with the cumin seeds, top up with the remaining rice. Cook in the same way as the plain rice.

Remove one ladle of the rice and mix with saffron. Serve with plain yoghurt and salad, garnished with the saffron rice.

CHERRY PILAF
Alubalu polov
❦

Fresh cherries are used when available, but as the season is short, sometimes the Persian housewife uses home-made cherry jam or dried or frozen cherries. If using fresh, 455g/1lb fresh cherries are enough for this recipe. Remove their stems, remove their stones with a stone remover (obtainable in large stores) and put the cherries in a small saucepan. Add a little sugar depending on your taste, plus 5–6 tablespoons of water, and simmer for about 7 minutes until they are a little soft and sticky. Remove from the heat and set aside to cool.

If using dried cherries soak them for a few hours before cooking, cook the same way, then remove their stones when cool.

315g/11oz rice
230g/8oz frozen black cherries
30g/1oz sugar
2 teaspoons lemon juice
685g/1½lb chicken breasts, cut into portions
salt and pepper
1–2 tablespoons oil
1 medium onion, chopped
½ teaspoon each ground cinnamon and saffron
60g/2oz each unsalted unroasted pistachio
and shredded almonds or just almonds
to make up the weight
3 tablespoons oil

TO GARNISH
a few fresh cherries

Clean, wash, and soak the rice as in the general instructions; parboil, rinse and drain the rice as in the recipe for plain rice.

Put the cherries in a bowl with the sugar and leave to defrost overnight. The next day put them in a small pan and simmer for 2 minutes, then, using a slotted spoon, transfer the cherries to a bowl. Add the lemon juice to the cherry juice in the pan and boil vigorously for 3 minutes until it is reduced to approximately 25ml/1floz. Remove from the heat.

Fry the onion in 1 tablespoon of oil until golden. Add the chicken and toss to brown, season with salt and pepper. Pour in 125ml/4floz water and simmer until tender. With a slotted spoon, transfer the meat to a plate. Increase the heat and boil the

RICE (Berenj)

gravy vigorously until reduced to about 4 tablespoons. Remove from the heat.

Grease the pan with two tablespoons of oil. Put
half the parboiled rice into the pan, top up with
the cooked chicken, half the cherries and sprinkle
on the cinnamon. Put the nuts in the corner, and
cover with the remaining rice and the oil. Steam
as in the recipe for plain rice.

Remove one ladle of the rice and mix with the
saffron. Serve the rice with salad, garnished with
the remaining cherries, saffron rice and put a few
cherries in the corner of the dish.

GARDEN PEA PILAF
Polov-e-nokhod farangi

315g/11oz rice
3 tablespoons oil
1 medium onion, chopped
455g/1lb lamb, beef or chicken, cut into
1 cm/¹/₂inch pieces
¹/₄ teaspoon each turmeric, ground cinnamon
and saffron
salt and pepper
115g /4 oz podded peas
25ml/1floz tomato purée

Clean, wash and soak the rice as in the general
instructions; parboil, rinse and drain the rice as in
the recipe for plain rice.

Fry the onion with the meat as in the recipe for
herb and lime pilaf, adding the peas and the tomato
purée, and the spices except the saffron. Simmer
to produce a thick mixture.

Swirl one tablespoon of oil in a large pan, add
half the semi-cooked rice, top up with the meat
and peas mixture, then add the remaining rice and
oil, cover the pan and steam as in the recipe for
plain rice. Mix a ladle of the cooked rice with the
saffron. Serve with plain yoghurt, garnished with
saffron rice.

For a variation make the following recipes:

RUNNER OR FRENCH
BEAN PILAF
Polov-e-lubia sabs

Substitute 230g/8oz runner or French beans, cut
into 1cm/¹/₂inch pieces, for peas.

CABBAGE AND MEAT
PILAF
Polov-e-kalam

Substitute 230g/8oz white cabbage, coarsely
chopped, for peas, and 455g/8oz minced meat, for
meat or chicken. Grate 60g/2oz onion over the
meat, add ¹/₄ teaspoon ground cinnamon, season
with salt and pepper. Prepare as in the recipe for
lentil with fruit pilaf.

Chop half a large onion and fry in 1 tablespoon
of oil. Take small balls of the meat mixture as big
as hazelnuts, make them smooth in your hands and
stir them in with the fried onion, until brown.
Remove them with a slotted spoon into a bowl.
Add the cabbage to the pan with 1 tablespoon of
oil and fry gently. Add 1–2 tablespoons of water,
and cook with the pan covered until soft. Stir in
one tablespoon of dill and sultanas (optional) and
season with salt and pepper. Remove from the pan.
Follow the instructions for steaming as in the recipe
for garden pea pilaf. Serve with plain yoghurt.
Garnish with the saffron rice prepared as in the
recipe for garden pea pilaf.

SAFFRON AND
YOGHURT BASE
Tahchin

This most elegant and tasty dish is usually seen at
family parties, or made for honoured guests.

117

315g/11oz rice
1 medium onion, chopped
4 tablespoons oil
455g/1lb chicken breast or lamb
salt and pepper
150ml/¹/₄ pint plain yoghurt
4 egg yolks
1 teaspoon ground saffron

Clean, wash and soak the rice as in the general instructions; parboil, rinse, and drain as in the recipe for plain rice.

Fry the onion in one tablespoon of oil, add the chicken and toss to brown, and cook as in the recipe for garden pea pilaf.

Set the oven to 180°C/350°F/Gas 4.

Beat the eggs with the yoghurt and the saffron in a large bowl, then add half the semi-cooked rice. Put 2 tablespoons of the oil in to a 900ml/1¹/₂ pint ring mould or 5cm/2inch deep, square baking dish and swirl it around so that it greases the inside well then dust with flour. Add the rice and yoghurt mixture, smoothing it out with a back of a spoon. Arrange the cooked and cooled chicken pieces on top, add the remaining rice and smooth out again, then pour over the remaining oil. Cover with foil and bake in the oven for one hour then reduce the heat to 170°C/325°F/Gas 3 and continue baking for a further 45 minutes, or until the rice is cooked. Loosen the edges with a palette knife and wrap wet kitchen towel around the base of the mould or dish to help release the base. Turn onto a serving platter, garnish with shredded lettuce and carrots, and put lemon slices all the way around. Serve with plain yoghurt and salad.

For variations make the following dishes:

SHIRAZI TAHCHIN
Polov-e-shirazi

Slice 4 medium aubergines, sprinkle with salt on both sides and leave for 30 minutes to extract the dark and bitter juices. Rinse under cold running water to remove the salt and dab dry with kitchen paper. Fry in shallow oil until light brown, then place in a colander to drain the excess oil.

Simmer 90g/3oz barberries in one teaspoon of sugar for five minutes, until soft. Or substitute sultanas for barberries, and simmer them with 2 tablespoons of lemon juice instead of sugar.

Arrange the aubergine slices neatly over the rice in the mould, sprinkle on the barberries and ¹/₂ teaspoon ground saffron, then follow the instructions for cooking as above.

BANANA AND CHICKEN MOULD
Kateh-e-ghablemeh-ie-ba-morgh

Clean, wash and soak the rice as in the general instructions; parboil, rinse and drain as in the recipe for plain rice.

Prepare the same amount of meat as in the recipe for saffron and yoghurt base, adding 230g/8oz skinned and quartered tomatoes. Simmer until thick.

Prepare a ring mould as in the same recipe.

Mix the yoghurt with the egg and saffron, and half of the parboiled rice. Place half into the mould, smooth it out with the back of a spoon, then add the remaining rice, smooth out again, and follow the cooking instructions as in the recipe for saffron and yoghurt base.

Turn the mould onto a serving plate and fill the centre with the cooked chicken mixture.

Slice one banana lengthways, coat in beaten egg and fry in oil until golden. Garnish the mould with the fried bananas.

SPINACH AND RICE MOULD
Tahchin-e-esfenaj

Fry a small onion, finely chopped, add 6 spinach leaves, and simmer for 3 minutes (or until wilted) with the pan covered. Remove with a slotted spoon and place in a colander to drain. Arrange the spinach and onion neatly in the prepared mould, add the mixed yoghurt rice, and top up with chicken mixture. Arrange 6–7 prunes (soaked and cooked with their stones removed) in a neat pattern over the meat, top up with the remaining rice and cook in the same way as in the recipe for saffron and yoghurt rice.

BOILED RICE
Kateh

Kateh is a method of cooking rice which is very popular in the Caspian littoral, one area of Iran where rice is its staple diet and a more substantial dish. Here it is often eaten for breakfast, lunch and dinner. Kateh is a family dish for an Iranian and never seen on a buffet table. The preparation is uncomplicated and does not require special skill. It is best to use a non-stick saucepan which has been greased well before the cooking stage begins.

3 tablespoons oil
2 cups long grain rice, cleaned and washed
4 cups water
a little salt (optional)

Grease a large saucepan with one tablespoon of oil, add the rice with the water, salt and remaining oil, and bring to the boil. Then reduce the heat and, with the pan uncovered, simmer for about 12–13 minutes, or until all the liquid is absorbed and little holes appear. Place the lid on tight and leave for about 30–40 minutes or until the rice is cooked.

Serve hot with any kind of khoresht and plain yoghurt.

For a variation make:

MILK PILAF
Shir polov

A very gilani dish (northern Persia), which is eaten at any time – breakfast, lunch or dinner – or the leftovers can be cut up for a picnic snack.

Cook the rice as in the recipe above (boiled rice), adding 1 cup of full fat milk with the water. When the liquid is absorbed and bubbles appear, scoop the rice into a dish. Heat 3 tablespoons of oil gently and mix with $\frac{1}{2}$ a generous teaspoon of ground saffron. Dip one lavash nan (obtainable in Persian supermarkets) or slice of white bread, into the saffron oil to coat well. Arrange this neatly in the bottom of the pan. Pour over any remaining saffron oil, add half the semi-cooked rice, and add 90g/3oz each of sultanas and chopped dates, and the same amount of blanched and stripped almonds (optional). Top up with the remaining rice and smooth this out with a back of a spoon. If necessary add $\frac{1}{2}$–1 tablespoon more oil.

Place the lid tight, reduce the heat as low as possible and cook for about 25–30 minutes. Serve with plain yoghurt or cold as a dessert. This dish can also be prepared in the oven: lower the semi-cooked rice into an ovenproof dish, follow the preparation as above, cover and cook for about 45 minutes. For variation I sprinkle half a teaspoon of ground cardamom and or cinnamon over the fruit and nut mixture.

STUFFED MEAT, FISH AND VEGETABLES (*Dolmeh*)

Hundred of years ago, before the birth of Christ, when the Macedonians conquered Persia, they were impressed with the extravagance of Persian banquets and how delicately they stuffed and cooked their lamb, poultry and vegetables.

The Zoroastrians or Parthians gave such a good impression that after the Macedonians returned to Greece they introduced the idea to their country and eventually into Rome, where it was known as the Zoroastrian or Parthian way of stuffing. The first book of its kind introducing the Zoroastrian/Parthian way of stuffing was written in the west in the 17th century.

Stuffed poultry and vegetables are as extravagant and popular today as they were in the days of the Sassanid Dynasty (AD 600).

These dishes are popular during rituals and celebrations, and more particularly during late spring to early summer, when vine leaves and most vegetables such as courgettes and aubergines come into season.

If a Persian does not grow the vegetables in their garden, they carefully select them from the greengrocers. They ensure that the produce is healthy, without any marks or dents, and is not too large, but of a regular size. Most Persians grow vines in their garden or orchard (bagh) not only for their own use, but also for their family and friends. If the vine leaves are chosen from the green grocers, especially fresh leaves are selected, which are young and shiny. Nowadays they can be obtained pre-packed, preserved in salt water.

The preparation for Dolmeh requires delicate handiwork and such talent is usually practised by more than one member of the family, although it is mostly uncomplicated and easy to prepare.

The stuffed vegetables can be cooked both on the stove and in the oven. If cooking on the stove choose a large non-stick or heavy aluminium saucepan, 2.25 litre/4 pints, with a well-fitting lid. If cooking in the oven, you will need a casserole or a glass ovenproof dish into which the vegetables will just fit neatly. There is no need to add liquid in the casserole dish, if cooking in the oven. Cooking on the stove is a more delicate process, and there is always a danger of over cooking the vegetables if the pan becomes too dry. To prevent the vegetables becoming soggy add liquid into the cooking pot a little at a time. At the end of cooking all the liquid should have been absorbed into the stuffed vegetables so that they are moist and juicy.

The basic ingredient for most Dolmeh is onion, finely chopped and fried in oil for a few minutes until golden, or transparent. If using turmeric, stir this in with the onion. Saffron and cinnamon can be mixed in the bowl with the other ingredients.

Long grain rice is also a basic ingredient which is simmered in water for about 4 minutes until semi-cooked, and drained well before mixing with the stuffing.

Herbs should be chopped fine, and you can substitute the green part of a spring onion or the young part of a leek for chives.

In most recipes finely chopped walnuts are used. Those bought in supermarkets are stale and I strongly recommend buying them from Persian supermarkets (see list at the back of this book). But you can substitute any nut of your own choice.

Substitute any dried fruit, such as finely chopped dates or apricots, for sultanas.

In most recipes saffron is one of the spices used, but substitute turmeric if you prefer (it is much cheaper). This must be fried with the onion as without frying it will give the dish a rather unpleasant aroma. Preparation for saffron is given on page 27.

If there is any leftover stuffing put it in the corner of the baking dish or pan, and spoon over about one or two teaspoons of oil.

Dolmeh can be eaten either as part of a dish or as a starter, and is best eaten hot, with yoghurt or chutney. The quantities here serve four people generously.

THE AUTUMN FESTIVAL OF MEHREGAN

According to Zoroastrian teaching, the angel of Mehr is the angel of promise – your word is your bond. The month of Mehr is the seventh month of the year in the Zoroastrian calendar, coinciding with September which is harvest time. It was a time of celebrating and family gathering, for remembering old people and the less well off. A few days before the celebration, crops were harvested and fruit and vegetables neatly displayed for all to see. On the morning of Mehregan, Bahman the old Zoroastrian baker, would call at our house, to make bread (nan) in our traditional oven (tanoor) and would make at least a hundred loaves. A whole lamb was roasted and cut into portions to cool, then garnished with cold slices of potatoes, onion rings, coriander leaves and a sprinkle of cumin. The lamb and garnish were sandwiched together between nan and distributed amongst the Zoroastrian community, rich and poor alike. It was a custom to make a bonfire in each street and the local people gathered round, offering each other roasted nuts from their hand-made silk bag (doolog). When the fire died down the crowd would return home to finish celebrating Jashn-e-Mehregan with their families.

ROAST LAMB WITH STUFFING
Barreh-e-too por shodeh

It is not so common to make a whole lamb for the family, but here is a recipe for weddings and celebrations.

275g/10oz long grain rice, cleaned and soaked
115g/4oz split yellow lentils, cleaned
2 tablespoons oil
3 large onions, chopped
175g/6oz minced lamb or chicken
6 cloves of garlic, crushed
1/2 teaspoon each ground cinnamon, turmeric and saffron
salt and pepper
1 egg
175g/6oz mixed chopped chives, parsley, coriander, tarragon and mint or 2 teaspoons dried of each
230g/8oz mixed blanched and chopped almonds and pistachios
140g/5oz each sultanas, chopped dried prunes and apricots
One whole lamb weighing no more than 20lb

Pour the water off the soaking rice. Simmer in a pan half filled with water for 3–4 minutes until semi-cooked. Drain well and set aside.

Simmer the lentils for about 30–35 minutes until tender, but not mushy. Drain well.

Heat the oil in a frying pan, add the onion and fry until soft and transparent. Add the meat with the garlic and stir for another minute to brown. Stir in the turmeric.

Put the mixture into a large mixing bowl, and when it is cool add the semi-cooked rice and split yellow lentils, the saffron, cinnamon and the chopped herbs. Break in the egg, season with salt and pepper, and add the dried fruit. Mix it all together with your hands.

Stuff the lamb with the resulting mixture, and sew the cavity with a large needle. Put the lamb on a baking tray in a preheated oven at 200°C/400°F/Gas mark 6, cover with kitchen foil and bake for about one and half hours. Then reduce the heat to 170°C/325°F/Gas 3 and bake for an additional 5–6 hours or until the lamb is tender. The lower the oven heat and the longer it takes the more tender the meat becomes. Baste from time to time.

Remove the foil 15–20 minutes before the end of cooking, to brown the lamb. Serve hot with any type of khoresht and rice, or cold with seasonal salad and nan.

STUFFED SHOULDER OF LAMB
Shaneh-e-bareh-e-porshodeh

115g/4oz dried apricots, soaked overnight
1/4 teaspoon each ground saffron and cinnamon
1 teaspoon sugar
salt and pepper

STUFFING
115g/4oz rice
salt and pepper
2 tablespoons oil
2 medium onions, chopped
115g/4oz minced lamb or beef
1/4 teaspoon each ground cinnamon, and saffron
60g/2oz chopped parsley or coriander
1 tablespoon chopped dill
60g/4oz each sultanas and chopped walnuts
l shoulder of lamb weighing about 1.5kg/3lbs

First make the stuffing, parboil the rice as in the recipe for roast lamb with stuffing.

Fry the onion, the meat and spices as in the same recipe, transfer the mixture into a mixing bowl, add in the remaining ingredients, season with salt and pepper, and mix well.

Preheat the oven to 200°C/400°F/Gas mark 6, spoon the stuffing on to the shoulder of lamb (with the flat side upwards) and place in a roasting tin. Cover with foil and roast in the oven for 30 minutes.

ESFAHAN

The Persians say that, including the outskirts, Esfahan is the largest city in the world. It is known as Esfahan Nesf-e-jahan ast (Esfahan is half of the world).

One of the major attractions of the city is its crowded Bazaar, with its delicate handicraft, such as silverware, rugs, and batik cloths.

The aroma of spices wafts throughout the long passage, with different pulses displayed in bowls and sacks. But the most famous produce is its sweet Gaz (nougat) made from a substance like thick treacle extracted from a low growing shrub, indigenous to Esfahan, sold and sent all over the world in a bed of flour, packed in small wooden or tin boxes, also wrapped in paper.

The city produces most of its own fruit and vegetables, irrigated from the melted snow from the Zagros mountains 400 kilometres away.

Winter is short, lasting only three months. Spring begins in February, when the weather becomes mild and a west wind blows gently over the bloomed gardens covered with flowers and blossoms on fruit and almond trees.

In the late 1970s, I visited this royal city with its palaces and buildings, with their ornate walls, and delicately coloured tiles, elegant columns hewn out of cedar wood, picked out by a thin ray of light filtering through a hole in the keystone and shining on the enormous cupola decorated with stars and arabesques.

The most fascinating feature of the city is its bridges, such as Si-o-se pol (the thirty-three bridges). Each coincides with a straight avenue running through the city from north to south. The most famous, which runs through the centre of town, is called Chaharbagh, meaning four gardens.

Many buildings were constructed by Shah Abbas of the Savafid dynasty, such as Chehel Sotoon (forty columns) with its gardens and peristyle reflecting in the pool in the morning sun.

My favourite was the 'shaking' minaret (monar jonban). Twin towers flank a very wide ogive. When you leaned out of an embrasure at the top of the tower and swayed your body regularly, the tower started oscillating in a perfectly visible manner, with the second minaret starting to move. This was put down to the power of the holy priest who was buried under the building.

The shaking minaret and the famous Ostrojan Mosque were built at the beginning of the 14th century. It was during this same period that books with different recipes were written in one volume, such as ash and other dishes.

I strolled through the streets of Esfahan on my very recent visit. It has grown since I was there, but Esfahan seemed as beautiful to me as it did many years ago. It was difficult to recognise the streets at first, but soon they became familiar. I went to visit the palaces again, they looked naked, with their coloured ornate tiles ripped off, hoping to be restored. I looked at the shaking minaret in despair, the place was deserted as the minaret ceased to shake.

Reduce the temperature to 170°C/325°F/Gas mark 3 and cook for a further 1½ to 2 hours until the meat is tender.

Meanwhile drain the apricots over a bowl. Put them in a small pan with about 150ml/5floz of the reserved drained juice. Add the cinnamon, saffron and the sugar. Bring to the boil, then reduce the heat and simmer uncovered for about 20 minutes until the apricots are soft. Add a little more of the reserved juice a little at a time if the pan becomes too dry.

Remove from the heat, and mash with a fork.

Remove the lamb from the oven, remove the foil, and pour on the apricot mixture. Return to the oven uncovered for a further 5–7 minutes. Serve with plain rice.

STUFFED MINCE
Rollet-e-goosht
❦

230g/8oz minced lean lamb, beef, veal or chicken
1 heaped tablespoon fine breadcrumbs
1 egg
salt and pepper
¹/₄ teaspoon each ground cinnamon and saffron
1 large onion, peeled
4 tablespoons oil

STUFFING
¹/₄ teaspoon turmeric
115 g/4oz chopped walnuts
1 tablespoon sultanas
1 tablespoon each chopped parsley and chives
¹/₄ teaspoon each ground cinnamon and saffron

Grate 2oz of the onion over the meat in a bowl, add the breadcrumbs, spices and the egg.

Knead to bind then chill.

To make the stuffing, chop the remaining onion, and fry in the remaining oil until golden, then stir in the turmeric.

Add the chopped herbs and stir. Transfer into a mixing bowl, add the remaining ingredients and mix.

Spread the prepared meat over the kitchen foil to about ¹/₂ to 1 inch thick. Add the stuffing lengthways at the edge, and roll up the meat. Press lightly at both ends to seal, lift with the foil, and lower into the pan with the fried onion (discard the foil) and fry gently on all sides (the meat will not break). Add 2 tablespoons of water if necessary, and cover the pan. Simmer for 45 minutes until the rollet is cooked, turning the meat from time to time. Serve with rice and plain yoghurt, and or salad.

For a variation, substitute lean fillet of lamb, beef or veal, for mince. Follow the instructions for stuffing. Roll the meat up and tie with trussing thread or string. Follow the cooking instructions as above.

HAKIM OMAR-E-KHAYYAM

During school holidays, and in the heat of summer, lunch was eaten in the cellar, sofreh style, the long cloth spread on thick Persian carpet, and everyone leaning against bolsters, or sitting on low seats around the octagonal pond.

We children often listened to my parents and the word games they used to play together. One of their favourite games was to think up sentences and poems starting with the last letter of the previous sentence.

Sometimes the poems were recited in a sing-song voice, especially if they were by the poet Hakim Omar-E-Khayyam, whose poems were about love, food and drink.

Much later in life I fulfilled my wish to travel to the city of Neyshapur to see the beautifully decorated minaret-style tomb of this great poet. The tomb was completely covered with his poems, written with different coloured tiles all over the high building.

Groups of people sat under the large apricot trees, shaded from the mid-June sun, resting their chins in the palms of their hands, as they stared up at the high minaret, their moving lips whispering the poems to themselves.

The atmosphere was one of utter tranquillity. The only sound that of the birds. Occasionally one of them would knock off a ripened fruit and it would land magically in our laps, ready to eat. It was one of the rare occasions in my life, when I was lulled asleep by the hypnotic atmosphere. I drifted back to when I was only a little girl of seven resting my head in BaBa's arms, in the cool cellar, as he read Omar-E-Khayyam's poems to me in his hypnotic voice.

ROAST STUFFED CHICKEN
Morgh-e-por shodeh

━◆━

90g/3oz long grain rice, cleaned and soaked
1 medium onion, chopped
2 tablespoons oil
60g/2oz each dried apricots and aloo bokahra, or
soaked prunes, or 115g/4oz fresh cherries, pitted
1/2 teaspoon each ground saffron and cinnamon
60g/2oz chopped walnuts
salt and pepper
1 chicken weighing approx. 2kg/4 1/2 lb

Parboil the rice as in the recipe for Roast Lamb with Stuffing and fry the onion in the oil as in the same recipe.

Put all the ingredients into a mixing bowl and toss to mix.

Stuff the chicken with the resulting mixture and sew up the cavity with a large needle. Place on a baking tray, cover loosely with kitchen foil and place in the preheated oven at 180°C/350°F/Gas mark 4 and roast for one hour. Then reduce the heat to 170°C/325°F/Gas mark 3 and cook for a further 1 1/2 to 2 hours or until the chicken is tender. Remove the foil ten minutes before the end of cooking to brown. Serve hot with any type of khoresht and plain rice or cold with seasonal salad. For a variation stuff a turkey the same way, but increase the ingredients if choosing a larger bird which takes longer to cook. Also substitute 2 tablespoons of pomegranate purée for the fruit.

HOT STUFFED FISH
Mahi-e-por shodeh

━◆━

A typical dish from the south (Bandar Abbas), the Persian Gulf or the Strait of Hormuz, this is a recipe which has stayed with me since my teenage days when I visited some friends in the oil fields region of Abadan.

The neighbouring country Iraq has great influence on the city of Abadan's eating habits and culture. The food becomes more peppery and hot, unlike the rest of the country where the ingredients are always prepared with subtle flavours. As tamarind is grown locally it is often substituted for pomegranate purée.

2 tablespoons oil
1 large onion, chopped
4 cloves of garlic, crushed
230g/8oz mixed chopped parsley, coriander and chives
1/4 teaspoon fenugreek (optional)
a few green or 1/2 a red chilli, chopped
(or 1/4 teaspoon chilli powder)
1/2 teaspoon turmeric
salt and pepper
200g/7fl oz thick tamarind fluid

FOR THE FISH
1 tablespoon oil
1 fish weighing about 1.25kg/2 1/2 lb, scaled, gutted and washed with the head left on

TO GARNISH
chopped parsley

Fry the onion with the garlic and spices in the oil as in the recipe for roast lamb with stuffing. Stir in the herbs, season with salt and pepper, and transfer into a mixing bowl. Add the tamarind fluid and toss well to mix.

Heat the oven to 180°C/350°F/Gas mark 4.

Place the fish in an ovenproof fish dish, stuff with the mixture, and sew up the cavity with a large needle or arrange the fish in a swimming position, if necessary curling the tail inwards. Brush on the one tablespoon of the oil. Cover loosely with kitchen foil. Cook in the oven for about 1 1/2 hours or until the fish is cooked and the liquid runs clear when the centre is pierced with a fine metal skewer. Remove the foil and drain off the cooking liquid into a sauceboat. Garnish with chopped parsley. Serve with plain rice.

GREY MULLET WITH CHESTNUTS, GRAPES AND HERBS
Mahi-e-por shodeh ba balut

Dried chestnuts are used in this recipe, but 230g/8oz fresh chestnuts can be used when available. Make as in the recipe for apple khoresht with chestnut and mint.

60g/2oz dried chestnuts or 115g/4oz chopped walnuts
4 tablespoons oil
1 medium onion, chopped
2 cloves of garlic, crushed
230g/8oz black and white grapes, halved or 60g/2oz sultanas
1 tablespoon chopped parsley or dried and crushed
1 teaspoon dried crushed tarragon or 1 tablespoon fresh chopped
½ teaspoon dried crushed mint or 1 tablespoon fresh chopped
salt and pepper
1 white fish e.g., grey mullet, weighing about 1.25kg/2½lb, scaled, gutted, and washed with the head left on, or salmon
lemon juice
1 tablespoon oil

TO GARNISH
Roasted flaked almonds
1 slice lemon (optional)
few black and white grapes, halved and seeded (or seedless grapes)

Prepare and cook the chestnuts as in the recipe for apple khoresht with chestnut and mint.

To make the stuffing, fry the onion with the garlic and herbs as in the recipe for roast lamb with stuffing. Transfer it to a mixing bowl with the cooked chestnuts, half the grapes and all the other ingredients except the lemon juice and 1 tablespoon of oil.

Preheat the oven to 180°C/350°F/Gas mark 4.

Rub the lemon juice inside the fish, and stuff with the ready mixture. Pour over the reserved oil and cook as in the recipe for hot stuffed fish. Serve with salad and or rice, garnished with the remaining grapes and flaked almonds. Place the lemon slice in the mouth if you like.

STUFFED QUINCE
Dolme-e-beh

〜・〜

60g/2oz long grain rice, cleaned and soaked
115g/4oz garden peas, cooked
3 tablespoons oil
1 medium onion, chopped
¼ teaspoon turmeric
115g/4oz lamb or beef, diced small
salt and pepper
½ teaspoon each ground cinnamon and saffron
the juice of one large lemon
1 tablespoon tomato purée
2 teaspoons sugar
4 medium quince

TO GARNISH
roasted almond flakes

Parboil the rice as in the recipe for roast lamb with stuffing. Fry the onion in 2 tablespoons of oil until golden. Add the meat and stir for 3–4 minutes. Add the spices, stir and cook with a little water until tender. Meanwhile dissolve the tomato purée in a little water, stir in to the meat mixture and season with salt and pepper. Leave to cool.

Remove the hairy parts from the quince, take a neat slice off each and set aside. Hollow the centre with an apple corer or a sharp-edged spoon.

Put the cooked and cooled rice and the meat mixture into a mixing bowl with the cooked peas and mix well.

Fill each quince with the resulting mixture. Replace the cap, then place them in a non-stick or heavy aluminium pan. Add three tablespoons of oil. Dissolve the sugar with 85ml/3floz water and pour over the quince with the lemon juice. Cover the pan, and simmer for about 30–40 minutes or until the quince are cooked. Serve with plain rice or as a side dish, or a starter, garnished with flaked almonds.

If cooking in the oven, put them into a casserole, pour 2–3 tablespoons of water over, cover and cook in a preheated oven at 180°C/350°F/Gas mark 4 for about 45 minutes to one hour or until the quince is soft.

For a variation substitute 60g/2oz split yellow lentils for peas, simmer for 30–35 minutes, drain and follow the instructions above for the stuffing.

STUFFED CABBAGE LEAVES
Dolmeh-e-barg-e-kalam

〜・〜

90g/3oz long grain rice
1 large white cabbage
20ml/4floz oil
1 medium onion, chopped
½ teaspoon each ground cinnamon and saffron
salt and pepper
230g/8oz minced lamb or beef
90g/3oz sultanas
60g/2oz chopped nuts

TO GARNISH
a few almond flakes

Parboil the rice as in the recipe for roast lamb with stuffing. Fry the onion with the minced meat and spices in 2 tablespoons of the oil, as in the same recipe. Put into a mixing bowl and add all the other ingredients. Toss well to mix.

Bring 900ml/1½ pints of water to the boil in a large saucepan. Meanwhile, remove any broken leaves from the outside of the cabbage and reserve. Remove the saucepan from the heat and lower the cabbage, stalk end down, into the water. Return to the heat, and bring back to the boil. Immediately reduce the heat, and simmer, uncovered, for 8 minutes. Remove from the heat and leave for 10 minutes, then gently pour off the water, holding the cabbage with an oven glove.

Place the cabbage on a board or work surface with the stalk end uppermost. Using a sharp knife, separate the leaves from the stalk. Roll back from the crown to gently loosen each leaf and then lift off. Repeat until there are 12 good leaves altogether.

If they are too brittle and stiff drop them one or two at a time into boiling water and simmer for another 2 minutes to soften a little. Leave to cool. Reserve the broken cabbage leaves.

Line a large saucepan with the reserved broken leaves. Place a ready prepared and semi-cooked cabbage leaf on a work surface and pare away the hard stalk with a sharp knife. Place two teaspoons of the ready cooked and cooled mixed stuffing in the middle of each leaf, fold the sides inwards and roll up. Repeat with the remaining leaves, placing them tightly side by side in the pan. If there is any stuffing left, place it in the corners of the pan and cover it with broken cabbage leaves. Pour the remaining oil over the stuffed leaves (dolmeh) then pour in 175ml/6floz cold water. Place the lid on tightly and place the pan on a high heat for one minute, then reduce the heat as low as it will go and cook for about 1½ hours. If cooking in the oven, arrange the cabbage leaves into a casserole dish, and pour 4–5 tablespoons oil over the stuffing. Cook in the preheated oven at 180°C/350°F/Gas mark 4 for about 35–45 minutes. Serve with plain yoghurt or sweet chutney.

STUFFED POTATOES
Dolmeh-e-sibzamini

Sir John Malcom (1769–1833) first visited Iran in 1799 as an envoy on behalf of Lord Wellesley, who was the Governor of India, in order to divert the attention of Afghan to Persia and to promote British trade. His second, short, visit was in 1810 when he was received well in Tehran. It was during his first visit that he introduced the first potato to the country. It was round like an apple and a low growing plant, so the Iranians named it Sib zamini, or the apple from the ground, now one of the major crops in fertile areas.

60g/2oz long grain rice, soaked
7 tablespoons oil
1 medium onion, chopped

½ teaspoon each ground saffron and cinnamon
salt and pepper
115g/4oz minced lamb, beef or chicken
2 teaspoons tomato purée
60g/2oz chopped walnuts
10 potatoes, each weighing 90–115g/3–4oz

Simmer the rice for 4 minutes, then drain well. Fry the onion in 2 tablespoons of the oil with the meat and spices as in the recipe for roast lamb with stuffing, and season with salt and pepper. Dissolve the tomato purée, add it to the mixture, and cook until thick. Put into a mixing bowl with the remaining ingredients and toss well to mix.

Preheat the oven to 200°C/400°F/Gas mark 6.

Scrub the potatoes, then carefully cut a 5mm/¼inch-thick slice horizontally off each one. Reserve the slices for lids. Using an apple corer or a sharp-edged teaspoon, hollow out the centre. Reserve the pulp in cold water to prevent it going black.

Fill the potatoes with the meat and rice mixture, replace the lids, then place the potatoes in a baking dish. Pour over 3 tablespoons of the oil and bake for about 1 hour or until cooked. Drain the potato pulps, dab dry, and fry them in hot oil until crisp. Serve with plain yoghurt and salad. Garnish with the fried pulps and chopped parsley.

AUBERGINE AND TOMATO DISH
Shekam pareh

100g/3½oz long grain rice, cleaned and soaked
4 aubergines, each weighing about 175g/6oz
salt and pepper
oil
1 large onion, chopped
230g/8oz minced lamb, beef or chicken
5 cloves of garlic, crushed
¼ teaspoon turmeric
1 teaspoon dried crushed mint

2 teaspoons tomato purée
230g/8oz walnuts
2 teaspoons chopped parsley

Parboil the rice as in the recipe for roast lamb with stuffing. Fry the onion with the garlic and spices in 2 tablespoons of the oil, as in the same recipe, dissolve the tomato purée and stir it in and season with salt and pepper. Put all ingredients into a mixing bowl with the cooked rice and toss.

Peel the aubergines lengthways at intervals of about 2.5cm/1inch, which gives a striped effect and helps to keep them intact during cooking. Cut lengthways through the middle, keeping the aubergine attached at the stem end. Carefully hollow out the centres of each half with a sharp-edged teaspoon, leaving about 5mm/¼inch of flesh all round. Sprinkle the aubergines with salt and leave to degorge for about 30 minutes.

Rinse under cold water and dab dry with kitchen paper towel. Heat 5 tablespoons of oil in a heavy frying pan, add the aubergines one at a time and fry for about 1 minute on each side until lightly coloured all over. Remove from the pan with a slotted spoon and set aside.

Preheat the oven to 180°C/350°F/Gas mark 4.

Fill the aubergine halves with the cooked and cooled mixture. Pour 2–3 tablespoons of oil in a baking tray and arrange the aubergine halves in the tray. Pour about one teaspoon of oil on each and cover loosely with kitchen foil. Bake for about 20–30 minutes or until cooked. Serve with plain yoghurt, garnished with parsley.

STUFFED COURGETTE
Dolmeh-e-kadu
➤❦

90g/3oz long grain rice, cleaned and soaked
4 tablespoons oil
1 medium onion, chopped
114g/4oz minced lamb, beef or chicken
¼ teaspoon each ground cinnamon, saffron and turmeric

140g/5oz mixed parsley, dill, mint, tarragon and chives, chopped
salt and pepper
¼ teaspoon cumin seeds
6 fat courgettes, total weight about 685g/1½lb

TO GARNISH
almond flakes

Parboil the rice, as in the recipe for roast lamb with stuffing. Fry the onion with the meat and spices in 2 tablespoons of the oil, as in the same recipe, stir in the herbs, season with salt and pepper.

Mix with all the remaining ingredients in a mixing bowl

Preheat the oven to 180°C/350°F/Gas mark 4.

Cut 5mm/¼inch slices off the stem end of each courgette and reserve. Using an apple corer or sharp-edged teaspoon, hollow out the centre of each. Discard the pulp.

Fill the courgettes with the meat mixture, place on the reserved cap and secure each with a cocktail stick. Then place them in a baking dish, spoon any leftover stuffing in the corner of the dish and pour over 1 tablespoon of the remaining oil. Cover and bake for 30–35 minutes or until the courgettes are soft. Serve with sweet chutney or plain yoghurt as a starter or side dish. Garnish with almond flakes. For a variation dissolve 1 tablespoon of tomato purée in 5–6 tablespoons of water, and add to the pan over the stuffed courgettes.

STUFFED ONION
Dolmeh-e-piaz
➤❦

60g/2oz long grain rice, cleaned and soaked
4 onions weighing about 240g/8oz each
3 tablespoons oil
90g/3oz minced lamb, beef or chicken
¼ teaspoon each ground cinnamon, and saffron and or turmeric
salt and pepper
1 dessertspoon each chopped dill and coriander

131

TO GARNISH
Few sprigs of fresh mint and tarragon

Parboil the rice as in the recipe for roast lamb with stuffing.

Peel the onion carefully and take a neat slice off the top and reserve. Using an apple corer gently hollow out the middle until only two rings are left. Reserve the centres. Place the hollowed onions into a saucepan and fill with water. Place on a high heat and bring to the boil. Cook moderately for about 3–4 minutes or until barely soft. Drain off the water and leave to cool.

Chop the reserved pulps from one onion, discard the rest and fry in 1 tablespoon of the oil with the meat and spices as in the recipe for roast lamb with stuffing. Put into a mixing bowl with the remaining ingredients and toss well to mix.

Preheat the oven to 180°C/350°/Gas mark 4. Fill the onion cases with the rice and meat mixture and replace the reserved caps. Arrange the onions neatly in a casserole dish and cook in the oven for 20–30 minutes or until soft. If cooking on the stove, place the dolmeh neatly into a 2.25 litre/4 pint non-stick or heavy aluminium based saucepan, into which 2 tablespoons of oil have been added. Pour 2 more teaspoons of oil over each dolmeh, and add 120ml/4floz water. Simmer for about 45 minutes, until the onions are cooked and the liquid has been absorbed. Garnish with a few sprigs of mint and fresh tarragon.

SWEET AND SOUR STUFFED VINE LEAVES
Dolmeh-e-barg-e-mo

This recipe gives instructions for preserved vine leaves which are easy to obtain. If using fresh vine leaves carefully choose young and shiny leaves and soak them in boiling water for 20 minutes until they become limp. They are now ready for stuffing.

230g/8oz preserved vine leaves in brine
115g/4oz long grain rice
7 tablespoons oil
1 large onion, chopped
230g/8oz minced lamb, beef or chicken
90g/3oz mixed chopped chives and parsley
1 heaped tablespoon chopped fresh dill
1/2 level teaspoon each dried crushed mint and tarragon or one tablespoon fresh mixed chopped
1/4 teaspoon each ground cinnamon, saffron, and turmeric
the juice of one large lemon or two tablespoons of vinegar
2–3 teaspoons sugar or to taste
salt and pepper

Put the vine leaves in a large bowl, pour over boiling water to cover and leave for about 20 minutes. Drain into a colander and rinse under cold running water, then pour boiling water over them and leave to soak overnight.

Cook the rice as in the recipe for roast lamb with stuffing. Fry the onion in 2 tablespoons of the oil with the meat, herbs and spices as in the same recipe. Put into a large mixing bowl and toss well to mix.

Put one vine leaf at a time on a flat surface, vein side facing towards you. Put 1 teaspoon of the stuffing near the stem end, then roll the leaf up tightly around the stuffing, and tuck in the edges to make a neat cigar shape. Swirl 1 tablespoon of the oil over the inside of a large saucepan, then line with the reserved vine leaves. Place the dolmeh side by side in one layer in the pan, pressing them down well with the back of your hands to ensure that they are packed in firmly. Pour over the remaining oil and about 225ml/8floz water. Simmer for 2 hours, adding 85–120ml/3–4floz water every 30 minutes or whenever the pan becomes too dry. Fifteen minutes before the end of cooking, mix the sugar in lemon juice or vinegar and add to the pan. Serve hot as a starter or as a main course with khoresht. It is also delicious cold. For a more savoury taste eliminate the sugar and the lemon juice.

PERSEPOLIS

It was in mid June that we joined a tour bus from Shiraz on its fifty mile journey to Persepolis, the ancient capital of the Persian Empire. We travelled through rocky barren land, along asphalted roads which wound deeper and deeper into desert plain. There were a few miles left to the end of the journey when the historical sight became visible, covering many hundreds of square yards at the foothill of the mountain. A monumental double staircase, with carved bas relief, depicting emissaries from foreign lands, paying tribute and homage to the king, led up to the Apadana, the king's audience chamber. Buried into the mountain sides were the tombs of Artaxerxes II and Artaxerxes III. Representatives of the many countries which made up the Persian Empire were engraved on the front entrance to these tombs with bas-reliefs of the king, standing in front of the fire altar after paying tribute to Ahuramazda.

We continued our short journey towards Pasargadeh, a rural community set on a treeless plain, where we saw the ancient site of the burial place of Cyrus the Great.

It was a short drive to visit Naghsh-e-Rostam, or the valley of the kings, where several Hakhamaneshian (Achaemenian) kings were interred, including Xerxes and Dariush the Great. The symbols of many bas-reliefs emphasised the importance of the Zoroastrian religion in these ancient times.

Before leaving Persepolis, everyone had a picnic out of their packed lunch boxes. The drive back to Shiraz was by way of the outskirts of Persepolis, passing through a vast area of desert plain, such a contrast to the city of Shiraz, with its colourful designed rose gardens and beautiful Bagh-e-Eram.

THE WATER INSPECTOR

One of my favourite walks was at night through the cobbled streets of Yazd, holding on to Baba's hand, towards my grandfather's bagh (orchard). Electric light lamps never interested me. I really preferred to see the niches in the wall, where cotton oil lamps used to sit, giving the street a cosy atmosphere.

Entering the bagh, the sloping path led down to where pulses, vegetables, herbs and melon and watermelon were grown. These plots were divided into strips, which were fed by irrigated water, which the family had to pay for, and around the edge were quince, pomegranate and all sorts of other fruit trees. Only a few feet away there was a constant running stream and like most people my family planted as many fruit trees as possible next to this stream, to take advantage of the free water.

Lunch was eaten under the shaded apricot tree, with food spread on the batik cloth. The water inspector Mr Sohrab always called unexpectedly, knocking the heavy wrought iron knocker for several minutes to make sure it was heard. His visit always seemed to coincide with our mid-day snack. Such perfect timing.

STUFFED AUBERGINE
Dolmeh-e-badinjan

Peeling aubergines at intervals to give a striped effect not only makes them look more attractive when served, it also helps to keep them intact during cooking.

90g/3oz long grain rice, cleaned and soaked
4 aubergines, each weighing about 175g/6oz
salt

133

7 tablespoons oil
1 large onion, chopped
4–5 cloves of garlic, crushed
230g/8oz minced lamb, beef or chicken
¼ teaspoon each ground cinnamon and saffron, or
½ level teaspoon turmeric
90g/3oz mixed chives, parsley, mint and tarragon,
chopped or ¼ teaspoon dried mint and tarragon
2 teaspoons tomato purée
2 teaspoons sultanas
salt and pepper

Parboil the rice as in the recipe for roast lamb with stuffing. Fry the onion in 2 tablespoons of oil with the meat, herbs and spices as in the same recipe. Dissolve the tomato purée in a little water, add to the mixture and cook until thick. Place the meat mixture in a mixing bowl with the cooked rice and all the remaining ingredients. Toss well.

Peel the aubergines at 1cm/½inch intervals, then cut a 1cm/½inch slice off the stem ends and reserve. Using an apple corer or sharp-edged teaspoon hollow out the centre, leaving the cases about 5mm/¼inch thick. Sprinkle the insides with a little salt and leave on a tray or a plate for about thirty minute to drain the dark bitter juices.

Preheat the oven to 180°C/350°F/Gas mark 4.

Rinse the aubergine cases under cold running water and pat dry with kitchen paper. Fill with the meat and rice mixture, replace the caps and secure with wooden cocktail sticks.

Heat 2 tablespoons of the remaining oil in a heavy frying pan, add the aubergines and fry gently until lightly coloured on all sides. Transfer to an ovenproof dish, spoon any left over stuffing into the corners of the dish and pour over the remaining oil. Cover loosely with foil and bake in the oven for 45 minutes to 1 hour or until the aubergines are soft. Serve with plain yoghurt.

STUFFED TOMATOES
Dolmeh-e-govjeh

115g/4oz long grain rice, cleaned and soaked
2 tablespoons oil
1 onion, chopped
2 cloves of garlic, crushed
150g/5oz minced lamb, beef or chicken
¼ teaspoon each ground saffron and cinnamon
1 tablespoon chopped dill
¼ teaspoon each dried and crushed mint and
tarragon
salt and pepper
4 large tomatoes, each weighing about 230g/8oz

TO GARNISH
sprigs of parsley

Parboil the rice as in the recipe for roast lamb with stuffing. Fry the onion with the meat, garlic and spices as in the same recipe, season with salt and pepper. Mix with all the remaining ingredients (except the tomatoes) in a large mixing bowl. Toss well.

Preheat the oven to 180°C/350°F/Gas mark 4.

Slice the top (stalk end) off each tomato and reserve. Scoop out the centres with a sharp-edged teaspoon and discard. Fill each tomato case with the rice and meat mixture, replace the caps, then place the tomatoes in a baking dish. Spoon any leftover stuffing into the corner of the dish and pour over the remaining oil. Cover loosely with foil and bake in the oven for 20 minutes or until the tomatoes are cooked. Serve as a starter or side dish with plain yoghurt, garnished with parsley.

APPLES STUFFED WITH CHICKEN AND NUTS
Dolmeh-e-sib

90g/3oz long grain rice, cleaned and soaked
2 tablespoons oil
1 medium onion, chopped
90g/3oz minced chicken, lamb or beef
30g/1oz each blanched almonds and pistachios,
finely chopped
2 teaspoons sultanas
¼ teaspoon each ground cinnamon and saffron
salt and pepper
6 crisp apples, each weighing about 115g/4oz

TO GARNISH
roasted flaked almonds

Parboil the rice as in the recipe for roast lamb with stuffing. Fry the onion in 1 tablespoon of the oil with the chicken and spices as in the same recipe. Add into a mixing bowl with all the remaining ingredients except the apple.

Preheat the oven to 180°C/350°F/Gas mark 4.

Slice the top (stalk end) off each apple and reserve. Using an apple corer, hollow out the centres (reserve for fruit salad). Fill the apples with the meat and rice mixture, replace the tops, then place any leftover stuffing in the corners of the dish and pour over the remaining oil. Cover loosely with foil and bake in the oven for about 30 minutes or until the apples are soft. Serve hot or cold as a starter or side dish garnished with flaked almonds.

PEPPERS STUFFED WITH MEAT AND RICE
Dolmeh-e-felfel

150g/5oz long grain rice, cleaned and soaked
30g/1oz split yellow lentils
4 green peppers each weighing about 230g/8oz each
3 tablespoons oil
1 large onion, chopped
150g/5oz lean minced lamb, beef or chicken
1 tablespoon mixed chopped dill and parsley
1 tablespoon fresh mint and tarragon chopped,
or ¼ teaspoon each dried crushed
¼ teaspoon each ground cinnamon and turmeric
salt and pepper

Parboil the rice as in the recipe for roast lamb with stuffing. Fry the onion in 1 tablespoon of oil with the meat and spices as in the same recipe, season with salt and pepper.

Simmer the split yellow lentils for 30–35 minutes until tender, drain well.

Put all the cooked and cooled ingredients into a mixing bowl.

Slice the top stalk end off each pepper and reserve, then scoop out the seeds and peel off the membranes inside. Blanch the pepper cases in boiling water for 3–4 minutes until barely soft. Drain and rinse under cold running water, then set aside.

Preheat the oven to 180°C/350°F/Gas mark 4.

Fill the peppers with the meat and rice mixture, then place them in a baking dish. Replace the caps. Spoon any leftover stuffing into the corners and pour over the remaining oil. Cover loosely with foil and bake in the oven for about 30 minutes or until the peppers are soft. Serve hot with plain yoghurt. To cook on the stove, dissolve 1 tablespoon of tomato purée in 150ml/¼ pint cold water, add to the pan and place the lid on tightly. Simmer for about 30–40 minutes. Serve with plain yoghurt.

VERY CASUAL

Giveh was sold in every shoe shop, as a casual pair of shoes. It was hand-knitted, often with really pretty patterns, especially for children. I loved mine; it had pictures of flowers and birds on it. All giveh were made with strong white cotton, very flat but comfortable. It was really summer shoes.

As an inquisitive child, I wanted to know everything, and loved the interesting stories told by Baba, mostly during evening after dinner. Baba was a slow eater – he took at least one hour to finish his meal, and never spoke during eating, as this was considered bad manners, because you may accidentally spit your food onto another person's plate.

We children all gathered around to hear the interesting stories of his childhood days. One such story was about the ancient Persian king, Kaykavous, who married a young girl after his wife's death. The girl's name was Soodabeh, and she quickly fell in love with the king's son, Prince Siyavash. The prince was a loyal son and ignored his stepmother's advances, so much so that she became angry with him and told tales about him to her husband.

As a punishment for his son and also to prove his innocence, Kaykavous ordered Siyavash to ride through fire on horseback.

The son obeyed his father, and rode through the fire. He escaped unharmed, but was so angry with his father that he did not turn back. He rode straight on until he eventually reached Tooran, which is north of Khorasan.

Afrasiyab, the king of Tooran, welcomed Siyavash and arranged for him to marry his daughter Farangis, making him heir to the throne.

But the king's brother naturally became jealous of Siyavash, and told tales about him to the king.

Afrasiyab became so suspicious that he ordered Siyavash to be beheaded.

The king of Persia heard the tragic news of his son's death, and that his daughter-in-law Farangis was expecting his grandchild. He sent a strong warrior called Giv to look for her and bring her to him.

So Giv set off on his long journey, he walked for many days, until eventually his footwear fell to pieces and his feet hurt. Giv knew that he still had a long way to travel, and he hit upon the idea of making stronger footwear by compressing old cloth and leather together, passing leather through the sole of the shoes to strengthen them and sewing the top with strong cotton.

Giv's invention worked, and from that day on this type of footwear was called giveh after Giv.

FISH, KEBABS, SALAD

TEST BEFORE BUYING

As a teenager, when I lived in Tehran, I spent a lot of time with my sister-in-law, a very talented cook whose name is also Shirin.

Every food item was carefully chosen before buying. The fishmonger called regularly at her apartment with his basket full of fish. Although they looked very fresh, my sister-in-law told me always to test the fish before buying: make sure the eyes are not sunken, press down on the flesh and make sure it does not make a dent and, when holding the fish in your hand, the whole fish should stay straight rather than droopy. The gills should look fresh and pink.

Never feel shy to smell the fish, even if buying from a shop.

HALIBUT IN ORANGE SAUCE
Mahi ba ab-e-porteghal

Traditionally sharp orange juice is used. But sweet orange juice can be substituted for this recipe.

1 medium onion, chopped
455g/1lb halibut, cut into four equal portions
300ml/^{1}/$_2$ pint orange juice
1–2 teaspoons rice flour
^{1}/$_4$ teaspoon ground saffron
115g/4oz chopped pistachios and blanched almonds

TO GARNISH
orange segments and sprigs of parsley

Simmer the chopped onion in 175ml/6floz cold water until soft, add the fish and simmer for 4–5 minutes until cooked.

Remove the fish with a slotted spoon and drain the liquid into a bowl.

Discard the onion, return the liquid back into the pan and add the fish. Dissolve the rice flour in the orange juice with the saffron and add to the pan along with the nuts. Serve the fish with rice garnished with orange segments and sprigs of parsley.

FRIED TROUT
Ghezelala-ye-sorkh shodeh

4 trout, each weighing about 230g/8oz, gutted, washed and slit in half, but intact
^{1}/$_2$ teaspoon ground saffron or turmeric
salt and pepper
2 eggs, beaten
oil

TO GARNISH
Orange rings

Wipe the fish dry, rub with saffron, salt and pepper, coat with the beaten egg and fry in moderately hot shallow oil until golden on both sides. Lift the fish out with a slotted spoon onto kitchen paper to drain the excess oil. Serve with rice garnished with orange rings.

BREAM FRIED IN LEMON AND EGG
Mahie-e-soof ba ab-e-porteghal

2 egg yolks
85ml/3floz sharp orange juice or the juice of one large lemon
salt and pepper
900g/2lb bream, cut into portions
plain flour for coating the fish
oil

Beat the egg yolks with the orange juice, season with salt and pepper. Marinate the fish cutlets in the mixture for a few hours.

Coat the fish with flour and fry for 3–4 minutes until golden and crisp. Remove to drain on kitchen paper. Serve with rice and seasonal salad, garnished with orange rings and sprigs of parsley.

For a variation substitute salmon for bream.

FRIED FISH CAKES
Cotlet-e-mahi

455g/1lb minced fish
1 egg
60g/2oz onion, grated
salt and pepper
2 tablespoons fine breadcrumbs
oil

Put all ingredients except the oil into a mixing bowl. Season with salt and pepper. Knead to bind. Take balls as big as walnuts, make them smooth in your hands, then flatten to about 1cm/½inch thick. Fry in shallow oil until golden on both sides. Serve hot or cold with salad or plain rice, or sandwiched between nan or bread.

FISH KEBAB IN POMEGRANATE PURÉE
Kabab-e-mahi-ba rob-e-anar

900g/2lb fish, cubed into 4 × 2.5cm/1½ × 1inch
thick pieces
150ml/¼ pint oil
3 tablespoons pomegranate purée, dissolved
in 150ml/¼ pint water or pomegranate
or orange juice
1 small onion, grated
salt and pepper

TO GARNISH
sprigs of parsley

Mix the oil, onion and pomegranate juice together and season with salt and pepper. Marinate the fish in the mixture for a few hours. Thread the fish on to a skewer.

Barbecue or grill until golden and crisp. Serve with rice garnished with sprigs of parsley and orange rings.

For a variations, simmer the juice of one large lemon with 2 tablespoons of tomato purée and 60g/2oz butter. Pour over the kebab when serving.

FISH COOKED IN FRUIT JUICE AND CLOVES
Mahi ba ab-e-miveh va mikhak

900g/2lb white fish, cut into 4 × 2.5cm/
1½ x 1inch pieces
115g/4 oz butter
450ml/15floz mixed pomegranate and orange juice
1 tablespoon tomato purée
½ teaspoon ground cinnamon
sprinkle of grated nutmeg
¼ teaspoon ground cloves
salt and pepper

TO GARNISH
orange rings and sprigs of parsley

Fry the fish in oil for 3–4 minutes.

Mix the juices with the spices, season with salt and pepper, pour over the fish and simmer for 4–5 minutes until the liquid is almost absorbed. Serve with rice, garnished with parsley and orange rings.

For a variation marinate the fish in 30g/1oz sugar mixed with 120ml/4floz vinegar and ¼ teaspoon saffron. Cook in exactly the same way and garnish with almond flakes.

SPICY PRAWNS IN HERB AND GARLIC SAUCE
Gholyeh-e-maygoo

—◦—

4–5 tablespoons oil
1 medium onion, chopped
685g/1¹/₂lb prawns, peeled and washed
4 cloves of garlic, crushed
1 teaspoon crushed ginger or ¹/₂ teaspoon
ginger powder
2 tablespoons each chopped parsley and coriander
1 tablespoon chopped chives
¹/₄ teaspoon each ground cinnamon and turmeric
1 teaspoon curry powder
pinch of chilli powder or to your liking
1 teaspoon sugar
300ml/¹/₂ pints tamarind fluid
(see basic recipes)
¹/₂ tablespoon tomato purée
salt and pepper

Fry the onion and garlic in oil until golden. Add the ginger with the chopped herbs, stir for two minutes, then add the prawns, spices and the sugar. Season with salt and pepper and stir in the tamarind fluid. Dissolve the tomato purée in a little water and add to the pan. Simmer until thick. Serve with plain rice. For a variation substitute fish for prawns.

FISH IN DILL SAUCE
Mahi ba shevid va govjeh

—◦—

6 tablespoons oil
1 medium onion, chopped
1 medium courgette, sliced into rings
¹/₂ teaspoon turmeric
285/10oz potatoes, coarsely diced
2 tablespoons chopped dill
salt and pepper
685g/1¹/₂lb white fish fillets

TO GARNISH
Grated carrots, tomato slices, and coriander leaves

Fry the onion in 2 tablespoons of the oil until golden, then add the courgettes and fry until lightly coloured. Remove with a slotted spoon. Stir in the turmeric, add the potatoes with the dill. Season with salt and pepper. Add 85–120ml/3–4floz water, cover and simmer until the potatoes are tender. Add the courgettes to warm for 2–3 minutes.

Meanwhile fry the fish in the remaining oil in another pan until golden.

Serve the fish with rice garnished with coriander leaves and the cooked vegetables from the pan.

STURGEON FISH KEBAB WITH TOMATO AND LEMON SAUCE
Kabab-e-mahi-e-ozunborun

—◦—

The sturgeon from the Caspian Sea is renowned for its rare and valuable caviar.

Caviar or sturgeon eggs have been known in England for more than 400 years. It was a kind of food popular during the Sassanian dynasty among the Zoroastrian rulers at the time, and still is today in Iran in the southern region of the Caspian. It is eaten by the majority of the area's population and is as popular as the less expensive fish roe (fish egg) obtainable in fish shops and Jewish delicatessens in the west.

The name caviar, or in Persian *Khaveeyar*, derives from the *Pahlavi* (Zoroastrian) language meaning egg. A chicken's (or any egg) egg is called *Khiya*.

The sale of caviar has increased in Iran since the revolution, replacing alcohol for sale in duty free shops.

The recipe given is for sturgeon, but you can substitute salmon and cook the same way.

1 small sturgeon weighing about 685g/1¹/₂lb, cut into 2-inch squares

140

TO MARINATE THE FISH
lemon juice
1 medium onion, grated
salt and pepper

FOR THE SAUCE
2 tablespoons tomato purée
3 tablespoons lemon juice
60g/2oz butter
salt and pepper

TO GARNISH
lemon rings and sprigs of parsley

Mix the lemon and the onion and season with salt and pepper. Marinate the fish in the mixture overnight.

Mix the tomato purée with lemon juice and butter, season with salt and pepper and melt over a gentle heat.

Thread the fish on to a skewer, and grill over charcoal, or under a hot grill. Brush the kebab at intervals of 3–4 minutes with the tomato and lemon mixture, turning them frequently. Serve with rice garnished with lemon rings and sprigs of parsley.

LEAF KEBAB
Kabab-e-barg
◆

As the meat is neatly cut and almost all the same shape and size, it is given the name of barg, meaning a leaf or rose petal.

685g/1¹/₂lb fillet of lamb, cut into 4 × 2.5cm/
1¹/₂ × 1inch pieces

TO MARINATE
1 large onion, grated
1 tablespoon olive or vegetable oil
salt and pepper

TO SERVE
1 egg yolk

cooked rice
sliced Spanish onion
grilled tomatoes
plain yoghurt
powdered somac (optional)

Mix the onion and olive oil and season with salt and pepper. Marinate the meat in the mixture for a few hours.

Thread the meat on to a metal skewer and grill over a preheated barbecue or under a hot grill for 10–15 minutes, turning them every 3–4 minutes, until tender.

Serve hot rice on a plate, add the egg yolk in the middle, cover with more rice. Place the kebab on the side, and sprinkle on the somac. Garnish with onion rings and grilled tomatoes and serve with plain yoghurt. For a variation make shish or (sikh) kebab:

Substitute 150ml/¹/₄ pint plain yoghurt for olive oil, add ¹/₂ teaspoon ground saffron to the marinated sauce and cook in the same way.

KEBAB IN A PAN
Kabab-e-hossaini
◆

Traditionally the meat is threaded onto small pomegranate twigs specially made for this dish, and cooked in a pan with a little water. But to be more practical, it is made without the skewers.

685g/1¹/₂lb fillet of lamb, cut into 4 × 2.5cm/
1¹/₂ × 1inch pieces
90g/3oz butter
2 large onions, peeled and made into rings
2 large peppers, seeded and quartered
275g/10oz tomato rings
salt and pepper

Add half the butter into a 1.25 litre/4 pint saucepan, arrange the meat with alternative layers of vegetables, add the remaining butter, and season with salt and pepper. Simmer for one hour with the pan covered, until tender. Serve with rice and plain yoghurt.

For a variation substitute minced meat for fillet, and leave out the butter from this recipe.

BIRYANI KEBAB
Kabab-e-biryani
◆

Arrange 685g/1½lb fillet of lamb, cut into small strips, neatly into a pan seasoned with salt and pepper, ½ teaspoon each ground saffron and cinnamon, 1 large onion, finely chopped, 60g/2oz butter and 2–3 tablespoons of water. Simmer with the pan covered until the meat is tender. Remove with a slotted spoon into a little hot oil and fry to brown. Serve with nan, bread or rice.

MINCED KEBAB
Kabab-e-koobideh
◆

If you are worried that the meat may fall off the skewer, just add one beaten egg before kneading. Instead of using the skewer press the meat onto a heavy griddle, to give the effect of a skewer, then after grilling for five minutes, cut them into strips, turning them frequently to brown.

685g/1½lb minced lamb
1 medium onion, grated
salt and pepper

TO SERVE
As in leaf Kebab

Knead the meat and onion, seasoned with salt and pepper, to bind. Take small balls as big as tangerines and press around the metal skewer to make them smooth, pressing down with the two middle fingers about 5cm/2inches apart to make indentations all the way down. Repeat with the remaining meat until all has been used. Cook over a heated barbecue

or on a rack under a preheated hot grill for 10–15 minutes, turning frequently.

Serve as in leaf kebab.

CHICKEN KEBAB
Jujeh kabab
◆

4 boneless chicken breasts, each weighing about
230g/8oz
1 large onion, grated
6 tablespoon plain yoghurt
1 tablespoon lemon juice
1 teaspoon ground saffron or turmeric

TO GARNISH
Lemon rings

Mix the onion and lemon juice with the yoghurt, season with salt and pepper, and add the saffron. Marinate the chicken breasts (with their skins on) in the resulting mixture for a few hours.

Thread the chicken pieces on to a skewer and cook over a preheated barbecue or on a rack under a pre-heated hot grill for 15–20 minutes, turning them frequently to brown. Serve with lime juice and a seasonal salad, garnished with lemon rings.

KEBAB IN A PAN No 2
Kabab-e-boshghabi
◆

This can be a quick snack with nan or served as a main meal for lunch or dinner with rice, grilled tomatoes, onion rings and plain yoghurt.

900g/2lb minced lamb or beef
1 medium onion, grated
salt and pepper

Put the meat and the onion in a large bowl, season with salt and pepper and knead to bind. Dampen your hands with water and take small balls as big as tangerines. Make them smooth in your hands then flatten them with the palm of your hand to 5mm/¼inch thick and place them into the frying pan. Cook slowly for 10–15 minutes, turning them every 3–4 minutes until brown and all the liquid has been absorbed. Best eaten hot.

ROAST LEG OF LAMB
Bareh-e-kabab shodeh
❧

1 leg of lamb weighing about 1.75kg/4lb
8 garlic cloves, quartered
1 teaspoon turmeric
salt and pepper

TO GARNISH
sprigs of mint

Preheat the oven to 220°C/425°F/Gas mark 7. Make deep incisions all over the joint with a sharp knife, and insert the pieces of garlic into them. Rub the turmeric and a little salt and pepper all over the joint.

Wrap the meat in foil and place in a roasting tin. Roast in the oven for 15 minutes, then reduce the temperature to 170°C/325°/Gas mark 3 and roast for a further 2½–3 hours or until tender. Garnish with sprigs of mint and serve with rice and plain yoghurt and any type of khoresht.

CRISPY SAFFRON CHICKEN
Morgh-e-sorkh shodeh
❧

4 chicken breasts or drumsticks
1 medium onion, chopped
½–1 teaspoon saffron or turmeric
¼ teaspoon ground cinnamon (optional)
salt and pepper
oil for shallow frying

Simmer the chicken, onion and the spices in 150ml/¼ pint water until half cooked. Remove the chicken with a slotted spoon, and drain in a colander. Fry in shallow oil until crisp and cooked.

LAMB POACHED IN SAFFRON
Bareh-e-ab-paz
❧

455g/1lb knuckle or any meaty part of lamb
1 medium onion, chopped
½ teaspoon ground saffron or turmeric
salt and pepper

Simmer the lamb with the onion, saffron, salt and pepper in water (about 85ml/3floz) until tender. Turn the lamb occasionally to cook evenly. Serve hot with rice.

APPLE AND WALNUT SALAD
Salad-e-sib ba gerdu
❧

175g/6oz rice, cooked
230g/8oz celery, trimmed and cut into 5mm/¼inch dice
5 eating apples, peeled, cored and cut into 1cm/½inch dice
140g/5oz walnuts, chopped
115g/4oz sultanas
300ml/10floz plain yoghurt or sour cream
salt and pepper

TO GARNISH
almond flakes
¼ teaspoon ground cinnamon

Mix all ingredients with half the yoghurt in a large mixing bowl. Serve drizzled with the remaining yoghurt, sprinkle on the cinnamon and garnish with the flaked almonds.

RED KIDNEY BEAN SALAD
Salad-e-lubia ghermez

140g/5oz red kidney beans, soaked overnight
1 medium potato, cooked and diced
3 hard-boiled eggs, chopped
90ml/3floz olive oil
juice of 2 large lemons
salt and pepper

TO GARNISH
Chopped parsley
1 large Spanish onion, cut into rings

Boil the beans vigorously for ten minutes, then simmer for one hour or until tender. Drain well.

Put all the ingredients into a mixing bowl, season with salt and pepper, and toss well to mix. Serve garnished with chopped parsley and onion rings. For a variation add half a large cucumber, sliced or diced small, and 3 large tomatoes, cut into quarters.

BROWN LENTILS AND SULTANA SALAD
Salad-e-adas ba keshmesh

140g/5oz brown lentils, cooked
115g/4oz basmati rice, cooked
1 small Spanish onion, finely chopped
60g/2oz sultanas
90ml/3floz olive oil
juice of 1 small lemon
salt and pepper

TO GARNISH
chopped parsley

Mix all the ingredients in a large bowl and serve as a starter or a main dish with nan, garnished with chopped parsley.

TRADITIONAL WELCOME

In early spring the trees were covered in blossom and the vivid green grass was damp with the early morning dew.

In the park in the early hours of the afternoon, groups of different family and friends gathered around their sofreh (picnic cloth) spread out with nan and fresh yoghurt, salad of spring onion, basil, mint and tarragon (sabsi khordan), with panir (fresh cheese). Food was dished out from aluminium containers (ghablemeh) placed along the long cloth, which looked as colourful as the table at home. Tea (chay) was served in small estekan glasses from a brass samovar, offered with sugar at the side on the saucer (ghand pahloo).

Many people strolled, enjoying the atmosphere, and then were asked to join in and sit down to the picnic. The hospitality of a Persian extended from a table at home to sofreh in the park. The word befermaind ('please join in' or 'after you') was heard in every corner of the park. Some sandwiched the food between nan and offered it to their walking guests to break the ice. It was a time to exchange addresses for a long friendship.

CHICKEN AND HERB SALAD
Salad-e-morgh ba sib zamini

1 medium potato, cooked and diced
140g/5oz cooked runner beans
175g/6oz peas, cooked and drained
685g/1½lb cooked chicken, diced small
1 teaspoon each fresh dill, tarragon and mint leaves, chopped

Grey Mullet with Chestnuts, Grapes and Herbs, and Orange and Yellow Heart Salad

Three variations of traditional crispy rice

An informal dinner including Turnip Soup

Delicacies for an informal gathering, including Pistachio Munchies, Coconut Drops, Chickpea Tears and Yazdi Cakes

Goodbye Meal-in-a-Bowl (top left); Sweet and Sour Fish (top right); Melon Surprise (bottom left); Fish in Dill Sauce (bottom right)

Cherry Pilaff

Minced Beef Kebabs and Lamb Kebabs; Lavash Nan and Turmeric and Cumin Nan; Stuffed Melon Dessert

Elephant Ears (top); Stuffed Fried Fingers (top left); Soft Syrup Fingers (top right); Sweet Syrup Circles (bottom left); Halva (bottom right)

Shirin displays a typical Persian buffet made of tantalising light dishes

2 teaspoons chopped parsley
juice of 1 lemon
salt and pepper
120ml/4floz plain yoghurt or sour cream or
mayonnaise

TO GARNISH
2 medium cooked beetroot, sliced into rings

Put all the ingredients into a mixing bowl and toss well to combine. Serve as a main meal garnished with beetroot rings.

OLIVIER SALAD
Salad-e-olivier

This dish of Russian origin became popular from the beginning of the 20th century. It is a popular feature of a dinner table from home to Hotel café and wedding banquet.

It is served as a main course or a side dish. Gherkins (khiar shoor) in brine are available in almost all supermarkets, especially Jewish delicatessens or continental shops.

1 medium potato, cooked and diced small
salt and pepper
230g/8oz carrots, cooked and diced
175g/6oz cooked peas
900g/2lb lean cooked chicken, diced
4 hard-boiled eggs, diced
3 medium pickled cucumbers, diced
115g/4oz olives, stoned
juice of 1 large lemon, or to taste
about 300ml/½ pint thick mayonnaise

TO GARNISH
radish rings and olives

Mix all the ingredients with half the mayonnaise. Serve on a large oval dish and smooth over the remaining mayonnaise Serve garnished with radish rings and olives.

RICE SALAD
Salad-e-berenj

For a pretty garnish, make radish roses by trimming both ends off the radishes then making thin cuts around each one to form petal shapes. Soak in iced water while preparing the salad so that the petals open out slightly.

140g/5oz each chick peas and long grain rice, cooked
230g/8oz celery, cut into 5mm/¼ inch dice
90–120ml/3–4oz olive oil
4 hard-boiled eggs, chopped finely
salt and pepper

TO GARNISH
10–12 radishes

Mix all the ingredients together and serve with nan as a main course, garnished with radishes.

POTATO AND YOGHURT SALAD
Salad-e-sib zamini ba mast

1 medium potato, cooked and diced
140g/5oz peas, cooked
285g/10oz celery, cut into 5mm/¼ inch dice
2 tablespoons chopped dill
50ml/2floz olive oil
115g/4oz chopped walnuts
juice of 1 large lemon
salt and pepper
300ml/10floz plain yoghurt

TO GARNISH
1 large beetroot, cooked, peeled and sliced
into rings

Mix all ingredients in a large bowl, season with salt and pepper. Serve as a starter with nan garnished with beetroot rings.

ORANGE AND YELLOW HEART SALAD
Salad-e-zard ba porteghal

❦

This pretty salad goes well with cold fish. For a dramatic effect, use both red- and green-skinned apples.

a few lettuce leaves
175g/6oz celery hearts, finely diced
2 canned artichoke hearts, drained
230g/8oz eating apples, cored and sliced into rings
squeeze of lemon juice
230g/8oz orange segments
175g/6oz cooked baby corn-on-the-cob

DRESSING
juice of 1 large lemon
85ml/3floz mayonnaise

50ml/3floz orange liqueur
2 teaspoons chopped fresh coriander
salt and pepper

To make the dressing beat the lemon juice, mayonnaise and liqueur together, add the coriander and salt and pepper to taste, then pour into a sauce boat.

Arrange the lettuce leaves on a serving dish and sprinkle the celery on top.

Dice one of the artichokes and add to the celery.

Arrange the apple rings over the salad and sprinkle with a little lemon juice to prevent discoloration. Arrange the orange segments in a circle on top of the apple slices, then place the remaining whole artichoke heart in the centre. Tuck the baby corn-on-the-cob around the edge of the salad, then spoon over a little of the dressing. Serve immediately with the remaining dressing served separately in the sauce boat.

BAKING AND SWEETS

BASIC NAN
Nan-e-sadeh

10g/¹/₄oz dried or 15g/¹/₂oz fresh yeast
1 teaspoon sugar
455g/1lb plain wholemeal flour
¹/₂ teaspoon salt
1 tablespoon oil

Dissolve the yeast and sugar in 85ml/3floz warm water and leave in a warm place to rise, which takes about 10 minutes.

Put the flour and the salt into a large mixing bowl and make a well in the centre. Add the frothing yeast and the oil, then slowly add about 225ml/8floz warm water and knead for about 5 minutes. Dust the dough with a little flour, cover with a damp cloth and leave for about one hour until it has doubled in bulk. Remove onto a slightly floured surface and punch for about 4–5 minutes. Leave in a warm place to rise again for about one hour.

Preheat the grill to hot. Heat a lightly greased 30mm/12inch cast iron frying pan.

Divide the dough into 9–10 equal balls and roll each to about 28cm/11inch round. Brush off any excess flour.

Place the nan in the hot pan, reduce the heat to very low and cook for about 3 minutes. Place the pan under the grill about 4 inches/10 cm from the heat and cook for a further 4 minutes until bubbles rise.

With a fish slice, transfer the nan to a wire rack and leave to cool. Repeat with the remaining dough, remembering to increase the heat between each cooking so that the pan is very hot when the nan is first put into it.

Bahman the Zoroastrian baker visited our house once a month, spending the whole day making nan in the clay oven (tanoor), and there was always some dough left to make Nan-e-Zardchoobeh or turmeric nan, then a whole lamb was put into the oven and friends and relations would come to share the feast.

GAHANBAR

Gahanbar is a traditional Zoroastrian custom, to commemorate the good deeds of a deceased member of the family, who had bequeathed part of their estate to the benefit of the poorer members of the community. The commemoration took place in every season, and the most important was that of five days before Nov Rooz (New Year), when a large assortment of dishes was placed in the most spacious room in the house, beautifully decorated with freshly cut flowers.

The dishes were spread out on a large table together with a large copper tray piled high with dried fruit such as figs, dates, sultanas, peaches, and apricots, and nuts such as pistachio, walnuts, almonds and roasted hazelnuts. The mixture was called lork.

In late morning the front door was left open as everyone was welcomed, and the gathering would reach a hundred or more. Everyone sat in silence listening to the Zoroastrian priest (Moobed) who was dressed in traditional white gown and cap. He recited passages from the Avesta, chanting away in a low musical voice. His eyes half closed and this chanting had such a hypnotic effect that some dozed off, while others waited, barely concealing their impatience to get at the tray of lork.

The ceremony lasted one hour with Moobed blessing members of the family and all those present. A sudden burst of laughter and activity broke the silence as the tray of lork was offered around.

At the end of the ceremony, when everyone had gone and only close members of the family and friends were left behind, trays of food which included the traditional Kolrabi and Quince soup (Beh-Va-Kalam) with large nan sandwiched with roast lamb, were taken around the community to both rich and poor alike, symbolising that all men are born equal.

TURMERIC NAN
Nan-e-zardchoobeh
——

Fry one medium finely chopped onion in 2 table-spoons of oil, stir in $^1/_4$ teaspoon cumin seeds with $^1/_4$ teaspoon turmeric and add into the dough when kneading. Follow the baking instructions for basic nan.

PIR-E-SABZ *(The green shrine)*

Going to Yazd only just recently brought many wonderful childhood memories back to me. I visited many places but my main wish was to see Pir-e-Sabz again. It was in October and the air was fresh and comfortable. The car journey began in the early hours of the afternoon, I had almost forgotten the neverending hills that we passed, set into a vast area of inhospitable, arid land. There was no sign of vegetation as we continued on our journey through the empty road, as the pale sun spread over the tranquil atmosphere.

The one way journey was at its end, when I was pointed to a small greenery at a distance in the lower slope of the mountain. It was exciting to reach the shrine. I climbed several hundred steep steps, and saw many candles burning, the scent of joss-sticks filled the atmosphere. I could hear the trickling water pouring from the giant rock into the pond, which was walled up since I was there as a child. I was entranced by the peace and tranquility, as I stood by the giant rock, absorbed by the magnificence of it all. I drifted back to my childhood days, I was only six, wearing a pink dress with small white flowers, my hair was tied in a pony tale, and I wore shiny black patent shoes.

I could almost hear the lady in her Zoroastrian costume, offering me a piece of fried nan (soorog), a sign of charity.

FRIED NAN
Soorog
——

10g/$^1/_4$oz dried or 15g/$^1/_2$oz fresh yeast
1 teaspoon sugar
455g/1lb plain white flour (preferably strong)
$^1/_4$ teaspoon salt
oil for frying

TO GARNISH
icing sugar and ground pistachios

Prepare the yeast as for basic nan. Prepare the dough in the same way, adding about 120–175ml/4–6floz water for kneading (mixing).

Heat 5–10mm/$^1/_4$–$^1/_2$inch oil in a large frying pan until moderately hot. Take balls from the dough (about the size of an orange) and roll them out on a slightly greased work surface to a circle about 18–20cm/7–8inches in diameter. Lift up the circle and make two holes in the dough with your fingers. Place the nan in the hot oil and fry over a moderate heat for one minute until golden. Lift with a fork and turn and cook the other side for a further one minute until golden. Drain on kitchen paper. Repeat with the remaining dough until all is used up. It makes about 7–8 soorog. Sprinkle with icing sugar and pistachio nuts.

CINNAMON AND NUT LOAF
Nan-e-darchin ba gerdu
——

10g/$^1/_4$oz dried or 15g/$^1/_4$oz fresh yeast
1 teaspoon sugar
685g/1lb plain wholemeal flour
$^1/_2$ teaspoon salt
2 tablespoons oil
1 heaped tablespoon sugar
$1^1/_2$ teaspoons ground cinnamon
90g/3oz walnuts or any nuts, coarsely chopped

149

a little milk to glaze
1 teaspoon sesame seeds

Prepare the yeast and the dough as in the recipe for basic nan, add the nuts in the final kneading.

Grease a 1½lb loaf tin and dust with flour. Place the dough in the tin and glaze with the milk. Sprinkle on the sesame seeds and leave in a warm place until double in bulk.

Meanwhile preheat the oven to 200°C/350°F/ Gas mark 6. Bake the loaf for 20 minutes at this temperature, then reduce the heat to 180°C/350°F/ Gas mark 4 and bake for a further 35 minutes. Turn onto a wire rack and leave to cool.

CAST AWAY THE BAD DREAM

In the small Zoroastrian community, every custom was carried out with charm, and one of them still in practice, was to cast away a bad dream by telling the dream to three small pieces of bread and then throwing them to a bird. The bird will eat the bread thus taking away the bad dream.

ZOROASTRIAN NAN
Hushva

Hushva nan is very similar to Sankak which is baked on pebbles commercially, in every corner of the back streets in the capital city, in the tanoor, with the heat spreading a few yards across the street.

Hushva nan was one of the family favourites and easy enough to be worth making at least three times a week, as it is best to eat it fresh (although it can be frozen). Delicious served hot with melted butter, honey or jam, or as a midday snack with feta cheese and golden syrup, or with fried egg, or for lunch and dinner with khoresht and polov (rice).

10g/¼oz dried or 15g/½oz fresh yeast
1 teaspoon sugar
455g/1lb plain wholemeal flour
½ teaspoon salt
1 tablespoon oil and a little more for brushing the pan

Prepare the yeast as in the recipe for basic nan.

Mix the flour and salt together in a large bowl. Make a well in the centre, add the frothing yeast, oil and slowly add 350ml/12floz warm water. Gather the flour into a dough with your hands, knead in the bowl for 4–5 minutes, then cover with a damp cloth and leave in a warm place until doubled in bulk. As this dough is looser than the rest it rises very quickly and needs checking frequently. It will take between 15 minutes and 1 hour depending on the warmth of the room.

Dampen your hands with warm water and knead the dough again, adding up to 50ml/2floz warm water until the dough becomes fairly loose but not runny. Cover with a damp cloth and leave in a warm place again until doubled in bulk (if the dough becomes loose at this stage don't worry – this is how it should be).

Preheat the grill to hot. Heat a lightly greased 30cm/12inch cast iron frying pan on the heat. Using both hands, remove one-third of the dough and place it in the middle of the hot pan.

Dampen your hands with water and pat the dough up and down with your fingers to spread it out with one hand only. Reduce the heat and cook for 2–3 minutes. Place the pan under the grill, about 4inches/10cm from the heat, and cook for 3–4 minutes. With a fish slice, transfer to a wire rack and leave to cool. Divide the remaining dough and repeat twice more, remembering to dampen your hands each time before handling the dough. Eat hot with melted butter and honey or cold with panir and fried egg or with khoresht.

BARBARY NAN
Nan-e-barbary

Barbary nan is made fresh and eaten fresh. Best served hot with butter, honey and or jam, it is a morning bread rather than an afternoon one for tea, lunch or dinner. It is heavier and thicker than any nan. If there is any leftover or frozen reheat it in a hot oven before using.

10g/^{1}/$_4$oz dried or 15g/^{1}/$_2$oz fresh yeast
455g/1lb plain strong white flour
1 teaspoon salt
^{1}/$_2$ teaspoon baking powder

TO GARNISH
sesame seeds

Prepare the yeast as in the recipe for basic nan.

Mix the flour and the salt together, add the frothing yeast, and slowly add about 100ml/4floz cold water. Gather the dough in your hands and knead it until it becomes soft and elastic – about 5–10 minutes. Cover with a damp cloth and leave in a warm place to rise to double the bulk.

Mix the baking powder with about 1 tablespoon of water, add into the dough and knead for a further 2–3 minutes. Turn the dough on to a well floured surface and knead well for another 5 minutes and allow to rest for another hour. Preheat the oven to hot: 240°C/475°F/Gas mark 9.

Divide the dough into four equal size balls. Working on one at a time, place it on a slightly floured work surface and flatten with your hand and stretch gently to make an oval shape about 5mm/^{1}/$_4$inch thick. With one hand make finger marks all the way down. Repeat the same with the rest of the dough, until all used up. Place them on a baking sheet giving a little space between each. Bake for 9–10 minutes until golden. These are best eaten hot.

LAVASH NAN
Nan-e-lavash

A little time consuming, but rather satisfactory once it is made, the recipe is just for you and not commercially made. A recipe which has been handed down to me by my mother, so try it as a change for your family if you have about half an hour to spare.

230g/8oz plain strong white flour
^{1}/$_2$ teaspoon salt
1 tablespoon oil
about 150ml/5fl oz yoghurt

Sift the flour and the salt in a large mixing bowl, add the oil and slowly add the yoghurt, mixing it with your hands into a soft dough. Add a little more yoghurt if necessary, a little at a time.

Turn the dough out onto a floured board and knead for about 4–5 minutes. Divide into 8 equal balls, then roll each ball to a 20cm/11inch round.

Preheat the grill to hot. Lightly grease a 30cm/12inch cast iron frying pan and place under the preheated grill until hot. Remove the pan from the grill, brush off any excess flour from the nan and place in the pan. Return to the hot grill and cook for 35–40 seconds or until bubbles rise. Turn the nan over and grill the other side in the same way.

Remove the nan from the pan and immediately wrap in a large sheet of foil (to prevent steam escaping). Repeat with the remaining 7 pieces of nan, piling them all up in the foil parcel. Leave to cool, then overwrap the foil in a polythene bag and freeze. Makes 8 nan.

CRISPY MILK BREAD
Nan-e-shir

❦

175g/6oz plain flour
1 teaspoon baking powder
tip of a teaspoon salt
60g/2oz caster sugar
½ teaspoon vanilla essence (or ground saffron
dissolved in half a tablespoon hot milk)
2 beaten egg yolks
4–5 tablespoons melted butter
2–3 tablespoons milk

Preheat the oven to 150°C/300°F/Gas mark 2 and dust a heavy, flat baking tray lightly with flour.

Sift the baking powder, salt and flour into a bowl. Stir in the sugar, egg, butter and vanilla essence, then slowly add the milk (if necessary) and mix with your hands.

Place the dough on a floured board and knead for 1 minute until soft. Dust the board with flour again, put the dough in the centre and roll out to a 30 × 18cm/12 × 7inch rectangle. Brush off the excess flour and lift the dough onto the floured tray. If not already slightly torn, make a small tear near the corner. Place on the bottom shelf of the oven and bake for 20 minutes. Reduce the heat to 130°C/230°F/Gas mark ½ and bake for a further 1¼ hours or until the bread is completely dry and can be lifted with one hand. Store in an airtight tin.

WEDDING CAKE
Cake

❦

4 eggs, separated
175g/6oz caster sugar
175g/6oz self-raising flour, sifted
2 tablespoons granulated sugar
2 tablespoons dark navy rum
4–6 tablespoons jam

350ml/12floz double cream
2 teaspoons cocoa powder
2/3 drops coffee essence
1 tablespoon caster sugar
1 teaspoon vanilla essence

TO DECORATE
grated chocolate
fresh strawberries

Preheat the oven to 200°C/400°F/Gas mark 6. Grease a 20cm/8inch round cake tin with a removable base and dust lightly with flour. Beat the egg yolks with the caster sugar until creamy and white, then fold in the flour. Whisk the egg whites in a separate bowl until stiff, then fold them into the flour mixture with a large metal spoon until thoroughly blended.

Pour into the prepared tin and bake in the oven for 30–40 minutes until risen and golden. Remove the tin from the oven, turn the cake out on to a wire rack and leave to cool. Put the granulated sugar in a small, heavy saucepan, add 175ml/6floz cold water and heat gently until the sugar has dissolved. Stir in the rum and remove from the heat. Set aside to cool.

Cut the cake horizontally into 3 layers.

Whip the cream until it will hold its shape and carefully add caster sugar and vanilla essence. Set 3 heaped tablespoons aside. Divide the remaining cream into 3 equal parts. Then mix the cocoa and coffee essence into the other portions. Place the base cake layer on a plate, sprinkle with two tablespoonfuls of the rum syrup and spread with the jam. Place another layer on top, sprinkle again with two tablespoonfuls of the rum mixture. Top up with some of the flavoured cream. Repeat with the other layers.

Finally spread the plain cream over the top and sides of the cake and decorate with grated chocolate and strawberries. Chill in the refrigerator until serving time.

YAZDI CAKE
Cake-e-yazdi

~ ~

2 eggs, separated
140g/5oz granulated sugar
90g/3oz margarine or butter
1floz each milk and rose water
1 teaspoon each baking powder, bicarbonate of
soda and ground cardamom
90g/3oz unsalted chopped pistachios
230g/8oz plain flour, sieved

Set the oven to 180°C/350°F/Gas mark 4.

Beat the egg yolk with the sugar until white. Mix in the butter, rose water, milk, baking powder, bicarbonate of soda and cardamom and beat. Reserve a few of the nuts, and add the rest to the mixture. Slowly add the flour and continue to beat. Beat the egg whites until stiff and with a large metal spoon fold into the mixture.

Put one dessertspoon of the mixture into individual cake cases and sprinkle on the nuts, place on a baking tray and bake for about 10–15 minutes, until the cakes are risen and golden.

HAMANTASCHEN
Goosh-e-hayman

~

60g/2oz chopped walnuts
30g/1oz sultanas
30g/1oz chopped dates
3 tablespoons red kosher wine
1 teaspoon ground cinnamon
1 tablespoon clear honey

OLD CITY OF SHUSH

The antique city that was the capital of King Darius (Dariush) was 700 miles south of Tehran. On the spot the site was very disappointing, since I was seeking fine ruins, and there was nothing in sight.

It was a matter of luck that on December 24th 1972, the first ever statue of an Achaemenian king was discovered. An inscription on its base soon revealed that it was Darius himself. The inscription on the 2.5 metre high statue reads, 'This is the stone statue that King Darius got made in Egypt so that those who saw it should know that the Persian has conquered Egypt.'

Only two years earlier marble tables with Cuneiform (Mikhi) characters engraved upon them were found. They were the foundation documents of Shush, an account of how it was built, how gold was brought from Sardes, cedar wood from Lebanan, stone from Hapirtush, ivory from Kush and India. The archaeological site was beautifully coloured and decorative, with enamelled bricks depicting soldiers, which can now be seen in the Louvre Museum in Paris and in the Tehran Museum.

The Jewish festival of Purim has its roots in the city of Shush, and in the book of Esther in the Old Testament you can read the story of the deliverance of the Jewish people in Persia from the hand of Haman the King who plotted their death. Purim is a joyful festival, an occasion for parties and celebration. Jacob, and his wife Parvin invited us to their typical Jewish home, where a traditional meal was served. After dinner we were shown to our bedroom, to sleep on thick mattresses laid on the floor. The eiderdown was hand made with a pale blue satin cover and large heavy bolsters as pillows, with their hand embroidered cases. We were suitably awed at spending the next few nights in a 4000 year-old city.

PASTRY
115g/4oz each plain and self-raising flour
1 teaspoon ground cinnamon
pinch of salt
30g/1oz icing sugar
115g/4oz margarine
1 egg yolk
a little beaten egg white, to seal and glaze

Put the nuts and fruit into a bowl, with the wine and cinnamon.

Warm the honey, add to the bowl and stir well to mix. Cover and leave to marinate for several hours.

Sift the flour, cinnamon and salt into a bowl and stir in the sugar. Add the margarine in small pieces and rub in with the fingertips. Make a well in the centre, add the egg yolk and 3 tablespoons of chilled water and mix to a soft dough. Leave to rest for about 15 minutes. Preheat the oven to 180°C/350°F/Gas mark 4.

Grease a baking tray and dust well with flour. Roll out the pastry on a lightly floured surface until 5mm/$\frac{1}{4}$inch thick and cut into 7.5cm/3inch circles with a plain pastry cutter. Put 1 teaspoon of the nut and fruit mixture in the centre of each circle, then brush all the way round the edge of each circle with beaten egg white. Fold the circle over and press to seal. Twist or crimp the edges. Brush the pastries all over with egg white to glaze. Bake in the oven for 20 minutes or until golden. Transfer to a wire rack and leave to cool. Makes 20–25.

ZOROASTRIAN CAKE
Komach

10g/$\frac{1}{4}$oz dried yeast or 15g/$\frac{1}{2}$oz fresh
60g/2oz brown sugar
455g/1lb plain wholemeal flour
teaspoon salt
1 heaped teaspoon each of ground cinnamon and cardamom
60g/2oz sultanas

60g/2oz each chopped walnuts and almonds, blanched and chopped
2 large eggs, beaten
50ml/2floz milk
2 tablespoons rose water
4 tablespoons oil

Prepare the yeast and the dough as in the recipe for basic nan, adding all the ingredients except the oil and knead the dough. Add 85–120ml/3–4floz warm water for kneading.

Meanwhile preheat the oven to 180°C/350°F/Gas mark 4, pour the oil into a 5cm/2inch deep, 20.5cm/8inch square dish. Place in the oven to heat for 7–10 minutes. Remove and add in the dough, bake for 40–45 minutes until risen and golden. Leave to cool a little, before removing from the tin.

ROSE WATER CAKE
Cake-e-zorati

FOR THE SYRUP
60g/2oz granulated sugar
50ml/2floz rose water
1 teaspoon lemon juice
$\frac{1}{4}$ teaspoon ground cardamom

CAKE
3 large eggs
150ml/5floz each oil and plain yoghurt
1$\frac{1}{2}$ teaspoons baking powder
$\frac{1}{4}$ teaspoon ground cardamom
230g/8oz semolina
115g/4oz caster sugar
flaked almonds for decoration

Put the sugar in a small heavy saucepan, add 50ml/2floz cold water and bring to the boil (about 5–7 minutes). When beginning to thicken add the rose water, lemon juice and cardamom and bring back to the boil. Boil vigorously for 3 minutes or until a thin syrup is formed. Test by dropping a little syrup onto a cold plate. If it doesn't spread it is ready. Remove to cool.

Meanwhile, preheat the oven to 180°C/350°F/ Gas mark 4. Grease a 28 × 18cm/11 × 7inch cake tin with a solid base, 4cm/1½inch deep, dust well with flour.

Beat the eggs in a bowl with the oil, yoghurt, baking powder and cardamom. Beat in the semolina and sugar to form a runny consistency, then pour into the prepared tin. Roll the flaked almonds in a little flour and sprinkle over the cake.

Bake in the oven for 17–20 minutes until risen and golden. Remove from the oven, cut into 4cm/1½inch squares but do not remove from the tin. Spoon on the cooked rose water syrup. Then leave to cool completely. Transfer the cake to a plastic container Store in the refrigerator and eat within a few days.

YOGHURT CITRUS CAKE
Cak-e-morabiyat

4 eggs, separated
175g/6oz caster sugar
finely grated rind of 1 lemon or orange
300ml/10floz oil
1½ heaped teaspoons baking powder
120ml/4floz plain yoghurt
230g/8oz plain flour
almond flakes to decorate

Preheat the oven to 200°C/400°F/Gas mark 6.

Grease an 18cm/7inch square cake tin with a removable base and dust with flour.

Beat the egg yolk with the sugar until creamy and white, then beat in the lemon or orange rind, the oil, baking powder and yoghurt. Slowly sift in the flour and beat until smooth.

Whisk the egg whites in a separate bowl until stiff, then fold into the flour mixture with a large metal spoon until thoroughly blended. Pour into the prepared tin and sprinkle with flaked almonds. Bake for 20 minutes, then reduce the heat to 180°C/350°F/Gas mark 4 and bake for a further

20 minutes, remove the tin from the oven, turn the cake out on to a wire rack and leave to cool. Store in an airtight tin for up to 1 week.

SWEET PASTE
Halva

If the flour and butter mixture becomes lumpy, simply pour it into a blender and work until smooth.

60g/2oz unsalted butter or 50ml/2floz oil
115g/4oz plain white flour
115g/4oz granulated sugar
1 heaped teaspoon ground cinnamon
85ml/3floz rose water
a few pistachios, finely chopped to decorate

Heat the butter or oil in a heavy frying pan, add the flour and stir over a gentle heat for 3–4 minutes until golden. When cool, sieve into a bowl and set aside. Put the sugar in a pan with 85ml/3floz cold water and heat gently until the sugar has dissolved. Cook on a moderate heat, then add the cinnamon. When bubbles appear, remove from the heat and pour in the rose water. Slowly stir in the sieved flour mixture until a thick paste is formed, then return to the heat and stir for 30–60 seconds. Pour the halva into a shallow dish (1cm/½inch deep) and smooth the surface. Leave to cool. Cut into diamond shapes and sprinkle with chopped pistachios before serving.

ICE IN HEAVEN
Yakh dar behesht

30g/1oz each corn- and rice-flour
300ml/½ pint milk
75g/2½oz sugar
75ml/3floz rose water
30g/1oz ground almonds
¼ teaspoon ground cardamom

TO DECORATE
chopped pistachio nuts and almonds

Whisk the cornflour and rice flour in 175ml/6floz cold water. Bring the milk to just below boiling point. Slowly stir in the water and flour mixture, stirring continuously until the mixture comes to the boil. Reduce the heat, add the sugar and continue stirring over a gentle heat for a further 4–5 minutes until the mixture thickens but does not become dry. Add the rose water, ground almonds and cardamom, stir for a further 2 minutes, then remove from the heat. Spoon into individual dishes, leave to cool, then chill in the refrigerator. Sprinkle with nuts. Serve chilled.

ROSE WATER STARCH
Masghati

As some recipes vary from family to family, so they do from district to district and region to region. Next to the Persian Gulf or Strait of Hormuz is the city of Abadan with its food and culture influenced by its Arab neighbour. Masghati is an Arab word which spread to other parts of Persia. This is one of many simple sweet recipes, which has long been a part of the Iranian diet.

60g/2oz cornflour
500ml/1 pint cold water
30g/1oz sugar
4 tablespoons rose water
30g/1oz clarified butter
1 tablespoon blanched and stripped almonds

TO GARNISH
1 tablespoon chopped pistachios

Mix the cornflour with half the water until smooth. Put into a pan and heat gently, stirring all the time. Add the rose water, sugar and the butter and continue stirring. Stir in the almonds, then remove the pan. When it has begun to cool, spoon into individual glass dishes and garnish with nuts.

CARDAMOM RICE
Halva berenji

30g/1oz unsalted butter
115g/4oz rice, washed
175ml/6floz rose water
1 heaped teaspoon ground cardamom
50–85ml/2–3floz golden syrup
2 teaspoon ground pistachios

Melt the butter in a heavy saucepan over a gentle heat and swirl it around. Add the rice with 600ml/1 pint cold water, simmer for about 45 minutes, then add the rose water. Cook until the rice is soft, add the syrup and cardamom. Cook for another minute. Serve as ice in heaven.

SAFFRON AND NUT PUDDING
Sholeh zard

Follow the recipe as above but substitute 200g/7oz caster sugar for syrup. Add 175ml/6floz rose-water and 1 teaspoon ground saffron, with 60g/2oz blanched almonds.

HAZELNUT SWEET
Shirini-ye-fandogh

155g/5$\frac{1}{2}$oz plain white flour
90g/3oz shelled hazelnuts
2 large eggs
65–85ml/2$\frac{1}{2}$–3floz oil
2 teaspoons cardamom
175g/6oz icing sugar
60g/2oz ground almonds

Stir the flour in a frying pan over a gentle heat for few minutes, until light brown.

BAKLAVA
Baghlava

SYRUP
140g/5oz granulated sugar
2 tablespoons rose water

PASTRY
55g/1³/₄oz plain white flour
¹/₄ teaspoon baking powder
1 egg yolk
1 tablespoon milk
1 teaspoon oil
a few chopped almonds or unsalted pistachios
to decorate

FILLING
345g/12oz ground almonds
230g/8oz sugar
2 teaspoons ground cardamom
1 tablespoon rose water
140g/5oz unsalted butter, melted

TO DECORATE
a few chopped pistachios

Roast the nuts under a hot grill, then rub with a towel to remove the skins. Then grind.

Break the eggs into a bowl, add 50–65ml/2–2¹/₂floz oil and the cardamom and stir well to mix.

Slowly add the sugar, hazelnuts and ground almonds and mix with your hands to form a dough. Stir in the cooled flour and mix in a further 12.5ml/¹/₂floz oil if necessary to give a soft dough.

Preheat the oven to 180°C/350°F/Gas mark 4.

Take hazelnut-sized balls from the dough and roll until smooth, gently press to 5mm/¹/₄inch thick in the palm of your hands. Place on the greased tray, allowing space for them to spread. Bake for about 12 minutes or until risen and golden. Transfer to a wire rack and leave to cool. Makes 90–95.

Put the sugar and 3 tablespoons of water into a small pan and bring to the boil. Add the rosewater and cook on a moderate heat until semi-thick. Set aside to cool.

Make the pastry. Mix the flour with the baking powder, add the egg yolk and the oil and mix with a fork. Put into a small bowl, cover and allow to rest for about one hour.

Choose a baking tray 28 × 18 × 4cm/11 × 7 × 1¹/₂inches. Divide the pastry in half. Roll out each piece on a work surface, and line the tin with one half.

Mix the nuts, sugar and cardamom, add to the tin. Press down well with the palm of your hand, then sprinkle on the rose water.

Preheat the oven to 170°C/325°F/Gas mark 3. Place the second rectangle of pastry over the filling. Pour over the melted butter, and cut into diamond shapes with a sharp knife. Sprinkle with almonds and bake for about 20–25 minutes until lightly golden. Remove and pour over the syrup, cover with a cloth and allow to rest until cold.

CARDAMOM, ROSE WATER AND NUT PASTIES
Ghotab

230g/8oz plain white flour
1 teaspoon baking powder
3 egg yolks
3 tablespoons plain yoghurt
115g/4oz butter, melted
icing sugar for dusting

FILLING
175g/6oz ground almonds
90g/3oz icing sugar
2 teaspoons ground cardamom
2 teaspoons rose water

Mix the flour and baking powder in a bowl, add the yoghurt and butter, and mix with your hands. Allow the pastry to rest for about 20 minutes. Meanwhile mix the ground almonds, sugar, cardamom and rose water. Preheat the oven to 180°C/350°F/Gas mark 4. Roll the pastry to 5mm/¼inch thick and use a round cutter to cut into circles about 5cm/2inches in diameter. Fill each with one teaspoon of the almond mixture, and brush with a little water or milk, press to seal and twist or crimp the edges. Place them on a greased baking tray, and bake for about 10–15 minutes or until golden. Remove and dust with icing sugar. Alternatively, deep fry and roll in icing sugar.

RICE CRUMBLE
Nan-e-berenji

245g/8½oz aerated margarine or white cooking fat
185g/6½oz icing sugar
1 egg, separated
25ml/1floz rose water
2 teaspoons ground cardamom
515g/18g rice flour
poppy seeds for decoration

Preheat the oven to 170°C/325°F/Gas mark 3.

Melt the fat over a gentle heat, put into a bowl and when lightly cool add the sugar and beat with a wooden spoon. Add the egg yolk, stir in the rose water and cardamom with the rice flour, then gather together with your hands.

Beat the egg white until stiff. Work into the dough with your hands until smooth. Take walnut-sized balls and press them in the palm of your hands to 1cm/½inch thick. Place them on a greased and floured baking tray, allowing space for them to spread. Sprinkle on the poppy seeds. Using the open end of a thimble or similar object, press a pattern on top of each biscuit. Bake for about 10 minutes or until risen and slightly golden. Transfer onto a plate to cool.

CRISPY ALMOND BITES
Haji badam

1 teaspoon ground cardamom
45g/1½oz icing sugar
1oz soft butter or margarine
90g/3oz ground almonds

Preheat the oven to 180°C/350°F/Gas mark 4.

Mix all the ingredients in a large bowl. Knead to a soft dough. Take hazelnut-sized balls in your hand and press down lightly to 5mm/¼inch thick and place on a greased baking tray and bake for about 10 minutes, until risen and slightly golden. Store in an airtight tin.

ROSE WATER FONDANT
Noghl

— ⬧ —

140g/5oz granulated sugar
3 tablespoons rose water
1 teaspoon glucose powder
about 30 blanched almonds, split in half
lengthways

Lightly grease a marble slab or heavy flat baking tray. Put the sugar in a small heavy saucepan, add the rose water and glucose and heat gently, until the sugar has dissolved. Bring to the boil and boil for 2½–3 minutes or until the syrup drops thickly from the tip of a spoon.

Pour the syrup immediately on to the greased slab or tray, leave to cool for 30–60 seconds, then gather together with a palette knife and, when cooled a little, knead well with your hands until cool.

Take chickpea sized balls of dough and roll in the palms of your hands until smooth. Push 1 piece of almond into the side of each piece of dough, then continue rolling the dough in your hands until the nut is in the centre. Place the fondants on a plate and leave to set for 1–2 days before serving. Makes about 60.

PISTACHIO MUNCHIES
Shirin-ye-pisteh

— ⬧ —

Thanks to my mother again for this wonderful sweet.

2 large egg yolks
75g/2½oz icing sugar, sifted
115g/4oz unsalted shelled pistachios,
ground to a paste
¼ teaspoon ground cardamom
1 egg yolk, to glaze
a few poppy seeds to decorate

MIDNIGHT FEAST
(Shab-e-yalda)

Shab-e-Yalda was the longest night of the year (eve of Yalda or Yuletide), celebrated by family and friends gathering to welcome the birth of the morning sun.

Our large walnut table was set with all kinds of fruit such as pomegranates, oranges and apples, and all kind of grapes. Summer fruit such as melon and watermelon were stored in the coolest part of the house for this occasion. Other dried fruit such as figs apricots, raisins and sultanas were mixed with roasted pistachios, almonds, hazelnuts, chickpeas, pumpkin and water melon seeds (Ajil). All different types of sweetmeats were piled high on large silver plates, laid out to be shared with visitors who called throughout the night to share in the celebration. The night was seen through by playing cards, and chatting until dawn, to celebrate the longest night of the year in the month of Day (December), which is named after the angel of creation and light in the Zoroastrian calendar.

Preheat the oven to 180°C/350°F/Gas mark 4.

Beat the egg yolks and icing sugar until white. Add the ground nuts and cardamom and gather together with your hands to form a soft dough. Take hazelnut-sized balls of the dough and press between your palms to flatten. Place on a greased and floured baking tray, spacing them well apart to allow for spreading. Glaze with egg yolk and sprinkle with poppy seeds. Bake for about 10–15 minutes until risen and lightly golden. Remove from the oven and leave to cool on the tray. Store in an airtight tin. Makes about 36.

TAKE THE LEFT OVER WITH YOU

There are many sweet memories of my childhood days living in Yazd amongst the small Zoroastrian community, where they kept their old traditions of many years ago. Did-va-basdid, or visiting each other during Novrooz, was one of my favourite.

Sometimes it began in the early hours of morning around breakfast time, everyone joined to eat fried smoked fish and sugar candies (pashmak), salad of fresh mint, tarragon, and spring onion with panir (feta cheese) and nan.

Those arriving mid morning were served chay in estekan glasses, held by their silver holders, along with nuts such as roasted pistachios, almond and hazelnuts. Different types of sweets such as baghlava, Ghotab, and cookies were offered around.

As a custom you had to take one of each and put it on your side plate showing that you were not refusing your host's offer. At the end of the short visit there was a polite gesture from the host wrapping the left-over sweets neatly to take home with you, something that you could not refuse and the excuse was that because it has been touched by your fingers you are the only person to eat it. At the end of the day, visiting so many family and friends, we all appreciated the carrier bag for carrying our share of sweets home. My bag always seemed heavier than anyone else's. Maybe I knew the custom too well.

RAISIN CRUNCHIES
Shirini-ye-keshmesh

60g/2oz margarine or butter at room temperature
60g/2oz caster sugar
75g/2¹/₂oz plain white flour, sifted
2 teaspoons seedless raisins

Preheat the oven to 180°C/350°F/Gas mark 4.

Put all the ingredients into a bowl and mix well with your hand until smooth. Gather the dough together with your hands then take hazelnut-sized balls and press into 6cm/2¹/₂inch rounds which are 5mm/¹/₄inch thick. Place on a greased and floured baking tray and bake for 10–15 minutes until lightly golden. Transfer to a wire rack and leave to cool. Store in an airtight tin. Makes 18–20.

SWEET SYRUP CIRCLES
Zolubia

230g/8oz each corn starch and plain flour
1 teaspoon soft butter
300ml/¹/₂ pint plain yoghurt
oil for deep frying

SYRUP
550g/1¹/₄lb granulated sugar
120ml/¹/₄floz rose water
2 teaspoons lemon juice

To make the syrup, put the sugar in a saucepan, add 300ml/¹/₂ pint water and heat gently until the sugar has dissolved. Bring to the boil and cook for 3–4 minutes, add the rose water and lemon juice and continue simmering until the syrup is thickened. Remove from the heat and set aside to cool.

Put the flour and corn starch into a mixing bowl, rub in the butter and mix well. Add the yoghurt very slowly, and mix until the mixture resembles cake mix.

Heat the oil in a small heavy saucepan. Pipe the Zolubia into the hot oil, and fry for just 30 seconds or until lightly golden. Remove with a slotted spoon and drop into the cooked syrup. Repeat with the remaining dough.

SOFT SYRUP FINGERS
Bamya

❧

2½ tablespoons oil
60g/2oz plain flour
1egg, beaten
oil for deep frying

SYRUP
230g/8oz granulated sugar
85ml/3floz rose water
2 tablespoons lemon juice

Make the syrup as in the recipe for sweet syrup circles, using 120ml/4floz water.

Put the oil in a small heavy saucepan, add 85ml/3floz cold water and bring to the boil over a high heat. Add the flour and stir with a wooden spoon to make a soft dough. Remove the pan from the heat, leave to cool slightly, then beat in the egg with a wooden spoon. Heat the oil in a deep-fat fryer. Put the dough in a piping bag fitted with a fluted nozzle and pipe one or two 5cm/2inch lengths into the hot oil. Deep fry for 45–60 seconds until golden. Then remove with a slotted spoon, and drop into the cooked syrup. Repeat with the remaining dough.

ELEPHANT EARS
Goosh-e-fil

❧

1 egg yolk
25ml/1floz milk
1 teaspoon oil
60g/2oz plain white flour

1 heaped teaspoon baking powder
a little beaten egg white to seal
oil for deep frying
icing sugar and ground pistachios to decorate

Beat the egg yolk and milk together, then stir in the oil.

Sift the flour and baking powder together and stir into the egg mixture to form a sticky dough and beat well. Allow to rest for 30 minutes.

Divide the dough into 15–18 pieces. Roll out each ball on a floured surface to a circle about 3mm/1/8inch thick. Brush all the way round the edge of each circle with beaten egg white, then fold the circle over and press to seal. Fry in moderately hot oil for 30 seconds, a few at a time. Remove with a slotted spoon. Drain on kitchen paper.

When cool, sprinkle with icing sugar and nuts.

CHRISTMAS PASTIES
Gata

❧

285g/10oz plain flour
2 teaspoons baking powder
1/4 teaspoon bicarbonate of soda
2 egg yolks
60g/2oz soft tub margarine or 50ml/2floz oil
60g/2oz caster sugar
50–85ml/2–3floz plain yoghurt
a little beaten egg white to seal

FILLING
8 heaped teaspoons jam or marmalade
45g/1½oz each ground almonds and walnuts
60g/2oz caster sugar
1 teaspoon ground cardamom

Beat one of the egg yolks with the margarine and the sugar, sift in the flour, baking powder and soda, then add the yoghurt slowly until smooth. Chill for 30 minutes.

Preheat the oven to 180°C/350°F/Gas mark 4.

Divide the dough into four equal pieces. Roll

CHRISTMAS IN THE CITY

The snow over the Alborz mountains, which overlooked the city of Tehran, spread to the streets of the capital, covering the naked branches of beech and plane trees bordering the steep avenues.

Winter birds flew over the deserted parks with their ponds now filled with frozen ice. Christmas celebrations took place on January 5th, the day the Christian Armenians in Persia believed Christ was born. Christmas was an international celebration as it is in the west. Elo, my Armenian friend, asked me to accompany her to the church on Christmas Eve. It was a short walk through the back streets of Tehran where every window glittered with Christmas decorations.

On entering the church we were confronted by the burning candles which gave the altar a cosy atmosphere. Every seat was taken and traditional Christmas songs were sung and Communion was received, many of the congregation taking home small pieces of bread to eat with wine before dinner as the head of the family conducted a small family service.

I was fortunate to join Elo and family for the traditional Christmas lunch. The food was a repeat of Christmas Eve dinner: plain rice, smoked fish and herb savoury cake followed by Gata, Yoka and Nazok, special Christmas sweets.

mixture over the jam on each piece. Fold the circle over and press to seal. Twist or crimp the edges. Brush the pasties with the remaining egg yolk. Place on a greased and floured baking tray and bake for 10–12 minutes until risen and golden. Transfer to a wire rack and leave until cold.

STUFFED FRIED FINGERS
Yoka

❧

175g/6oz plain flour
1 heaped teaspoon baking powder
2 egg yolks
60g/2oz butter, melted and cooled,
or 50ml/2floz oil
50ml/2floz milk
oil for frying

FILLING
60–75g/2–2¹/₂oz each ground almonds
and ground walnuts
60g/2oz caster sugar
1 teaspoon ground cardamom
1 tablespoon rose water
icing sugar for dusting

Prepare the dough as in the recipe for Gata, adding milk to knead the dough.

Roll out each ball on a floured surface to a triangle, about 5mm/¹/₄ inch thick. Brush all the way round the edge of each triangle with beaten egg white. Mix together the ground nuts, sugar and cardamom and moisten with rose water.

Place a small almond-sized ball of the filling in the centre of each triangle, then gently roll the dough up around the filling to make a cigar shape. Seal with more egg white.

Deep fry the rolls a few at a time for about 1 minute until lightly golden, then remove with a slotted spoon. Drain on kitchen paper and dust with icing sugar. Makes 24.

out each quarter on a floured surface to a 15 cm/ 6inch circle about 5mm/¹/₄inch thick. Spread 2 teaspoons of the jam over each piece of dough, leaving a 1 cm/¹/₂inch margin all around. Brush all the way round the edge of each circle with beaten egg white.

Mix together the ground nuts, sugar and cardamom and sprinkle 1¹/₂ to 2 teaspoons of this

LET IT GO

Winter was a month to look forward to. It seemed the family gathered together more then than in any other season. The thick snow looked so pretty on the naked trees, around the sunken garden. Our life revolved around Bokhari, the stove fire with its chimney going through the ceiling. Baba would often place his bowl of ash on the round stove, when telling us children stories of his childhood days. Often I would ask Baba to repeat exciting stories, which was never tiring to me. One such story was about a young man named Shahpour, rather stout and strong, he often impressed the community with his bravery, to the extent that he arranged to walk down hundreds of the slippery steps of the dark tunnel, where the washerwomen did their washing.

The water was crystal clear, and they carried some sort of lighting with them. The steps were very old and wearing out.

A day was arranged that Shahpour would walk down the steps, in the dead of the night without any form of light, and to prove his bravery, he had to hammer a nail into the ground. Shahpour wore a long creamy coloured quilt coat, matching scarf and gloves, and heavy hand-knitted giveh (shoes).

He began to walk down the few hundred steps with a brave face, feeling his way along the steamy and very slippery passage, until eventually he reached the bottom.

The air was really steamy and hot down there, you could hear the sound of water as the stream gushed down from underneath, and trickling water, as the steam hit the ceiling.

He hammered the nail into the ground and thought his achievement was greater than anyone else's so far. He got himself off the ground slowly and tried to stand, but someone was holding on to his coat and would not let go. Shahpour was relaxed at first, and asked gently to release his coat, but there was no reply. He continued begging, but still whoever it was would not let go. Eventually he lost consciousness, and fell onto the steamy floor.

Several hours passed, his family and friends became anxious and with great difficulty they took the journey down the slippery tunnel. They found Shahpour unconscious with his coat nailed into the floor.

CHRISTMAS THIN ROLLS
Nazok

—◆—

3 eggs
1 tablespoon rose water
115g/4oz soft tub margarine
25ml/1floz milk
230g/8oz caster sugar
2 teaspoons baking powder
1/4 teaspoon bicarbonate of soda

2 teaspoons ground cardamom or cinnamon
1 teaspoon ground mixed spice
120ml/4floz plain yoghurt
685g/1 1/2 lb plain flour, sifted
beaten egg white to seal
2 teaspoons sesame seeds to decorate

FILLING

12 heaped teaspoons jam or marmalade
155g/5 1/2 oz each ground almonds and ground walnuts
60g/2oz caster sugar
1 teaspoon ground cardamom

163

Beat 2 of the eggs with the margarine. Add the rose water, milk, sugar, baking powder, soda and spices and beat. Add the yoghurt slowly with the flour and mix until smooth. Chill for 30 minutes.

Preheat the oven to 180°C/350°F/Gas mark 4.

Divide the dough into 6 equal pieces. Roll out each piece on a lightly floured surface to a 23 × 12.5cm/9 × 5inch rectangle. Spread 2 teaspoons of jam over the centre of each piece of dough, leaving a 2.5cm/1inch rectangle all round the edge. Brush all the way round the edges of each rectangle with beaten egg white. Mix together the ground nuts, sugar and cardamom and sprinkle 3–4 teaspoons of this mixture over the jam on each piece of dough. Roll the rectangles up like Swiss rolls from one long end, then place on a greased and floured baking tray. Beat the remaining egg and brush over the pastries to seal. Sprinkle over the sesame seeds. Bake the pastries for about 10–15 minutes until risen and golden. Remove from the oven, leave to cool on a wire rack, then cut each into six 4cm/1½inch pieces. Makes 36.

CARDAMOM SWEET
Sohan-e-ardi

The nearest ingredient for this sweet obtainable in the west is chapati flour and jaggory sugar, both obtainable in Indian supermarkets.

115g/4oz clarified butter
115g/4oz fine chapati flour
105g/³/₄oz jaggory sugar
1 teaspoon freshly ground cardamom
roasted pistachio nuts for garnishing

Heat three-quarters of the butter in a heavy frying pan, add the flour and cook on a moderate heat until it changes colour and you can start to smell the aroma. Add the ground cardamom and the sugar to taste, continue stirring for another 2 minutes. If necessary, add the remaining butter to form a dough-like consistency. Remove the pan from the heat,

pour the mixture into a lightly greased baking tray, and garnish with the nuts cut into shape while still warm. Or mould in to shape with a biscuit cutter. Store in tins and eat within a few days.

BURNT SUGAR ALMONDS
Badam sookhteh

115g/4oz granulated sugar
60g/2oz blanched and shredded almonds
½ teaspoon ground saffron
grease a sheet of foil

Melt the sugar in a small non-stick or heavy aluminium frying pan over a gentle heat until the sugar has melted and is turning a caramel colour. Stir in the saffron and the almonds and stir once or twice until completely coated in the toffee mixture. Remove the pan from the heat. With a teaspoon immediately put small blobs of the mixture on to the greased tray, spacing them well apart to allow for spreading. Leave until cold and hard, then transfer to greased foil. Eat within a day or two.

ALMOND TREAT
Shirini-e-badam

2 large egg whites
115g/4oz caster sugar
1 teaspoon almond essence
175g/6oz ground almonds
almond flakes to decorate

Preheat the oven to 150°C/300°F/Gas mark 2.

Whisk the egg whites until stiff. Gently fold in the sugar with a large metal spoon, add the almond essence with the ground almonds and stir until evenly incorporated.

Place ½ a teaspoonful of the mixture on a greased and well-floured baking tray, allowing space for them to spread. Place one almond flake on each. Bake for 10–11 minutes until risen and lightly golden. While they are still hot, remove them with a palette knife and place on a plate to cool. When cold store in an airtight tin.

THE JOY OF BURNING

School was a happy place. I loved the playground which was in the centre with classrooms built around it. There was also a small sunken garden, with pine filling the atmosphere with their scent, and fruit and nut trees in the middle fed by irrigated water.

There were several almond and pistachio trees. I loved pistachios, they looked beautiful with their green branches and bright red nuts. When the nuts were ripe, the outer shell would open to release the nut, which would then be slit open ready to be picked, and during break we were allowed to pick and eat them.

The almonds, like the pistachio, were harvested in the autumn. They were different, their branches laden with the green nut, and rather hard to crack open.

Even as children we had cookery hours at school. I remember the exciting moment of my very first lesson making Badam Sokhteh (burnt almonds). We all had to get a mark for our cooking, and Memeh was so proud when I presented her with my very first sweet that she offered them to her friends with pride!

MARZIPAN AND ROSEWATER MULBERRIES
Toot

90g/3oz ground almonds
75g/2$^{1}/_{2}$oz icing sugar
1 tablespoon best quality rose water
about 48 strips of pistachio nuts
or blanched almonds

Mix the ground almonds with 45g/1$^{1}/_{2}$oz of the icing sugar and stir. Blend in the rose water with a fork to form a sticky mixture. Roll out small amounts of dough between your palms until slightly larger than a pea. Taper each one slightly at the end, then roll in the remaining icing sugar until evenly coated. Insert a strip of nut into the thicker end to resemble a mulberry stalk. Place well apart on a flat plate and leave uncovered in a cool place for at least 1 hour. Store in a single layer in an airtight tin.

THE WATERFALL RESTURANT

The choice of restaurants and night clubs in the capital city of Tehran was most impressive. The restaurants, whether in the back streets of the city or a chalet in the slopes of the mountain, looked cosy during winter months. But my favourite was situated in the lower slopes of Shemiran, the mountain region, only one hour's drive from the capital city. The setting for this restaurant was one of the most magnificent: the dinning area was out in the open under the blue sky, with millions of stars above. There was the sound of a waterfall gushing from the nearby mountain adding to the special cool evening breeze. It was a contrast to eating on the flat roof of our house in Yazd.

THE SINGING BIRD

The air became mild, there was no more snow on the ground, the black crows had almost flown away, and the sparrows and nightingales flew around the garden from one tree to the next. Roses had begun to bloom, and the fruit and nut trees were covered in pink and white blossoms, with the mild wind scattering their petals over the small octagonal pond in the open-style house.

It was approaching mulberry time, forty days after novrooz, when the first fruit ripened. The legend says that birds love the mulberry (toot) so much that they sing 'Chelhom Chelmon Toot to Delom' meaning forty days after Novrooz the berries are in my tummy!

A large strong white cloth was held beneath the mulberry tree, by several people each holding on to the edge. One man was up the tree, shaking each branch hard, to release the ripened small creamy-coloured fruit, pouring down into the large cloth. The fruit was then sorted out, some to be eaten fresh and the rest to be dried and stored for winter. Whenever I buy sweet dried mulberries in the Persian supermarket in the west it brings back joyful memories of time in Yazd.

THE FROZEN WINE

Friday was a general holiday, as Sunday is in the west, and come late evening, our cousins would join us for dinner dressed in their woollen clothes. My favourite outfit was a full length red dress which had been knitted by Memeh. All the rooms in our house were built around an open inner courtyard, with a small pond in the middle. Food had to be carried from the kitchen out into the open to the living room, where we would eat sitting around the stove fire (bokhari). I remember vividly one harsh winter evening with thick snow on the ground. A large number of relatives were invited for dinner and the walnut table was set with the most tantalising dishes and home-made bottles of wine. Baba asked me to fetch an extra bottle of wine for him from the store room. I was astonished when entering the room to find that several of the bottles placed on the shelf near the door had burst, but the frozen wine had retained the shape of the bottle and was still standing on the shelf. It was very cold to hold the block of ice in my hands but I was determined to lift the solid content and carried it to the dinner table with my bare hands.

COCONUT DROPS
Ghatreh-e-nargil

2 large egg whites
90g/3oz icing sugar
¼ teaspoon vanilla essence
90g/3oz desiccated coconut

Preheat the oven to 150°C/300°F/Gas mark 2. Beat the egg whites until stiff, then fold in the icing sugar with a metal spoon. Fold in the vanilla essence and the coconut. Place small knobs on a grreased baking tray, spacing them a little to allow for spreading. Bake for 10 minutes until risen and slightly golden. While they are still hot remove them with a palette knife and place on a plate to cool. Store in an airtight tin when cold.

166

THE MAGICAL SOUND

Manshad was almost uninhabited, with the exception of a few families spending their summer holidays in their apartments. The family often took a walk in the early hours of the afternoon to avoid the midday sun, heading towards the water fall which gushed down, cascading over a flat piece of stone, glistening in the reflection of the sun.

The slopes were rocky and uneven, making them difficult to climb. There were numerous almond and walnut trees growing on each side of the path. You could only hear the sound of the mountain spring, pouring into the reservoir irrigating the surrounding lands. Often the sound of a soft flute would break the silence, coming from the shepherd who sat under a large almond tree, looking straight ahead in deep thought. He wore old brown trousers, a matching long coat and old felt hat. His batik cloth spread in front of him, his working hands looked rough as he broke the thick nan and his home-made panir (cheese) with a bite from the home grown onion.

His drink was the crystal clear water from the nearby spring which ran just underneath the rock. He took his time over his lunch, folding his empty batik cloth and placing it behind his head, resting against the trunk of the tree. Then he would take his old wooden flute out of his pocket and play hypnotic music. With the animal bells echoing as background music the combination would give such a magical sound that everyone took their seats along the slope to listen to the free concert.

The shepherd did not talk very much, only nodded with a smile, when he said, 'goodbye (khodahafez), God be with you' to his audience. The young man was such a familiar face to everyone.

The sound of his music followed us for a long way up to the waterfall where everyone relaxed before returning home.

GINGER NIBBLE
Shirini-ye-zanjafil

7 tablespoons oil
60g/2oz icing sugar
1 teaspoon ground ginger
60g/2oz shelled walnuts, finely chopped
115g/4oz plain flour
1 egg yolk, beaten, to glaze
a few chopped nuts to decorate

Mix the icing sugar and oil with a fork until smooth, mix in the ginger, walnuts and the flour. With your hands gather the dough until smooth. Chill for 30 minutes.

Preheat the oven to 180°C/350°F/Gas mark 4. Take hazelnut-sized balls of the dough and roll until smooth. Press gently to 5mm/¼inch thick.

Put them on a floured baking tray and brush with the beaten egg. Bake for 16 minutes until risen. When cool remove and store in an airtight tin.

SWEET CINNAMON
Biscuit-e-darchin

6 tablespoons oil
45g/1½oz icing sugar
1 heaped teaspoon ground cinnamon
90g/3oz plain flour
1 egg yolk, beaten, to glaze
poppy seeds to decorate

Mix the oil, sugar and cinnamon with a fork until smooth. Stir in the flour and knead to a soft dough. Chill for 15 minutes.

167

Preheat the oven to 180°C/350°F/Gas mark 4. Take hazelnut-sized balls of the dough and roll until smooth. Press gently to 5mm/¼inch thick, then place on an ungreased baking tray. Brush with the beaten egg and decorate with poppy seeds. Bake for about 10 minutes. Remove from the tray when slightly cool. Store in an airtight tin.

THE SUNSHINE
Shirin-ye-khorshid

————

½ teaspoon ground saffron
1½ teaspoons freshly ground cardamom
50ml/2floz oil
90g/3oz icing sugar
1 large egg, beaten
175g/6oz rice flour
30 shelled pistachios, or blanched and halved almonds
poppy seeds for decoration

Mix the saffron with 1 tablespoon boiling water in a mixing bowl. Add the cardamom, 50ml/2floz oil and the icing sugar. Mix until smooth. Blend in the egg and rice flour. Knead to a soft dough, cover and chill for 15 minutes.

Preheat the oven to 150°C/300°F/Gas mark 2. Take small balls as big as hazelnuts, make a hole in the centre and insert 1 pistachio in each. Close up the hole, then press in the palms of the hand to 5mm/¼ inch thick. Place on a greased and floured baking tray. Using the open end of a thimble, or a similar small object, press a pattern on top of each ball of dough. Sprinkle on the poppy seeds, and bake for about 15 minutes or until risen. Leave to cool on the tray then store in an airtight tin.

MOON AND THE SUN

My father's bed-time stories were educational, and in one of which I learned that the winter moonshine is the summer sunshine.

It was a cold winter evening with the forecast of snow. I remember quite vividly waking up in the night, looking out of my window and seeing the ground covered in white. I was delighted the snow was so deep that I wouldn't have to go to school the next day. I went back to a warm bed and contented sleep.

It seemed just a few moments later that my mother called me saying that I'd be late for school.

I opened my eyes sleepily, puzzled that I was expected to go to school in such thick snow. Then I realised that what I had seen had been bright moonshine and not snow.

When the heavy snow really did fall and there was a full moon and a clear sky it was easy to imagine the garden was bathed in summer sunshine.

FLOWER BUD BISCUIT
Ghand-e-shekoofeh

————

6½ tablespoons oil
60g/2oz caster sugar
½ teaspoon baking powder
115g/4oz plain flour
1 egg white, beaten, to glaze
poppy seeds to decorate

Mix the oil, sugar and baking powder together, then add the flour. Gather the dough in your hands and knead to make it smooth. Chill for 15 minutes.

Preheat the oven to 180°C/350°F/Gas mark 4. Take hazelnut-sized balls of the dough and press to 5mm/¼inch thick.

Bake as in the recipe for sweet cinnamon, remembering to glaze with beaten egg. Store in an airtight tin.

THE LAST OF THE SASSANIAN

When the capital of Persia was Tisfoon, or Madaen, now situated in Iraq, there were many battles, due to the Arab invasion.

Yazdgerd-e-Sevom, king of the Sassanians (Zoroastrians), had his last encounter at Nehavand, to the west of the country. Forced to flee from his enemies to Khorasan in the east, he came across a windmill and decided it was a suitable place in which to spend the night. It was a fatal mistake. Khosrov the miller recognised the king and murdered him so he could steal his elaborate clothes and jewellery. This was the origin of the word 'assassinate' and the end of the Sassanian Zoroastrian dynasty.

Four of Yazdgerd's daughters ran away, accompanied by their old nannies. After a long and exhausting journey they came to the outskirts of the city of Yazd, and they passed away within a short distance of each other, comforted by their trusted nannies. Legend has it that the spirit of the princesses told a local shepherd that this was their resting place and from then on these sites became holy Zoroastrian shrines. To this day Zoroastrians from all over the world visit these holy places at a special time of the year during summer, where they cook many dishes for everyone to share.

HERBAL MEDICINE

The practice of herbal medicine is still very much in evidence amongst Zoroastrians. If someone is unwell, two close relatives will arrange a cure for the patient. Secretly they will boil borage, then strain and sweeten it to make a pleasant drink. One of the relatives will then rush excitedly to the patient and break some (false) news in order to give the patient a shock. At the same time the other one will give him or her the herb to drink. You would be surprised how effective these herbal cures are. Borage for example is especially good for curing coughs and colds.

COCONUT BISCUITS
Biscuit-e-nargil

7 tablespoons oil
60g/2oz icing sugar
60g/2oz dessicated coconut
90g/3oz plain flour
1 egg white, beaten, to glaze
poppy seeds to decorate

Mix the oil, sugar, coconut and the flour in a mixing bowl, gather the dough with your hands to make it smooth. Chill for 20 minutes.

Preheat the oven to 180°C/350°F/Gas mark 4.

Take hazelnut-sized balls from the dough and press them gently to 5mm/¼inch thick. Put them on a greased and floured baking tray, glaze with the egg white and bake for 8–10 minutes until risen. Remove from the oven and when slightly cool remove the biscuits from the tray. Store in an airtight tin.

CHICKPEA TEARS
Nan-e-nokhodchi

◆

60g/2oz butter (at room temperature)
45g/1½oz icing sugar
1 heaped teaspoon cardamom
80g/2¾oz chickpea flour

Preheat the oven to 150°C/300°F/Gas mark 2.
Whisk the butter, sugar and cardamom with an
electric mixer until smooth. Stir in the chickpea
flour and whisk again until creamy (don't worry if
the dough is crumbly). Gather the dough with your
hands and roll out to 1cm/½inch thick and cut
with different small shapes. Place on an ungreased
baking tray and bake for about 15 minutes. Leave
to cool before removing. Store in a tin.

DATE AND NUT ROLL
Shirini-ye-khorma

◆

PASTRY
175g/6oz self-raising flour
1 heaped teaspoon ground cinnamon
90g/3oz butter or margarine, cut into small pieces
2 teaspoons lemon juice

FILLING
140g/5oz stoned dates, soaked overnight in
175ml/6floz cold water
15g/½oz butter or margarine
1 heaped teaspoon ground cinnamon
juice of one large lemon
30g/1oz ground almonds
icing sugar for dusting

To prepare the pastry, sift the flour and cinnamon
into a bowl. Rub in the butter with your finger
tips until the mixture is crumbly. Add the lemon
juice and about 37ml/1½floz ice-cold water to
make a soft dough. Cover the bowl and chill in the
refrigerator for 20 minutes.

SOFREH-E-ABOLFAZL

I could often hear my Muslim Nanny Malog
calling 'Abolfazl', brother of Emam Hussain,
the son of Ali, to find a fiancé for her
daughter Sakineh who was 24 years old and
still unmarried.

The custom to grant her wishes was to lay
out 'Abolfazl sofreh', on a rectangular white
cloth.

On the arranged day, as a girl of only
seven, my Nanny dressed me up in a chador
to join in the feast in her house.

At the entrance to her house was a large
cobbled terrace, where many guests, all
women dressed in different coloured
chadors, stood chatting and pouring tea out
of the brass samovar. The dinning room was
prepared with sofreh the day before and was
locked as it was forbidden for anyone to
enter the room for 24 hours.

Everyone waited outside impatiently
until Malog unlocked the door. The long
cloth which was laid over the old Persian
carpet looked extremely colourful laden
with many different dishes of Ash, yoghurt,
fruit, sweets, shelled nuts and Halva.

A large plate of dates with bowls of flour
was the main attraction, as Malog explained
to me that it is believed that overnight
Abolfazl had entered the room and touched
the flour to make it holy. Of course everyone
took turns to see the amazing Abolfazl finger
print then later the flour was made into
Halva for everyone to taste for good luck.

Many women added more dates to the
sofreh, to make their wishes come true.
Afterwards the lady priest (Akhond) recited
prayers from the Qu'ran.

Finally all the guests helped themselves
from the appetising dishes and wished
Sakineh luck in finding a fiancé in the near
future.

Meanwhile, put the dates and their soaking liquid into a small, heavy saucepan. Bring to the boil, then reduce the heat and simmer until soft and creamy, stirring with a wooden spoon. Add the remaining ingredients except the icing sugar and stir to mix.

Remove from the heat and stir in a further 25ml/1floz cold water if the mixture is too dry. Set aside to cool.

Preheat the oven to 180°C/350°F/Gas mark 4.

Divide the dough into 2 equal portions. Roll out each portion on a lightly floured board to a 32.5 × 12.5cm/13 × 5inch rectangle. Spread the filling to within 1cm/½ inch of the edges. Roll the pastry up like a Swiss roll, then cut into ten 2.5cm/1inch pieces with a sharp knife. Lift onto an ungreased baking tray lightly dusted with flour, leaving about 1–2.5cm/½–1inch between each. Bake in the oven for 12–15 minutes until risen and lightly golden. Remove from the oven, dust the rolls with icing sugar, then transfer to a wire rack and leave to cool. Store in an airtight tin. Makes 20.

ROSE WATER AND NUT ICECREAM
Bastany

➤━✦

115g/4oz granulated sugar
2 tablespoons rose water
2 teaspoons lemon juice
300ml/½ pint double cream
60g/2oz blanched almonds or pistachios, finely chopped

Put the sugar, rose water and lemon juice in a small heavy saucepan, add 1 tablespoon cold water and heat gently until the sugar has dissolved. Bring to the boil and boil for 3–4 minutes or until the syrup sets into a ball when a little is spooned onto a cold plate. Remove from the heat, pour into a bowl and leave to cool. Whip the cream until it will stand in soft peaks. Fold in the nuts, then slowly stir in the cooled sugar syrup. Put the mixture in a freezer container and freeze for at least 4 hours, beating the mixture every 45 minutes. Cover the container and freeze overnight.

ROSE WATER FRUIT SALAD
Salad-e-miveh

➤━✦

2 large fresh oranges, cut into segments
4 tangerines, cut into segments
3 eating apples, cored and diced
2 bananas, sliced into rings
175g/6oz black and white grapes, halved and seeded
1 teaspoon caster or brown sugar
juice of 2 large oranges
6 tablespoons rose water
300ml/½ pint plain yoghurt or lightly whipped cream
1 tablespoon ground unsalted pistachios

Mix all the fruit in a mixing bowl. Mix the sugar and orange juice with the rose water, add to the fruit mixture and toss well. Spoon over the yoghurt. Sprinkle with the pistachios when serving.

JAMS, PICKLES AND DRINKS

JAM (*Moraba*)

One of the early immigrants from India to Persia two and half thousand years ago was sugar.

Sanskrit Sakara (in the ancient language of Hindus) was known as shikar is Persia. After the Arab invasion one century later, during the ninth century, the cultivation of sugar was introduced to north Africa where it found its way to Spain and then on to Europe, replacing honey, the sweetener of the time.

Confectionery shops in Persia were known as Ghanadi after the sugar lamp (ghand), and so confectionery became known as candy in English. These solid sugars, some in the form of cones weighing several kilos, were often placed on the serving table nearest to the entrance to the shop.

In Zoroastrian rituals such as engagements and weddings, these sugar cones are wrapped in green shiny paper and presented with other items. But the most popular of all were served as ghand pahloo. The sugar cones are broken down into small pieces and served with black tea on the saucer.

Often it was given to babies dissolved in water for digestion.

The jams and preserves are mostly home-made with fruit from the orchard or from the nearby farm, with preserving or white sugar. The recipe I have given is in a small quantity, which can be doubled or more.

It is best to use an enamel or non-stick pan, and a wooden spoon to stir.

Jam is a typical family breakfast, spread over butter on nan or bread, eaten with chay (black tea).

Once the jam has reached the setting point, remove the pan from the heat and allow to cool uncovered, to prevent the danger of any condensation from the lid.

Store in dry, warm, sterilised jars with well-fitting, air-tight lids.

The most popular speciality of the Caspian littoral, is orange blossom jam: Moraba-ye-bahar-e-naranj. It is not a very common jam to be made by a housewife in Tehran or any other city, but is frequently bought in shops.

ORANGE BLOSSOM JAM
Moraba-ye-bahar-e-naranj

◆━◆

115g/4oz orange blossom
115g/4oz sugar
the juice of 1 medium lemon

Simmer the blossoms in water for 2–3 minutes, drain, simmer them again, then drain again. Put them in cold water to soak for several hours, preferably overnight, changing the water 2–3 times. This will ensure that any bitterness is completely removed.

Bring 50ml/2floz water to the boil with the sugar, reduce the heat and allow the sugar to dissolve. Add the lemon juice and cook moderately until thick. Add the blossoms and cook for a further minute. Remove from the heat and pour into warm sterilised jars. Leave to cool, then cover and store.

CINNAMON CHERRY JAM
Moraba-ye-gilas

◆━◆

For a better flavour it is best to cook the cherries with their stones in then remove the stones at the end of cooking.

230g/8oz fresh cherries
2 tablespoons lemon juice
230g/8oz preserving sugar
1 teaspoon ground cinnamon

Put the cherries in a heavy saucepan, add the lemon juice and 3 tablespoons cold water and bring to the boil. Reduce the heat, cover and simmer for 15 minutes. Remove the pan from the heat, add the sugar and cinnamon and stir well with a wooden spoon. Return to the heat and boil vigorously for 3–4 minutes or until the ingredients are soft and

setting point is reached. Pour into warm sterilised jars, leave to cool, then cover and store. Makes 350g/12oz.

CARROT JAM
Morab-ye-havij

◆━◆

230g/8oz grated carrots, or carrot pulps
285g/10oz preserving sugar
4 tablespoons lemon juice
60g/2oz blanched almonds, finely chopped
3 tablespoons rose water

Put the carrots in a saucepan, add 120ml/4floz cold water and bring to the boil. Reduce the heat, cover and simmer for 10–15 minutes or until the carrots are soft. Remove the pan from the heat, add the remaining ingredients and stir well to mix. Return to the heat and boil vigorously for about 12 minutes or until setting point is reached. Store as in cherry jam. Make 455g/1lb.

APPLE JAM
Moraba-ye-sib

◆━◆

230g/8oz finely grated eating apples
230g/8oz preserving sugar
2 tablespoons lemon juice
2 tablespoons rose water
1/4 teaspoon ground cardamom

Put the apples in a heavy saucepan, add 120ml/4floz water and bring to the boil. Reduce the heat, cover and simmer for 10–12 minutes or until the apples are stewed.

Remove the pan from the heat, add the remaining ingredients and stir well with a wooden spoon. Return to the heat and boil vigorously for 10–15 minutes or until setting point is reached. Store as in cherry jam. Makes about 285g/10oz.

PUMPKIN JAM
Moraba-ye-kadu zard

230g/8oz finely grated pumpkin flesh,
or pumpkin pulp
230g/8oz preserving sugar
2 tablespoons rose water
finely grated rind and juice of 1 large lemon
1 teaspoon ground cinnamon

Put all the ingredients in a heavy saucepan and heat gently until the sugar has dissolved. Bring to the boil, then reduce the heat and cook moderately for 25–30 minutes or until setting point is reached. Store as in cherry jam. Makes about 350g/12oz.

CUCUMBER JAM
Moraba-ye-khiyar balang

230g/8oz thinly sliced, peeled cucumber
175g/6oz sugar
50ml/2floz rose water
3 tablespoons lemon juice

Put the cucumber in a saucepan, cover with about 300ml/$\frac{1}{2}$ pint cold water and bring to the boil. Reduce the heat, cover and simmer for about 10 minutes or until the cucumber is soft, drain and mash. Add the sugar, rose water and lemon juice and stir over a moderate heat for about 5 minutes. Bring to the boil and boil vigorously for about 8–10 minutes or until setting point is reached. Store as in cherry jam. Makes 175–200g/6–7oz.

AUBERGINE ROSE WATER JAM
Moraba-ye-badinjan

400g/14oz aubergines
230g/8oz sugar
50ml/2floz rose water
3 tablespoons lemon juice

Bring a heavy saucepan of water to the boil. Peel the aubergines and slice thinly. Drop them immediately into the boiling water (to prevent them turning black) and simmer for 8–10 minutes until soft. Drain, then mash until smooth and return to the rinsed-out pan. Add the sugar, rose water and lemon juice and stir over a moderate heat for about 5 minutes. Bring to the boil and boil vigorously for 8–10 minutes or until setting point is reached. Store as in cherry jam. Makes about 375g/13oz.

QUINCE JAM
Moraba-ye-beh

140–175g/4–6oz quince, peeled and finely chopped
150g/5oz sugar
juice of 1 large lemon
50ml/2floz rose water
$\frac{1}{4}$ teaspoon ground cardamom

Put the quince in a large saucepan, cover with about 325ml/11floz cold water and bring to the boil. Reduce the heat, cover the pan and simmer for 30–35 minutes or until soft.

Add the sugar, lemon juice, rose water and cardamom. Cover and boil vigorously for 2–3 minutes or until setting point is reached. Store as in cherry jam. Makes about 175–200g/6–7oz.

ORANGE AND CARROT MARMALADE
Moraba-ye-porteghal va havij

230g/8oz coarsely grated carrots
285g/10oz sugar (preferably brown)
2 small oranges
2 tablespoons lemon juice

Put the carrots in a heavy saucepan, cover with 50–85ml/3–4 floz cold water and bring to the boil. Reduce the heat, cover and simmer for 8–10 minutes or until the carrots are soft.

Remove the pan from the heat and stir in the sugar. Remove the rind from the oranges with a zester or canelle knife. Rinse under cold water. Halve the oranges and squeeze the juice (there should be 85ml/3floz) and add it to the pan with the lemon juice.

Bring to the boil and boil vigorously for about 12–15 minutes, or until setting point is reached. Store as in cherry jam. Makes 375–400g/13–14oz.

TOMATO JAM
Moraba-ye-govjeh farangi

455g/1lb soft tomatoes
345g/12oz sugar
the juice of half a large lemon

Put the tomatoes into a large bowl, add boiling water and after one minute remove the skins, then chop. Simmer with the pan covered until soft, then mash and stir in the sugar and lemon juice. Bring to the boil and cook on a moderate heat until setting point is reached.

Store as in cherry jam.

RADISH AND GINGER JAM
Moraba-ye-torobcheh va zanjafil

A very unusual combination of ginger and radish makes a very special family jam.

To choose radishes, press between fingers to be sure they are firm.

345g/12oz small cherry red radishes, topped and
tailed and sliced in thick round pieces
30g/1oz fresh ginger finely grated
or pulped in a blender
175g/6oz sugar
the juice of half a large lemon

Simmer the radishes in 225ml/8floz water until soft. Remove the radishes with a slotted spoon and chop them finely. Meanwhile simmer the ginger in the same liquid until soft. Add the chopped radishes, lemon juice and the sugar and stir once or twice. Cook on a moderate heat until setting point is reached. Store as in cherry jam.

WATERMELON JAM
Moraba-ye-hendavaneh

275g/10oz watermelon skin with the green part
removed, cut into small pieces
230g/8oz sugar
the juice of half a large lemon with the bits

Simmer the watermelon skin in 250ml/8fl oz water for 6–7 minutes until tender. Drain over a bowl, and reserve 200ml/6–7floz of the liquid.

Grind the cooked flesh coarsely and return back to the pan with the reserved liquid. Add the sugar and stir until it dissolves. Add the lemon juice and cook for another 5–7 minutes, until setting point is reached. When cool store as in cherry jam.

GARLIC RELISH (JAM)
Torshi ya moraba-ye-sir

This most delightful typical family recipe, a cross between relish and jam, has been given to me by Dr and Mrs Dinyar Hakhamaneshi.

1kg/2.2lb garlic cloves, peeled
½ litre vinegar (any kind)
750g sugar
5–6 whole cardamom pods
½ teaspoon ground cardamom
1 teaspoon ground cinnamon
¼ teaspoon ground cloves
½ teaspoon each fennel, onion and cumin seeds
1 dessertspoon mixed basil, dill, tarragon and mint, dried and crushed
1 dessertspoon chopped chives

Simmer the garlic in water for 2–3 minutes (no longer), drain well and pierce each with a cocktail stick.

Meanwhile cook the vinegar with all the other ingredients for 4–5 minutes until thick. Put the garlic in a large sterilised jar. Pour over the syrup, and when cool cover and store for at least six months to one year before using (the longer it is kept the tastier it becomes).

LAKE REZAIYEH

I was a girl of eight when I first visited Lake Rezaiyeh, the birth place of prophet and philosopher Zaratrostra (Zardosht) 300 kilometres from Tabriz. Our friend Bijan drove a short distance from the salt water lake, to show us how he produced his own salt. We could see many holes deep into the ground, belonging to individual families. It is said that the three wise men of biblical times passed through this area of western Persia on their way to Bethlehem.

PICKLES (*Torshi*)

Another strong feature of the table at home is pickles and preserves. With herbs, fruit and vegetables all equally playing a major part in the recipes made by every housewife in Persia.

Like other dishes, recipes for pickles are handed down from one generation to the next using crops mostly picked from the garden or nearby farm.

The longer the pickles are kept, the better and tastier they become.

Pickle-making does not need special skill, just choose the spices to your own liking: peppery and hot or the delicate taste of sweet chutney with cinnamon and cloves.

Choose an enamel or non-stick pan for cooking.

Use only vinegar, rather than mixing it with water.

At the end of cooking, allow the mixture to cool with the pan uncovered, so there is no danger of condensation.

Do not allow any liquid to mix with the ingredients once it has reached the final stage of cooking.

All jars should be completely dry with well-fitting lids for storing.

PICKLED ONION
Torshi-ye-piaz

345g/12oz pickling onions
350ml/12oz malt vinegar
3 garlic cloves, crushed
1 teaspoon dried and crushed mint
$^1/_4$ teaspoon salt or to taste

Put the ingredients in a heavy saucepan and bring to the boil over a high heat. Boil vigorously for 1 minute, then remove from the heat and set aside to cool. Store in airtight jars.

ORANGE RELISH
Torshi-ye-pust-e-porteghal

230g/8oz thinly pared orange peel
7 cloves of garlic, crushed
60g/2oz sugar
$^1/_4$ teaspoon salt
300–350ml/10–12floz malt vinegar

Simmer the orange peel for 2 minutes, drain, repeat this once more. Spread on kitchen paper and leave overnight.

The next day, grind the orange peel in an electric grinder and place in a heavy saucepan with the garlic, sugar, salt, and enough vinegar to cover. Boil vigorously for 2 minutes, then remove from the heat and set aside to cool. Store in airtight jars. Makes about 1$^1/_4$ lbs.

PICKLED AUBERGINES
Torshi-ye-badinjan

455g/1lb very tiny pickling aubergines, stem removed
1 teaspoon salt
300ml/$^1/_2$ pint malt vinegar

1 head of garlic, crushed
4 teaspoons sugar
4–5 sprigs each fresh mint and tarragon, finely chopped, or 1 teaspoon each dried
a little pepper to taste

Cut a small lengthways slit in the centre of each aubergine. Simmer in water with 2 teaspoons of the salt for 5–6 minutes, drain well.

Put the aubergines in a heavy saucepan with the remaining ingredients, and boil vigorously for 4–5 minutes. Remove from the heat and set aside to cool. Store in warm airtight jars.

PICKLED AUBERGINES WITH HERBS
Torshi-ye-badinjan va sabsi

285g/10oz aubergines
salt
115g/4oz chopped mixed herbs: basil, coriander, dill, mint and tarragon
1 head of garlic, crushed
1 teaspoon cumin seeds
120–150ml/4–5floz malt vinegar

Put the aubergines under a preheated hot grill for about 15 minutes, turning them every 3 minutes, until softened and wrinkled. Leave until cool enough to handle, then peel, place on kitchen paper, sprinkle with a little salt and leave to degorge for 2–3 hours. Chop the aubergine and place in a heavy saucepan. Add the herbs, garlic, cumin seeds and $^1/_4$ teaspoon salt and enough vinegar to cover. Boil vigorously for 3–4 minutes, remove from the heat and set aside to cool. Store in airtight jars.

PICKLED GARLIC
Torshi-ye-sir

455g/1lb garlic cloves, peeled
300–350ml/10–12floz malt vinegar
1 teaspoon salt

Place the garlic cloves in a pan and add enough vinegar to cover. Add the salt and bring to the boil. Remove from the heat, set aside to cool. Store in airtight jars. The longer it is kept the better is the pickle.

DATE AND TAMARIND CHUTNEY
Torshi-ye-khorma

230g/8oz pitted dates, ground
300ml/¹/₂ pint tamarind liquid
(see index for preparation)
50ml/2floz lemon juice
1 head of garlic, crushed
60g/2oz sultanas
30g/1oz ground mixed spice
a pinch of cayenne pepper
a little salt

Put all the ingredients into a pan and simmer with the pan covered for 30 minutes until thick, stirring occasionally. Pour into warm sterilised jars, leave to cool, cover and store. Makes 565g/1¹/₄ lbs.

PICKLED CHERRIES
Torshi-ye-gilas

455g/1lb fresh black cherries, pitted
¹/₄ teaspoon salt
about 175ml/6floz malt vinegar

Wash the cherries and pat dry with kitchen paper. Spread them out on a cloth and leave to dry for 2 days. Put the cherries in a warm jar, sprinkle with the salt. Heat the vinegar and pour over the top. Seal and store.

DRINKS
Nooshabeh

Whichever part of the country you are in, hospitality plays a very big part. On arriving at the house, a tray of drink is always ready to offer to guests.

Drinks vary according to season: during summer, freshly squeezed or extracted fruit juice is served with scraped melon, or grated cucumber, scented with rosewater, also all different kind of home made syrup. The Zoroastrians' favourite rose water drink with basil seeds is served during happy occasions such as engagements and weddings. During winter hot black tea is served in small estekan glasses. Doogh is an all-year-round drink. It is very popular during hot summer at home and in restaurants served with chelow kebab.

YOGHURT DRINK
Doogh

300–350ml/10–12oz plain yoghurt (best sharp)
salt
ice cubes
dried crushed mint

Beat the yoghurt with the salt and the mint, add 600ml/1 pint iced water. Serve in individual glasses with ice cubes.

HAMADAN

One of the early lessons I learned at school was about the ancient city of Hamadan and it was not until very recently that I visited the city founded by the legendary Jamshid Shah, as the poet Ferdowsi says.

It took just over eight hours by car to drive 435km south of Tehran, via Saveh, to reach Hamadan. We were welcomed by our friend Navid and his wife Aghdas to their typical Hamadan home, to join the eighty guests for welcoming their parents, who had just became Haji, back from Mecca. The table was already set with an assortment of dishes: starters, khoresht made from home-grown vegetables with meat and chicken, plus different types of rice dishes.

The low coffee tables were set with various nuts and sweets. Soft drinks and water were served. There was a sound of joy and laughter amongst the guests, who were invited by their hosts to share this special occasion.

The tour began the next morning, to see the cuneiform (MiKHI) rupestral inscriptions engraved on a cliff at the bottom of the green valley, about 10 kilometres west of the city. The site is called Ganj Nameh, meaning the letter of treasure.

The famous tomb of Abu Ali Sina (called Avicenna in the west) is in Hamadan, where he died in 1037. Today he would have been called, a 'pluridisciplinary' scientist. But he was above all a mathematician. His theories were taught in universities until the 19th century. As a poet and philosopher, his work is still studied by Iranian and orientalists.

Baba Taher (better known to the Persians as Baba Taher-e-oryan), the famous poet, is honoured in Hamadan. His monument was built during the 20th century. The interior is decorated with a long spindle, shaped ceramics and a rotunda covered with green marble flag-stones, upon which are inscribed the finest verses of the poets.

I leaned against the cool marble wall, listening to the sound of flute-playing and the hypnotic voice of the old man reciting verses, dressed in his dark brown suit and felt hat. I was so completely absorbed by the peace and tranquility, I did not realise one hour had passed. I then went to visit the most curious monument of the Jewish mausoleum reputed to contain the tombs of Esther and Mordecai.

Esther was a young Jewish girl, who came to Xerxes for help, for just treatment and protection for the Jewish people. She succeeded so well, that she became queen of the Hakhamaneshian. Her uncle Mordecai was invited by her to the king's palace and facilitated the settlement of Jewish colonies in Persia, especially in Hamadan, where now several thousand Jewish people are settled.

CUCUMBER AND MINT DRINK
Nooshabeh-e-sekanjabin ba khiyar

4–6 tablespoons mint drink (see index)
285g/10oz finely grated peeled cucumber

Mix all the ingredients with 600ml/1 pint iced water. Serve chilled with ice cubes.

CUCUMBER AND ROSE WATER DRINK
Nooshabeh-e-khiyar ba golab

285g/10oz finely grated, peeled cucumber
4–6 tablespoons rose water, to taste
4 teaspoons sugar

Mix all ingredients with 600ml/1 pint iced water. Serve with ice cubes.

181

VARIATION

MELON AND ROSE WATER DRINK
Nooshabeh-e-kharbozeh ba golab
———

Substitute half a large melon, scraped, for cucumber.

APPLE AND ROSE WATER DRINK
Nooshabeh-e-sib ba golab
———

Substitute 4 eating apples, peeled and grated, for melon.

WATERMELON DRINK
Nooshabeh-e-hendavaneh
———

*½ a ripe, sweet watermelon
sugar (optional)
ice cubes*

Work the water melon flesh in a mouli-legumes to extract the juice. Discard the flesh and the seeds. Serve with ice cubes.

ROSE WATER DRINK
Sharbat-e-golab
———

This Zoroastrian drink is traditionally served at weddings and New Year (Nov rooz) celebrations, or sometimes during early spring when there is no fruit in season.

*8 sugar cubes or 5–6 teaspoons granulated sugar
50ml/2floz rosewater, or to taste
1 teaspoon white basil seeds*

Dissolve the sugar in 600ml/1 pint water. Add the rosewater and the basil seeds. Serve chilled with ice.

MINT DRINK
Sekanjabin
———

*175g/6oz granulated sugar
85ml/3floz malt vinegar
6–8 sprigs of fresh mint*

Put the sugar in a heavy saucepan, pour in 225ml/8floz water and bring slowly to the boil. Reduce the heat and simmer for 10–15 minutes, then add the vinegar and simmer for a further 20 minutes, or until the syrup is formed (drop a little onto a cold plate, it should barely spread). Add the mint, then remove the pan from the heat. Leave to cool uncovered (do not leave the lid on the pan or the condensation will spoil the syrup) and discard the mint. Store in airtight bottles. Serve chilled with iced water.

SEASONAL DRINK

The Persian New Year (21st of March, 1st of Farvardeen) was a time for everyone to enjoy. A time for over-eating and indulging themselves with food and various sweets.

Dried fruit juice was recommended to clear the system after such heavy eating. Dried fruit such as apricots, peaches, cherries and plums were soaked for 2–3 days covered with cold water. Turn the fruit in water every day then serve the juice in large lemon tea glasses, with a few pieces of the dried and soaked fruit.

ORANGE DRINK
Sharbat-e-porteghal

~ ~

300ml/$\frac{1}{2}$ pint orange juice, freshly squeezed
thinly pared rind of 2 medium oranges
4 tablespoons lemon juice
90–115g/3–4oz granulated sugar,
or to taste

Put all the ingredients in a small heavy saucepan. Heat gently until the sugar has dissolved, then simmer for about 30 minutes until thick. Drain in a sieve over a bowl when cold. Store in airtight bottles.

VARIATION

CHERRY DRINK
Sharbat-e-albaloo

~ ~

Make as for orange drink above, with 300ml/$\frac{1}{2}$ pint cherry juice (use pitted fresh cherries and extract the juice in a juice extractor), 4 tablespoons lemon juice, 90g/3oz granulated sugar and a few drops of vanilla essence.

QUINCE AND LEMON DRINK
Sharbat-e-beh-limoo

~ ~

Make as for orange drink above, with 120ml/4floz quince juice (made in juice extractor), 2 tablespoons lemon juice, 140g/5oz granulated sugar and $\frac{1}{4}$ teaspoon ground cardamom.

BASIC RECIPES

POMEGRANATE PURÉE
Robb-e-anar

Pomegranate purée is obtainable in Persian supermarkets throughout the year, but here is a recipe if you wish to make your own. Seed the pomegranate first then extract the juice.

1.2 litres/2 pints sour pomegranate juice
(made in juice extractor)
1 medium uncooked beetroot, peeled and diced
1 teaspoon ground cinnamon

Put all the ingredients in a heavy saucepan, simmer uncovered for 1½–2 hours, stirring occasionally, until thick. When cool store in airtight jars. Makes about 230g/8oz.

HOT MINT
Naana dagh

1 tablespoon oil
1 teaspoon crushed dried mint
2 garlic cloves, peeled and crushed

Heat the oil in a small heavy frying pan, add the garlic and stir once or twice. Add the mint then remove from the heat.

TAMARIND LIQUID
Ab-e-tamr

Tamarind pods are available from Persian and Indian shops. The liquid which is produced by soaking them is dark and rich, with a sweet-sour flavour. If you prefer you can use concentrated tamarind liquid. Dilute it with water in the proportion of 25ml/1floz to 175ml/6floz cold water.

285g/10oz tamarind pods
1.25 litres/2¼ pints cold water

Wash the tamarind pods, place in a bowl and cover with 1.2 litres/2 pints of the water. Leave to soak overnight.

The next day, crush the pods with a fork, then place in a large saucepan with the soaking liquid. Simmer for 2–3 minutes until fairly soft.

Place a colander over a bowl and pour the contents of the pan into it. Stir with a spoon and let the liquid drain through into the bowl, then return the pods to the pan and add the remaining cold water. Stir and, if cool enough, squash the pods with your hands to extract as much liquid as possible. Drain into the colander again. If necessary, repeat with cold water to extract more dark liquid until only the pulp remains. Then discard the pulp. Makes about 1.5–1.6 litres/2½–2¾ pints.

YOGHURT
Mast

1 litre/1¾ pints milk
1 generous tablespoon plain yoghurt

Bring the milk to the boil. As soon as the froth rises remove from the heat and pour into an oven proof earthenware or glass dish. Leave for about 35 minutes depending on room temperature, until tepid. Put the yoghurt into a separate small bowl and add two tablespoons of the milk. Beat vigorously, then add to the remainder of the milk. Agitate with a fork from the edge inwards. Put a warmed plate over the bowl to reduce condensation and place in a warm place. Put a thick cover such as a towel over the plate and bowl and leave for 5–8 hours (no longer or the yoghurt will turn sour). Very gently tilt the bowl to see that it is set. If a slight coating of liquid does remain, carefully spoon it off into a glass.

To avoid curdling when adding yoghurt to a

hot liquid during cooking: beat 1.2 litres/2 pints yoghurt with 1 egg white. Slowly add it to the hot liquid by stirring with a wooden spoon in one direction only. Lower the heat to barely simmer and as soon as a thick sauce forms, remove from the heat.

An alternative method to prevent curdling is to whisk plain flour into the yoghurt in the proportion of 1 teaspoon plain flour to 150ml/¼ pint yoghurt. Mix well then add to the pan.

FRESH CHEESE

When I was a child, Soghrab, the Muslim lady, called every day to deliver us fresh herbs. She packed the herbs in a large batik cloth with fresh cheese packed in the middle, which she carried on her shoulder, holding the heavy cloth with one hand and in the other she held a deep pottery pot with freshly made yoghurt. A taste I will never forget.

THE NATURAL ALARM

Our holiday house in Manshad was built on the lower slope of the mountain, with the running stream below giving the place a tranquil atmosphere. Everything about the place was natural, and my favourite was waking up in the mornings to the sound of the cockerel, from the terrace below.

Opening my eyes, I would see the bubbling samovar (tea urn) in the corner on a small walnut table, fresh eggs from the barn down the stairs, and nan and panir freshly made by Masoomeh, our holiday home keeper. Standing on the balcony, looking through the thick branches of the walnut trees which overhung the building, we could spot visitors at a distance, at least a mile away, walking up the steep slope towards the house, giving us time to fold away the mattresses (doshak) and eiderdowns, leaving the Persian rugs visible, and welcome them for breakfast. Thanks to the cockerel for waking us on time.

PERSIAN CHEESE
Panir

Panir is eaten in every Persian house from morning until night – for breakfast, lunch, dinner and supper. In summer it is delicious with nan, watermelon or other melons, in autumn with grapes, and in winter it is eaten with nan, dates and walnuts. It is both nourishing and satisfying.

Here are two recipes for panir. The first uses yoghurt and is so quick that it can be made in minutes. The second has a creamier texture and softer taste which is acquired by using rennet rather than yoghurt. Traditionally, panir is made with goat's milk, but nowadays it is equally often made with cow's milk. Only use pasteurised milk not homogenised or skimmed.

PANIR 1

1.2 litres/2 pints pasteurised milk

Bring the milk to the boil. Beat the yoghurt and pour it into the milk, which will curdle. Stir once and remove from the heat. Line a colander or sieve with a large piece of muslin. Ladle in the curdled milk, tie the ends of the muslin tightly to make a bag, then place on a tilted kitchen board by the sink. Place a heavy object on it and leave for 30 minutes or until the excess water has drained away. If the panir is not to be eaten straight away dissolve 2 teaspoons salt in 600ml/1 pint boiling water. Leave until cold, then gently drop in the panir. Keep it in the refrigerator for up to 3–4 days. Makes 200–230g/7–8oz.

PANIR 2

1.2 litres/2 pints pasteurised milk
2 tablespoons rennet essence

Warm the milk in a heavy saucepan to 37°C/98°F (or just warm to the finger – if hot it will curdle). Add the rennet essence. Stir once or twice, then immediately remove from the heat. Pour into a dish and cover with a warmed lid to reduce condensation. Put it in a warm place, such as an airing cupboard or by a radiator. Leave to stand for 3–5 hours, depending on the temperature, until set.

Gently pour off the excess whey and discard, then leave until really cool. Line a colander or sieve with a large piece of muslin. Ladle in the set milk. Tie the end of the muslin tightly to make a bag, then hang over the sink for 3–4 hours or until the panir stops dripping. Gently squeeze the bag to check. This cheese can be stored in the refrigerator in brine water as prepared above. Makes 175g/6oz.

NOODLE
Reshteh

50g/2oz plain white flour
pinch of salt

Sift the flour and salt into a bowl. Slowly add 2 tablespoons warm water and knead for 2–3 minutes to make a soft dough. Cover and leave to rest in a warm place for about 20 minutes to make a soft dough. Roll out the dough on a floured surface to a 35–40cm/14–15inch circle. Fold in half to make a semicircle, then fold again. Cut into very thin matchstick strips. Dust with flour to prevent the strips sticking together.

RUE AND MINT SAUCE
Sir va sedab

Traditionally this sauce is made rather runny and poured over the bread in a bowl. This version is thicker and excellent with fish dishes. It is used for a special dish for Zoroastrian rituals.

1 tablespoon oil
5 garlic cloves, crushed
1 teaspoon turmeric
leaves of one mint sprig, finely chopped
2 teaspoons chopped fresh rue
1 teaspoon crushed dried mint
2 heaped teaspoons sugar
85ml/3floz vinegar
salt and pepper

Fry the garlic in the oil for one minute, add the turmeric and herbs and stir for another two minutes. Remove the pan from the heat.

Dissolve the sugar in the vinegar, stir into the pan, then return to the heat and season with salt and pepper to taste. Simmer gently for 2–3 minutes until thick. Serve with fish.

ORANGE RINDS
Khalal-e-porteghal

2 large or 4 small oranges
2 teaspoons sugar

Remove the rind from the oranges with a canelle knife or zester and rinse it under cold water to drain the bitter taste. Place the rinds in a small heavy saucepan with the sugar and, if using, nuts, e.g. almonds/pistachio, and 50ml/$\frac{1}{2}$floz water. Bring to the boil, then reduce the heat to moderate and cook for 10 minutes or until the ingredients become fairly dry.

ROSE WATER
Golab

Golab or rose water is one of the specialities of Persian cuisine usually used in sweets or sweet dishes, such as sholeh zard (rice pudding) or used as a cool summer drink. It is also delicious when mixed with paloodeh (noodle or starch sweet), a drink Zoroastrians use on happy occasions mixed with white basil seeds. It is also used with scraped melon or grated cucumber. There are different types of rosewater or Golab, obtainable in Persian supermarkets and in Armenian grocers. Do not confuse it with the rose water sold in the chemist's.

SOUR GRAPE JUICE
Ab-e-ghooreh

Sour grape juice is seasonal. Many freeze the freshly picked, unripe grapes for later use when not in season.

The juice is also bottled and ready for sale in Persian supermarkets throughout the year. Here is a recipe for a simple version to make yourself.

Cover 455g/1lb sour grapes with 200ml/8floz water and simmer until soft – about 5 minutes. Drain over a bowl, and with the back of spoon extract as much juice as possible. You can substitute gooseberries for sour grapes and cook in the same way.

SUMAC
Sumagh

Sumac has a very pleasant sharp taste, and is a speciality of Persian restaurants served with Kabab (kebab) dishes. It is red-brown powder with an astringent quality, which is ground from the drupes of sumac shrubs, grown in most parts of Persia. In Yazd some woman used it as an old-fashioned remedy for relieving stomach problems such as diarrhoea.

TRADITIONAL DRIED WHEY
Kashk

Dried whey, or kashk, is seen in large sacks displayed in containers along the bazaar all over Persia. These white salty balls are made by boiling large quantities of whey for many hours, to produce these traditional balls which are used in vegetable and ash dishes. In Yazd on a hot summer's day kashk was soaked, then liquidised and poured over crispy bread with grated cucumber and crushed garlic, to which ice cubes were then added and eaten as lunch or mid-morning snack. (It is best to have on a relaxing day as it brings drowsiness) Kashk is rather high in price because of the amount of whey being used and the many hours taken for preparation. It is obtainable in Persian supermarkets both in the form of a ready-to-use paste, or in balls. If in the form of a ball, put these in a bowl, cover with water and leave for several hours to soak, then put them through a blender and work until smooth. Use as directed.

TURMERIC
Zardchoobeh

Turmeric is a very deep yellow root, seen packed in large sacks along the bazaars of different cities in Iran, which then has to be ground for use. It is also available in powder form, and is the major spice used in Persian cooking.

Because of its colour and pleasant aroma it gives a gentle flavour in all dishes and sometimes can be substituted for saffron in khoresht and ash dishes, but by no means should be substituted for saffron if mixed uncooked, direct with rice dishes as the aroma of turmeric will become obvious, with an unpleasant taste. Turmeric is much cheaper than saffron and can be found in large quantities in Persian supermarkets and in Indian shops.

If too much is used the flavour becomes obvious and rather unpleasant: $1/4$ to $1/2$ a level teaspoon is sufficient for a dish for four people.

DRIED LIME
Limoo omani

Limoo Omani or dried lime is believed to originate from Oman, but this most unusually delicate and flavoured dried fruit is widely used in Iran, as there is no comparison in flavour between fresh lime or lemon. These should by no means be mistaken with the green lime in the shops, which you buy over the counter, as limoo omani are a different species and professionally dried. They are usually packed in a small polythene bag, and are obtainable in Persian and some oriental shops. There are two kinds of lime, one with dark, and the other with light skin, both with the same flavour. The lighter skinned lime is used for certain dishes such as Khoresht-e-ghimeh to keep it light, and the darker version for ghormeh sabsi, to give it a dark colour. If the lime is used whole, as the seeds have rather a bitter taste, make 2–3 insertions with a sharp knife around the dried fruit, to infuse their flavour during cooking.

Powdered lime is available in Persian super-markets, which is more economical.

For making whole limes into powder, set the oven to hot for about 5 minutes then turn the heat off. Spread the limes on a baking tray and place in the switched-off oven and leave for 2–3 minutes. This will make them crisp and easy to handle. Slit them open and remove the bitter seeds, then while still crisp and warm grind them in a coffee grinder and store in airtight jars (do not wash the limes or get them wet – they are already clean).

DOOGH
Yoghurt drink

Doogh is one of the most popular summer drinks, prepared at home and served in resturants. It is as popular today as it was in ancient Persia, and is also drunk throughout the Middle East and India, with slight variations. Doogh is named after a farmer's daughter who used to milk the goat regularly (or shir dooshidan). Shir means milk and dooshidan means milking. So doogh derives from the second verb dooshidan.

Doogh is usually served chilled, and sometimes over crushed ice. The most famous bottled spring water is from Ab Ali or Ab-e-ali, situated just over 70 miles north-east of Tehran, along the valleys of the Alborz mountains, and the most popular Doogh sold in Iran is named after this valley as Doogh-e-Abali. There are no actual measurements for making Doogh – it varies according to taste. But the recipe given here is a guide line. Never use lemon juice as this will take away the natural flavour. Instead use yoghurt which has been standing for about 2 days which has turned sharp.

300–350ml plain yoghurt, preferably sharp
in flavour
salt according to taste
$1/4$ teaspoon dried crushed mint
ice cubes

Beat the yoghurt in a large bowl, add a little salt according to your taste and continue beating. Stir in the dried mint, beat, add 600ml/1 pint iced water and beat well. Serve in individual glasses and garnish with a little dried mint. Serve with Chelov Kabab (Rice and Kebab) or as a cool drink.

THE ANCIENT REMEDY

The storage room was large, really large, built by my late grandfather at the other end of the garden. It had several windows, some just underneath the vine trellis. During winter the dried twigs were heavy with snow, covering the windows, their glass stained with old winter leaves. There was no heating in the room, with shelves all along the side, packed with many many jars and containers, all filled with diffrent herbs, fruit, syrup, and many other things, which was stored during summer for winter use. There were all sorts of different shaped barrels, filled with pulses and grains. Also some bags, with nuts in their shells, dried fruit and vegetables which were not in season during winter. Everything was individually labelled. A small hand-written book of several pages was placed on a low, highly polished coffee table in the corner of the room. Some pages had already faded, and parts were torn. The book was read by many friends over the years who visited the room. It contained the brief history of where the original belief came from describing the significance of it all. The belief goes back many thousands of years to Zaratrostra, the founder of the Zoroastrian religion around 600 BC, who believed in one God. He believed that Fereshteh (the angel) should fight ahriman (the evil), and believed a healthy body meant a healthy mind. At the same time the physicians of those days proved that to retain good health, it was essential to cosume the right kinds of food, such as someone bad tempered or with a fever should eat cold food. The cure for stomach ache which had accrued within one or two days was hot food. It was one century after the birth of Zaratrostra that the Greek physicians built on the idea and brought the influence of Zoroastrian eating habits into western civilization. Then similar ideas spread into China, such as Yin and Yang.

It is common practice when visiting the doctor in Iran to be asked about your diet for the last two or three days. If the patient is sick and suffers with stomach ache, a brief diagnosis is that she or he has consumed too much cold food: fruit such as cherries, apricots, citrus fruit, plums, barberries and watermelon. But melon is hot and the stringy bits from the seeds are good for the kidneys. Mulberries are hot, especially when dried, and are warming and nourishing for cold winter days. Pomeganate, and sour or unripened grapes, are cold, but when ripened and sweet grapes are hot. The most common cold fruit are cherries and unripened grapes and it is recommended that these are avoided by women in early pregnancy to avoid miscarrages. Figs (when dried) and dates are hot. Fresh dates stuffed with walnuts are nourishing and a typical winter snack.

Generally vegetables are neither cold nor hot, except for onion, which is hot when fried, and spinach, which is cold.

All home-made fruit syrups are neither hot nor cold as they contain boiled sugar. Grains such as rice and barley are considered very cold, wheat neither hot nor cold. Generally all kind of pulses are cold food (but not very) with the exception of some such as mung beans, which are hot and nourishing. Nuts are all considered hot when dry, but neither hot nor cold when picked fresh from the tree (except walnuts, which are considered very hot). Lamb, veal and cockerel are cold, whereas hen, duck and beef are hot (but not very). Rose water is very hot. Spices are generally hot. Dairy produce such as yoghurt is cold, but cheese is neither hot nor cold (whey from fresh yoghurt is good for relaxation, and causes drowsiness when it is drunk before bed time). Eggs are very hot. Herbs such as mint and tarragon are hot.

Nabat is very hot, and often melted in a small heavy aluminum pan without any liquid and given to the patient if he or she has consumed too much cold food such as cherries. It was a custom that the lady of the house would call on neighbours to ask if they could spare a bowl of their dinner (if cooked without any spice) for her sick child, such as nokhodab (meaning chickpeas with water) Very lean lamb is boiled with one chopped onion and a handful of chickpeas, sometimes with no salt.

If someone had developed spots on their face it was a sign that they had consumed too much hot food. Fruit dishes such as plum ash were made or they had to eat a large quantity of fresh fruit. If an old lady in the Zoroastrian community suffered with a headache, before consulting her doctor, lettuce oil or lightly boiled egg yolk was rubbed on the forehead to be left for several hours then washed clean. If someone had a fracture, beaten egg and a teaspoon of turmeric were the dressing. Pregnant women were advised by their family to eat only hot rich food, such as one piece of baklava (baghlava) a day, nuts and plenty of pulses for natural protein. Fruit, in particular apples, but not too much citrus, were highly recommended as a good source of vitamins.

THE JOURNEY

The city of Yazd is in the centre of Persia, surrounded by small scattered villages. This desert province, with its population of more than sixty-six thousand, still has a small number of Zoroastrian inhabitants as well as Muslims, Jews and others.

Historically, there are several interesting buildings and ruins connected with the Zoroastrian religion, which has its roots in Yazd. The outskirts of the town are green and fertile as they are irrigated by purchased water (Ghanat) and from shirkooh, the mountain of milk. A special feature of the buildings is the domed roofs. These are typical of old Islamic architecture, some with tall ventilation chimneys to catch the cool breeze.

Factories and local cottage industries produce top-quality woollen blankets and materials for things such as suits. Copper jewellery is also produced in Yazd. But perhaps the most famous export is traditional sweets – baghlava, ghotab, sohan – which are sent all over the world.

I was in my very early teens when I left Yazd. It was an exciting experience, travelling the 500 miles to Tehran. I was one of the first to arrive at the bus depot, accompanied by my friends and relations. After saying goodbye, I climbed aboard the blue and white coach. Being the first passenger I took the window seat, with my packed lunch prepared by Memeh.

It was a long journey, with passengers falling asleep in their seats, then trying to wake up when we passed through various small towns such as Ardakan, Nain and Natanz. In each one there was a small café where black tea was served in small estekan glasses on floral patterned saucers with a sugar lump at the side. Everyone chose their own corner in which to eat their packed food. I remember how carefully my mother had packed my sofreh (white cloth) so that I could have a different snack at every stop.

Kashan was our major stop before passing through the Muslim holy city of Qum. I drank black tea most of the time, keeping some of the food for my brother Kumars, who had not tasted Memeh's cooking for a long time.

The 500 mile journey from Yazd was coming to an end. The blue and white coach with its tired looking passengers approached the city of Tehran.

My body suddenly woke up and I raised myself in my seat. The city took me by surprise. Completely the wrong image for an eastern city. Looking through the window, misty with the road dust, I stared, amazed, as the coach drove along endless avenues and boulevards. There were government offices and monuments surrounded by colourful gardens and fountains. Bustling crowds wearing the latest fashions were shopping in self-service supermarkets and going to restaurants. Others were queuing up to see the latest film at a cinema matinee. There were children just starting school in their smart uniforms, playing in the modern school grounds. Avenues and pavements looked spotlessly clean, just sprinkled with autumn leaves from the high beech and plane trees on each side. Each had been nurtured by the steady stream of melted snow running down from the Alborz mountains that shadowed our coach on its journey through the heavy traffic. I was deep in thought knowing Yazd was many miles away.

It was on a very recent visit back to Tehran that I walked slowly up the steep hill of Pahlavi avenue (as it is known to me, although the name has changed since the revolution). This is the longest avenue in town – about 10 miles. It was difficult to recognise the place, but the streets were typically of Tehran, with water channels in every main and back street gushing down from the melted snow from the Alborz mountain. There were many more shops and cafés, the confectionery shops as always spreading their aroma along the street. There was heavy traffic with bustling crowds, the women and girls all in Islamic clothes, the men with open-neck shirts and long sleeves.

Halfway I took a bus ride to Shemiran in the mountain region and found the café I used to visit as a teenager. I wore a long overall and a scarf as is the regulation. The owner was the same but old now and did not recognise me. I left with a thank you, rather than a smile which is not allowed.

GLOSSARY

avishan or abishan	thyme	maveez	raisins
ard	flour	mikhak	cloves
ard-e-berenj	rice flour	namak	salt
ab	water	naana	mint
ab-e-angoor	grape juice	neshasteh	cooking starch
ab-e-limoo	lemon juice	piaz	onion
ab-e-porteghal	orange juice	rayhan	basil
barg-e-boo	bay leaf	razyooneh	fennel seed
barg-e-mov	vine leaves	seer	garlic
darchin	cinnamon	sib	apple
felfel	pepper	sib-zamini	potatoes
gard-e-limoo(omani)	dried lime powder	sheved/sheveed	dill
geshniz	coriander	shanbalileh	fenugreek
golab	rose water	somagh	sumac
hel	cardamom	shekar	sugar
jaafary	parsley	tokhmeh-e-sharbati	white basil seed
jovz-e-hendi	nutmeg	tarkoon	tarragon
kashk dried	whey	tokhm-e-geshniz	coriander seed
keshmesh	sultanas	tarreh	Persian chives
kalal-e-badam	almond strips and slivers	torobcheh	radishes
kalal-e-pesteh	stripped pistachios	torob-e-koohi	horseradish
kalal-e-naranj	orange rinds	tareh tizak	water cress
khmir torsh	yeast	zireh sabs	cumin seed
kash khash	poppy seed	zaaferan	saffron
limoo omani	dried (Persian) lime	zardchoobeh	turmeric
marzeh	oregano	zereshk	barberries

THE NAMES AND ADDRESSES OF ALL PERSIAN SUPERMARKETS IN THE UK

NINA
103 Alcester Road, Moseley,
Birmingham, B13 8DD
Tel: 0121 442 4205

GOOLCHIN
132 Western Road, Brighton, BN3 1DA
Tel: 01273 32451

SUPER ATLAS
275 Upper Brook Street, Manchester,
M13 0HR

VICTOR HOGO
26–27 Melville Terrace, Edinburgh,
EH9 1LP
Tel: 0131 667 1827

SUPER BAHAR
349A Kensington High Street, London,
W8 6NW
Tel: 020 7603 5083

SARA FOODS
7 Hereford Road, London, W2 4AB
Tel: 020 7229 2243

MSOOD
9A Hammersmith Road, London,
W14 8AJ
Tel: 020 7602 1090

TEHRAN
555 Finchley Road, London, NW3 7BJ
Tel: 020 7435 3622

KHAYAM
149 Symore Place, London, W1M 5TL
Tel: 020 7258 3637

HOMA
473 Finchley Road, London NW3 6HE
Tel: 020 8435 2370

HORMOZ
5 Ashbourne Parade,
Temple Fortune, Finchley Road,
London, NW11 0AD

BIJAN
180 Cricklewood Lane, London,
NW2 2DX
Tel: 020 8208 3858

INDEX